N
914
>6
737
990

Barcode on next page

D1430386

The Newsmakers:

The Media's Influence on Canadian Politics

161134576

David Taras

University of Calgary

HUMBER COLLEGE
LAKESHORE CAMPUS
LEARNING RESOURCE CENTRE
3199 LAKESHORE BLVD WEST
TORONTO, ONTARIO M8V 1K8

Nelson Canada

© Nelson Canada,
A Division of Thomson Canada Limited

Published in 1990 by
Nelson Canada,
A Division of Thomson Canada Limited
1120 Birchmount Road
Scarborough, Ontario
M1K 5G4

All rights reserved. No part of this work covered by the copyrights hereon may be reproduced or used in any form or by any means—graphic, electronic or mechanical, including photocopying, recording, taping or information storage and retrieval systems— without the prior written permission of the publisher.

Illustration credits: p. 117, © Raleigh News and Observer. Distributed by Los Angeles Times Syndicate; pp. 199-202, courtesy of the National Archives of Ontario.

Every effort has been made to trace ownership of all copyrighted material and to secure permission from copyright holders. In the event of any question arising as to the use of any material, we will be pleased to make the necessary corrections in future printings.

Canadian Cataloguing in Publication Data

Taras, David, 1950-
  The newsmakers

Includes bibliographical references.
ISBN 0-17-603444-7

1. Reporters and Reporting — Canada. 2. Mass media — Canada — Influence. 3. Journalism — Political aspects — Canada. 4. Politicians — Canada. 5. Canada — Politics and government. I. Title.

PN4914.P6T37   1990   070.4'493240971   C90-094139-1

Printed and bound in Canada
1 2 3 4   WC   93 92 91 90

Preface

The main argument in this book is that newsmaking is a struggle for power. Mao Tse Tung once said that power comes out of the barrel of a gun. While that is still true, power also comes out of the lens of a camera and from published words. The battle is over the messages that are communicated to Canadians through the mass media. Owners, regulators, audiences, and readers—but especially journalists and politicians—have potential influence over news content. The contest is often waged at close quarters within newsrooms and between journalists and their sources, with a variety of interests, agendas, and egos having to be accommodated. As each major news event summons up different actors and perspectives, the battlelines are constantly shifting.

This book focuses in particular on the relationship between journalists and politicians. The first section examines the changes that have taken place within Canadian journalism as journalists have gone from being relatively powerless to being significant wielders of influence. It also focuses on the traditions, routines, and forces at work within the Ottawa Press Gallery. The power of television and the demands of television's infotainment agenda are described at length. A second section analyses how political leaders have adapted to and make use of the mass media and communications technologies. Media management techniques, public opinion polling, direct mail campaigns, and political advertising have become the bread and butter of political survival. At stake is the ability to promote policies, sway opinion, and create and maintain images. A concluding section suggests five ways in which modern communications and media reporting have altered the fabric of democracy. A new Canadian politics has emerged under the intensity of the television spotlight and the harsh critical gaze of Canadian journalists.

The most pleasurable task in the writing of a book is to thank those who have contributed to its development. There were many people who gave of their time, shared thoughts, experiences, and ideas, and offered guidance and advice. Without grants from the Research Grants Committee of the University of Calgary, none of the field work for this book could have been conducted. I am grateful for their generous support. Elly Alboim, Arnold Amber, Dalton Camp, Vince Carlin, Ken Colby, Jim

Coutts, Keith Davey, Jeffrey Dvorkin, Allen Garr, Joyce Fairbairn, Doug Fisher, Alan Fryer, David Halton, Romeo Leblanc, Marc Lortie, Charles Lynch, Arch Mackenzie, Ian Mckinnon, Patrick Martin, Jason Moscovitz, David Nayman, Don Newman, Terry O'Grady, Peter O'Malley, Terry O'Malley, Graham Parley, George Radwanski, Gordon Robertson, Jeff Sallot, John Sawatsky, Tom Scott, Robin Sears, Val Sears, Hugh Segal, Brian Smith, Mark Starowicz, Geoffrey Stevens, AnnaMaria Tremonti, Norman Webster, Anthony Westell, W. A. Wilson, and Hugh Winsor were among those interviewed for this study. Not all of those interviewed wished to be identified. Most spoke freely about their values and experiences, frustrations, and triumphs and how they viewed the many faceted world of political reporting. I often left interviews feeling that doors had been opened, allowing in the fresh air of new ideas.

Dale Thomson of McGill University and Anthony Westell of Carleton University read parts of the manuscript and saved me from making errors. I am especially thankful to my friend and colleague, Leslie Pal, for his incisive and thought-provoking critique. Two referees, assigned by Nelson Canada, W. H. N. Hull of Brock University and Gerald Sperling of the University of Regina, gave me stimulating and important perspectives and were enormously helpful. Daphne Gottlieb Taras also read the manuscript with a keen eye and offered valuable suggestions for improvement. Any errors that may exist, however, are mine alone.

Dianne Fox typed the manuscript through its various stages, numerous changes, and continual revisions. I am thankful for her patience, good humour, and endurance.

Dave Ward at Nelson Canada offered encouragement, enthusiasm, and good advice, and copy editor Margot Lettner did a masterful job sharpening words and ideas.

The Newsmakers is dedicated to my wife, Daphne Gottlieb Taras, who has enriched my life in so many ways and gave me the confidence to believe that I could write this book. Our two boys, Matthew and Joel, have little understanding of why their father was not there to read to them about dinosaurs on so many weekends. I promise to make it up to them.

PART 1

INTRODUCTION

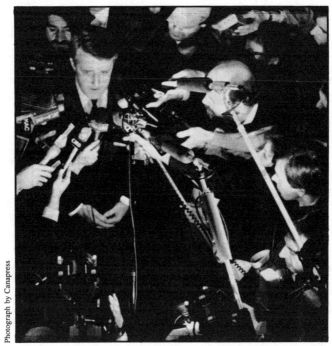

Photograph by Canapress

1

Contending Theories of News: Influences and Effects

This book is about newsmakers, with the title intended to reflect a double meaning. It is first about journalists whose job it is to witness, fashion together, and report the news, and second about the politicians who are often the subjects or the sources for what is being reported. That news in Canada is to some extent the product of an on-going struggle for power and control between the two estates is a central argument of the book. The battle is over who will set the conditions and determine the issues for public debate, a contest intrinsic to careers and prestige on both sides and to public life in Canada. The sharpness of the struggle is softened to some degree by a recognition that each side needs the other in order to succeed, and by habits of coexistence and co-operation that have developed based on these needs. Journalists need access to politicians, whether simply for a quote to be used for newspaper stories, or television or radio clips; or for a deeper probing, perhaps off the record, of what is taking place behind the scenes. Journalists need politicians in order to give their reports legitimacy and credibility. Politicians, in turn, need journalists to get their messages to the public, to explain their actions and build popular support for their policies and, of course, for themselves. In the 1990s, power often comes through the lens of a television camera. Politicians have to be on television to be visible to their publics; without that visibility, their prestige and level of recognition, if not their importance, will diminish. The battlefield on which news is created involves rituals of combat and co-operation, strategies for gaining ascendency, and has an enormous impact on shaping Canadian politics.

The reason that the struggle among "newsmakers" is so critical is that news, especially television news, is a powerful conduit (some might say the most powerful) of basic images and information, facts, and values to the general public. News plays a vital role in setting the political agenda, the issues, events, and people that become part of the public's consciousness. To argue that the media do not have considerable power in shaping public perceptions and, in so doing, influencing government policies and priorities, is the equivalent of arguing that the earth is flat or that Tinkerbell and the Tooth Fairy are real. It's just not so.

Canadians are mediaholics to an extent that most observers find astonishing. A typical Canadian spends approximately nine years of his or

3

her life in front of a television.[1] By age twelve, Canadian children will have been bombarded by 12,000 hours of television and will have spent more time watching television than they have been in school.[2] Canadians are exposed on average to a mind-spinning 1,560 advertisements per day, whether in newspapers, on radio, on signs or billboards, or on television, and most Canadians will see a newspaper and hear radio at least once a day.[3] News permeates Canadian life; information, images, fast-breaking stories flow steadily through the country's bloodstream.

The book will explore the many ways in which news reporting and modern information technologies have affected Canadian politics. Indeed, almost all of politics has changed because of the changes that have taken place in the media. The breathtaking speed of modern communications has quickened the pace of political decision-making. Political leaders are often forced to respond at a moment's notice to news about dramatic events that have just occurred, whether in Canada or on the other side of the globe. In these situations they are deprived of the time needed to think through policies, to consult, or to build consensus. The visual nature of television has made political leaders into performers in front of a mass audience, where the ability to perform for the cameras may be as critical to success as mastering the details of government organization and policy. The rise of critical journalism, with its harsh cynicism and devastating critiques of politicians, may have made it more difficult for politicians to govern effectively, as well as undermined the dignity and attractiveness of high office and affected the credibility of public institutions. Political leaders are imprisoned in a fish bowl where their every move can be observed. In addition, public opinion polls have become the score-card of politics and the life-blood of political survival. Instead of looking at the long-term effects of policies and believing that, as political leaders, they should lead rather than follow, politicians have become obsessed by the latest gusts of public opinion as measured by public opinion surveys.

The book pays considerable attention to the power of television, in particular, to how the format of television news and its "infotainment" agenda have conditioned political behaviour. Television news, it will be argued, has to some degree become its own reflection as politicians have geared their own images and agendas to the routines and requirements of television news. Television is the context for much of the interchange that takes place between politicians and journalists, including print journalists whose roles have changed because of television.

This introductory chapter will review the principle theories and explanations about the nature of news and how news is created. The central proposition will be that while each of these models has some validity, and can be the determining factor in particular situations, they do not adequately cover the media-political battlefield that is the source and mainspring of so much of what constitutes news in Canada. A second section will describe contending theories about the effects that the media have on their audiences. Although the scholarly debate about media effects is rife with controversy and disagreements, I argue that a preponderance of evidence clearly supports the view that the media have an agenda-setting role. The media have the capacity to prime their audiences about the ways in which the world should be viewed.

Chapters Two, Three, and Four examine how forces within journalism have brought about fundamental changes in the relationship between journalists and politicians. Changing values in journalism, the dynamics of news reporting in the Ottawa Press Gallery, and the requirements of the television news "frame" are described in detail. Chapters Five through Eight focus on how politicians have changed their priorities, strategies, and behavior to meet the challenges presented by the new media environment. The often stormy relationship between prime ministers and journalists, the techniques used by politicians to manage the media, and the new technology of election politics are discussed and evaluated in this section. A concluding chapter discusses some of the problems that have emerged in an era where television has become a main instrument of democracy. To some degree, the political system has still not adjusted to the dramatic changes that have taken place because of the power of television. The stakes for the Canadian political system and for the Canadian public, however, are exceedingly high. For as Todd Gitlin has written about the impact of the media, "They name the world's parts, they certify reality as reality."[4]

THEORIES ABOUT NEWSMAKING

The Mirror Model

The mirror model contends that news mirrors reality and that it reflects issues, events, and people as they really are. Journalists hold a mirror to the world and the mirror reflects back the reality of everyday life, life as it really is. This is a view that seems to be widely accepted among journalists. News is not twisted or invented or crafted together out of dark shadows. Rather, it is obvious, self-evident, and intrusive. Reality imposes itself on journalists. New taxes, an airplane crash, political scandal, Middle East terrorism, or the evitable fascination of human interest stories—man bites dog—must be reported regardless of the personal views of journalists, newspaper owners, television news executives, or advertisers. Journalists often brag about having a nose for stories, a sixth sense about where and how stories are developing and which behind-the-scenes machinations are about to become news, yet in most cases news is so obvious that it hits them squarely between the eyes.

This argument is usually a journalist's first line of defence when confronted with angry complaints about coverage from politicians, protests by interest groups, or reactions from disgruntled readers or viewers. The news, they argue, reflects reality, however painful that reality might be to some people. For instance, when the Canadian media's coverage of Israel's handling of the Palestinian uprising in its occupied territories brought heated condemnation from Canadian Jewish groups, the response from journalists was that their obligation was to depict reality whether particular groups liked that reality or not. As David Bazay, a CBC news executive, explained to a Jewish audience in Toronto, "It is patently untrue to say we distort the news. If there are pictures of Israeli soldiers beating Palestinians, it's because that is reality."[5] *Toronto Sun* reporter/ photographer Stuart McCarthy had the same message: "What's happening in Israel is ugly, but the images are factual. What is seen on the nightly news or in pictures is true and I can't apologize for it."[6] Most journalists would argue that what's true for the Middle East is also true for Canadian politics; the camera doesn't lie, ultimately, inevitably what we are seeing, what we are told, what we read reflects cold reality. While a particular story might be slanted in a certain way or may have missed some pertinent details, in the end the media's mirror is self-correcting. Political leaders such as Brian Mulroney, John Turner, Audrey McLaughlin or Jean Chrétien are seen by Canadians as they really are, with all their warts and blemishes. The varnish of image politics and clever techniques of manipulation eventually wear off before the glare of the media mirror.

The mirror model was celebrated by David Brinkley in a documentary about American society in the 1960s. Brinkley asserted that "What television did in the sixties was to show the American people to the American people. . . . It did show them people, places and things they had not seen before. Some they liked and some they didn't. It wasn't that television produced or created any of it."[7] An important scholarly study of the media's coverage of the war in Vietnam by Daniel Hallin contends that media criticism of the American war effort did not lead or prime American public opinion but, instead, reflected a breakdown of consensus among political leaders and in the public at large that had already occurred.[8] The media again reflected reality.

The Fowler Committee on Canadian Broadcasting elevated the mirror concept to a transcendent national mission when it reported in 1965. Fowler saw the entire broadcasting system as a mirror reflecting the full length and breadth of Canadian culture and identity. The report made the following eloquent appeal:

> When we declare that broadcasting should be a major instrument for the development of a distinctive Canadian culture, we use that most abused word "culture" in its broadest and original meaning. It is the reflection of life itself, in all its variety—its beauty and ugliness; its significant artistic achievements

and its unimportant daily occurrences; its big people and its little people; its important and often inscrutable messages, and its light insignificant interests; its great opinions and its amusing anecdotes; tragedy and comedy, laughter and tears, criticism, irony, satire and sheer fun and amusement—all are essential.[9]

The vision remains firmly embedded in the CBC's sense of mission and priorities. An extended and heart-rending interview with a woman dying of cancer on CBC radio's *Morningside*, a graphic portrayal of AIDS victims dying in a hospice reported on *The National*, a terrifying portrait of a burn victim shown on CBC television's *The Journal*, or a glimpse into the sordid underside of Canadian life on CBC's *The Fifth Estate* are meant to show life in stark relief rather than as a "sugar-coated" fantasy.

The mirror model is also encased in the CBC's guidebook on journalistic policy, which stipulates that news and current affairs programs "present the general flow of ideas prevalent in our society. . . . In performing this role, those responsible for journalistic programming must avoid a cumulative bias or slant over a period of time and must be mindful of the CBC's responsibility to present the widest possible range of ideas."[10] Indeed, Mark Starowicz, the producer of *The Journal*, has described his program as a kind of Parliament: "We are the perpetual emergency debate, and we ascertain what the spectrum of debate should be. But unlike the politicians, we have no legislative agenda."[11] Starowicz sees journalists as neutral professionals managing and reflecting the many spectrums of opinion in Canadian society.

The firmest anchor for the mirror principle is in the emergence of journalism as a distinct profession grounded in specialized training and an ethic of societal service and responsibility. Many Canadian journalists believe that through an education in journalism, the heat of experience, and a constantly refined sense of judgement they are able to discern objective reality. Objectivity is central not only to the credibility of individual journalists but also to journalism's claim to professional status. That journalists are "to provide a truthful, comprehensive, and intelligent account of the day's events in a context that gives them meaning" is the first requirement in fulfilling the ideal of journalistic responsibility.[12]

THE DISTORTED MIRROR MODEL

A second model contends that journalists and news organizations are not passive, neutral reflectors of reality but active agents that change the reflection in some way. Events in the real world are transformed to fit journalistic needs and criteria. News stories are chosen according to a rigid set of media requirements and processed to meet the needs of owners, news organizations, or individual journalists. Some events are ignored entirely or downplayed because they don't have the characteristics necessary to make them leading news items. As discussed in Chapter Four, television news stories in particular must have these characteristics: they must be dramatic and sensational, easily labelled and condensed, and be visually appealing; and involve well-known individuals and clear pro and con positions. Events that make the news have therefore been twisted out of shape and, in the process, have become something alien and artificial. They have been taken out of their context in the real world and recontextualized to fit the media's needs.

Proponents of the distorted mirror perspective have different views about the ways in which the mirror is distorted. Some believe that what is reflected in the mirror is the power of the people who own news organizations, while others argue that the need to gain large audiences in order to attract advertising dollars is now so overwhelming that news is driven by audience demand; what the audience is seeing is its own reflection. Others take the view that news is shaped by the organizational dynamics of individual news organizations, "the pulling and hauling" imposed by their external and internal environments, or that national cultures and identities tilt the mirror in a certain direction. Yet another perspective is that news is journalist-centred and largely the product of the interplay between journalists and their sources that occurs at the flash-point of a story's development. Politicians, government officials, and interest group representatives are the main sources with which journalists have to contend. This interplay produces much of what becomes news. This does not mean that there are not other powerful forces at work in creating and processing the words and pictures that constitute the news. News is, in fact, the product of a complex mix of factors, any one of which can be decisive in a particular circumstance.

The Ownership Model

One third school of thought holds that news is dictated primarily by the interests of the huge corporate empires that own so much of the Canadian media. Enormous corporations, headed by tycoons or controlled by a particular family, dominate the Canadian media landscape. While consumers in the 1990s appear on the surface to have a veritable smorgasbord of choices available to them—a proliferation in the number of television channels that can be accessed on basic cable, pay-TV, and satellite; an explosion in magazines, journals, and newsletters; and the mushrooming of video outlets and products—ownership of the media remains in relatively few hands. To paraphrase Michael Parenti, there are many songs, few voices.[13] This is especially the case with newspapers, where family-owned chains have divided the spoils of the Canadian marketplace much as feudal barons once carved up England and France. Edward Herman and Noam Chomsky state the proposition this way:

. . . the dominant media firms are quite large businesses; they are controlled by very wealthy people or by managers who are subject to sharp constraints by owners and other market-profit-oriented forces; and they are closely inter-locked, and have important common interests with other major corporations, banks and government. This is the first powerful filter that will affect news choices.[14]

A.J. Liebling's famous quip was that "freedom of the press belongs to the man who owns one."[15]

Canada's largest communications company, and the third largest in the world, is the Thomson Corporation of Toronto. The family-run corpo-ration is headed by Kenneth Thomson, the son of founder Roy Thomson and ranked by *Fortune* magazine as the world's ninth richest person. The Thomson empire owns forty daily newspapers in Canada, which together control over 20 percent of Canada's newspaper circulation, including *The Globe and Mail*, the jewel in the crown of the Canadian newspaper industry.[16] Thomson is also the second largest owner of newspapers in the United States with over 140 dailies and weeklies, most of them small-town operations. It also publishes 23,000 trade and professional books, newsletters, and magazines. Real estate, travel companies and depart-ment stores—The Bay, Simpsons, and Zellers—are also part of the Thom-son conglomerate.[17]

Roy Thomson founded the dynasty in 1931 when he bought a radio station in North Bay, Ontario. His first newspaper was *The Timmins Press*, which was purchased with a down payment of $200 in 1934. A tough, hard-nosed, irascible figure, Thomson was difficult to work for; he payed the lowest wages in the industry, and working conditions were often dismal. James Winter reports that even today, "The Thomson chain has a reputation for running a penny-pinching, profitable business, where reporters have been asked to buy their own copies of the newspapers, and memos have been circulated about too much toilet paper being con-sumed in the women's washrooms of the newspaper buildings."[18] For Roy Thomson, news was simply a commodity to be sold. He once bragged that "editorial content is the stuff you separate the ads with."[19]

The public relations image is that Ken Thomson, a more refined and distant figure than his father, maintains a "hands off" attitude towards editorial content, seeing newspapers as a business from which sizable profits are expected. It's argued that control and even supervision are impossible with such vast and diverse holdings. There are suggestions, however, that Ken Thomson "felt compelled to produce a more conser-vative *Globe and Mail*" and, in 1988, that he gave publisher Roy Megarry the green light to institute sweeping changes in the news-room, changes to make the paper more appealing to an upscale, business-oriented readership.[20] To many, Ken Thomson is the very epitome of the Canadian corporate establishment. He sits on over forty boards of directors; owns a private art collection that includes close to 200 paintings by Cornelius Krieghoff, some which are national treasures; is a fixture in Toronto's charitable and social events; and presides over companies that bring in over $5 billion in revenue annually.[21]

Conrad Black, the chairman of Hollinger Inc., is considered a less benign figure. Sometimes viewed as the *enfant terrible* of the Canadian corporate world because of his outspoken views on politics and aggressiveness in business, Black currently owns 207 newspapers and seems bent on acquiring more at a phenomenal rate. In 1988 alone, he bought twenty-one dailies and fifty-nine weeklies. Black's specialty is small-town monopoly newspapers that record high profits. Hollinger's "herd of tiny cash cows" helps finance the purchase of prestigious properties that bring influence and power. Britain's *Daily Telegraph*, Israel's *Jerusalem Post*, *Saturday Night* magazine, and a 15 percent interest in *The Financial Post* give Hollinger political muscle. In addition, Black has cultivated powerful connections: former British Foreign Secretary Lord Carrington, former U.S. Secretary of State Henry Kissinger, Allan Gottlieb, Canada's former ambassador to Washington, and corporate magnets Peter Bronfman and Paul Reichmann all sit on Hollinger's Board of Directors. Hollinger Vice-Chairman Peter White was once chief of staff for Prime Minister Brian Mulroney. It was White who described Black as a modern press baron, observing that "the true nature of the press baron is that he is part businessman, part media figure and part politician—though without the vagaries involved in dealing with an electorate."[22]

Black, who has written columns for various newspapers, has unabashedly conservative views. He seems to admire strong men such as Franco, Degaulle, and Duplessis and enthusiastically supported Reagan's and Thatcher's policies. He also believes that journalists need to be ruled by a strong hand. As Black once put it, "My experience of the working press is that they're a very degenerate group. There is a terrible incidence of alcoholism and drug abuse. The mental stability of large elements of the press is more open to question than that of many other comparable groups in society. A number of them are ignorant, lazy, opinionated, intellectually dishonest and inadequately supervised."[23] He takes an even harsher attitude towards investigative reporting. In a column written for *The Toronto Sun* (which he does not own) in 1989, he described investigative reporters as "swarming, grunting masses of jackals."[24]

Another media giant is Southam Inc. of Toronto. Its fifteen newspapers account for roughly 38 percent of total daily circulation in Canada, approximately 1.5 million newspapers sold each day.[25] The Southam chain includes some of the old lions of English-Canadian journalism: *The Ottawa Citizen*, *The Gazette* (Montreal), *The Hamilton Spectator*, *The Windsor Star*, *Calgary Herald*, *The Edmonton Journal*, and both *The*

Vancouver Sun and *Province*. Southam's Business Information Group publishes magazines, directories, and newsletters and runs trade and consumer shows, among other ventures. It also owns Coles Books, Canada's largest chain of bookstores, and polling and research firms through the Angus Reid Group of Winnipeg. The current president, John Fisher, is the great-grandson of founder William Southam, whose first purchase was *The Hamilton Spectator*, bought for $6,000 in 1877.[26] Control over Southam remains in family hands. Once described by William Thorsell, *The Globe and Mail's* current editor-in-chief, as "a flabby, rambling underproductive old soldier of a corporation," Southam is now considered a ripe takeover target.[27] It beat back at least one hostile takeover attempt in 1985 by swapping shares with Torstar, publisher of Canada's largest daily circulation newspaper, *The Toronto Star*, and Harlequin Books, which produces fantasy romance novels. The deal that allowed Torstar to own 22.4 percent of Southam and Southam to have a 30 percent non-voting block of Torstar's shares came to an end in 1990. There is some speculation about a full-scale Southam-Torstar merger, one that would create a media giant large enough to play on the global stage. Still another possibility is that Southam will fall prey to a hungry corporate predator and be broken apart or restructured.

Another large communications company is Maclean Hunter Ltd. of Toronto, which owns a dizzying array of media properties. These properties include more than 200 magazines, among them *Maclean's* magazine and *Chatelaine*; several clutches of radio stations in Alberta, Southern Ontario, and Atlantic Canada; cable companies in Canada, the United States and Britain; television station CFCN; the CTV affiliate servicing Calgary and Lethbridge; and The Toronto Sun Publishing Company. Toronto Sun Publishing owns the Toronto, Calgary, Edmonton, and Ottawa *Suns*, all of which are cheeky and sensational tabloids; *The Financial Post*, which is austere and dignified; and a string of small dailies and weeklies in Ontario, Western Canada, and Florida.

The most flamboyant of Canada's media moguls is Pierre Péladeau, the founder of Quebecor Inc. Among Quebecor's ventures are *Le Journal de Montréal*, which has the largest daily circulation in Quebec, four other dailies, dozens of weekly newspapers, a bevy of magazines and magazine stores, and over twenty printing plants. In 1988 Quebecor launched *Super Hebdo*, a forty-page weekly that is distributed free to over 800,000 Montrealers. Péladeau has also been a principal backer of Quebec's most prestigious and influencial newspaper, *Le Devoir*, which is presently run by a non-profit foundation teetering close to bankruptcy. Should *Le Devoir* collapse, Quebecor has first claim to the paper's accounts receivable.[28] A self-proclaimed "bad boy," Péladeau's "long-standing reputation for drinking hard and chasing women is the stuff of legends," as are his lavish parties and generosity to various charitable causes.[29] But he is a man of contradictions. Although his own tastes are for Beethoven's symphonies and literary classics, his newspapers specialize in "gossip, girls and gore."[30] A one-time supporter of Quebec separatism, Péladeau became chairman of the 1987 Canada Day activities in Montreal.[31] While he apparently does not interfere with daily operations at *Le Journal de Montréal*, he does "have ideas he'll pass on."[32] He became embroiled in controversy in 1990 when he reportedly wrote a memo to *Le Journal de Montréal* "urging it to promote francophone designers instead of English-speaking Jewish designers" in its fashion section.[33] Péladeau also, according to at least one account, "chews up executives at an incredible rate" and "gives golden handshakes as often as a traffic cop hands out parking tickets."[34] Péladeau's ambition to build a communications empire that includes everything "from the timber to the postal stamp,"[35] however, is no mystery. With twenty acquisitions in 1988 alone, Péladeau is setting a frenetic pace.

In Atlantic Canada, the Irving family has long been "the Kingdom and the power." Based largely on oil and real estate but spread over some 300 companies, K.C. Irving's holdings are estimated to be worth $5 billion.[36] Ownership of the newspapers and television stations in Saint John's, Moncton, and Fredericton gives the family an iron grip on New Brunswick's media. They also have important media properties in other centres in the Maritimes.

Table 1.1
The Media Giants
Canada's Top 9

	Company	1988 Revenue
1.	The Thomson Corp.	$5.00 billion
2.	Southam Inc.	$1.65 billion
3.	Maclean Hunter Ltd.	$1.30 billion
4.	Quebecor Inc.	$1.29 billion
5.	Torstar Corp.	$956 million
6.	Hollinger Inc.	$683 million
7.	Rogers Communications Inc.	$358 million
8.	Groupe Transcontinental GTC Ltée	$326 million
9.	Canadian Broadcasting Corp.	$326 million

Source: *Maclean's,* 17 July 1989.

CTV is the most watched television network in Canada. The network is a federation of twenty-four affiliate stations stretching from NTV in St. John's to CHEK in Victoria. Critics claim that CTV's commitment to quality Canadian programming has been soft, and that the network has become little more than a consortium to purchase expensive but highly lucrative American programs. Baton Broadcasting, which owns CFTO in

Toronto, CJOH in Ottawa, and the Saskatchewan affiliates, is the largest of CTV's eleven ownership groups. Baton is controlled by the Eaton family, owners of the department store chain, with a sizable interest also maintained by the Bassett family.

The growth of large media conglomerates in Canada seems to be part of a world-wide trend. The West German giant Bertelsmann AG, American companies such as Time-Warner, Capital Cities–ABC, General Electric–NBC, and the communications empires built by former Australian Rupert Murdoch and Britain's Robert Maxwell span continents and encompass virtually every medium of communications from magazines to motion pictures, from books to television. Murdoch, whose newspapers account for one-third of total newspaper circulation in Britain, also owns powerful dailies in Australia's major cities as well as Twentieth Century Fox, Metromedia, Harper and Row, the Fox television network, and a phalanx of newspapers and magazines in the United States. He is particularly noteworthy because of his direct intervention in the editorial process; according to John Pauly, "Murdoch is not at all shy about using his papers to support candidates he likes, sometimes even by slanting news coverage."[37] The ultraconservative Murdoch has used his papers to scourge liberal politicians and has not been afraid to create political dust storms.

John Porter and Wallace Clement, as well as other scholars working within the Canadian political economy tradition, have argued that the owners of media empires are part of a larger fabric of societal control. Tied to the country's corporate and governmental elite and through a tight social network to each other, media owners represent, in Porter's words, a "confraternity of power."[38] Clement's argument is that while owners do not share an all-encompassing ideology, the media are nonetheless "biased in favour of existing arrangements of power."[39] Audiences and readers may be exposed to a variety of media viewpoints but virtually all views are conservative. In their editorial stances, news organizations may attack individual politicians, support one political party over another, or criticize particular government policies; the legitimacy of the institutions themselves, however, are never questioned. Indeed Herbert Gans, among others, contends that by focusing on political leaders, by using them as authoritative producers of news, the media in fact celebrate their power.[40]

Richard Ericson, Patricia Baranek, and Janet Chan make the case that the news media maintain social control by exposing deviant behaviour.[41] Most of the events reported in the news—crimes, scandals, airplane crashes, strikes, drugs, trials, and political or diplomatic clashes—are about the upholding of societal norms, and the punishment of those who have violated those norms. As Ericson has written:

Today we no longer parade deviants in the town square or expose them to the carnival atmosphere of Tyburn, but it is interesting to note that the "reform" which brought about this change in penal policy coincided almost precisely with the development of newspapers as media of public information. . . . [N]ewspapers (and now radio and television) offer their readers the same kind of entertainment once supplied by public hangings or the use of stocks and pillories. An enormous amount of modern "news" is devoted to reports about deviant behavior and its punishment.[42]

One can thus argue that former cabinet ministers such as Sinclair Stevens and Robert Coates, who were enveloped by scandal, or a besieged president like Richard Nixon endured an "ordeal by public spotlight" that had elements of a medieval ritual. Fallen TV evangelists Jim Bakker and Jimmy Swaggart endured a similar trial by public spectacle; journalists, among others, were administrators of justice and retribution. By showing disorder, news contributes to maintaining order.

The key question is the extent to which owners dictate editorial content. While there is little evidence to suggest that Canadian owners exercise direct control, there is wide suspicion that power is wielded subtly and indirectly. It is argued that owners inevitably hire media managers who share their values, beliefs, and priorities; managers presumably use the same criteria in hiring journalists. Although journalists may be given wide autonomy in choosing which stories to cover and how these stories are reported, limits—"red lines," if you will—almost certainly exist. Articles or reports that take a viewpoint radically different from that of the owner or that criticize the owner's business operations are unlikely to be tolerated. Mark Hertsgaard, who wrote a book on media coverage of Ronald Reagan, was told by one source that if a journalist was inclined to buck the rules of conventional news coverage, he would find himself blocked by barriers invisible to the naked eye but impenetrable nonetheless. As one journalist told him, "If you go outside the parameters, it's like bumper cars. . . . You hit the wall and get bounced back."[43] But direct intervention by owners is rare. The sting of control is felt through a self-censorship that comes from anticipating the reactions of management. As Michael Parenti explains, "The anticipation that superiors might disapprove of this or that story is usually enough to discourage a reporter from writing it, or an editor from assigning it. . . . This anticipatory avoidance makes direct intervention by owners a less frequent necessity and leaves the journalist with a greater feeling of autonomy than might be justified by the actual power relationship."[44] In addition, journalists operate in an organizational culture where promotions, higher salaries, and top assignments require a certain amount of team play.

In a 1986 report to the Centre for Investigative Journalism, CBC producer Nick Fillmore claimed that "some reporters are having serious problems with the new conservative values that have swept through many news organizations" and that journalists "quietly accept censorship within their own news organizations."[45] He cited instances in which reporters weren't allowed to pursue stories that would be critical of the business community. News organizations would deny that such barriers exist.

✳ Concentration of newspaper ownership is much more extensive in Canada than in the United States. Where in the United States 149 chains control approximately 70 percent of daily circulation, in Canada two chains, Thomson and Southam, account for 60 percent of circulation;[46] moreover, one chain can dominate an entire region. According to the 1980 report of the Royal Commission on Newspapers (Kent Commission), "In seven provinces – all but Ontario, Quebec and Nova Scotia— two-thirds or more of provincial circulation is controlled by a single chain."[47] Rival chains compete against each other in only eight cities: Edmonton, Calgary, Winnipeg, Toronto, Ottawa, Montreal, Quebec City, and St. John's. The market in these cities tends to be segmented along income and educational lines, with "low brow" papers such as the *Suns* appealing to a different constituency than the "middle brow" papers owned by Thomson and Southam. Papers carve out their own niches, leaving little in the way of real competition. In most centres, however, a single paper, usually part of a large chain, enjoys a newspaper monopoly.

The conventional wisdom is that monopolies disfigure the democratic process. If a monopoly newspaper avoids covering local issues or controversies, they are likely to remain unreported. If the newspaper takes a strong editorial position about a particular subject, there may be little opportunity for opposing views to emerge. Corporate priorities can also smother editoral independence. According to Dennis Hale, this point was emphasized in the work of the Kent Commission:

> No one who has been close to newspapers can doubt that, in fact, the power exercised by a chain, shaping the editorial content of its newspapers, is pervasive. Head office appoints the publishers, who appoint everyone else. They control budgets and, in some cases, control expenditures in fine detail. They operate with a string of interchangeable publishers and understood administrative norms. To suggest that they foster editorial independence is, as is said in French, to dream in colour.[48]

Lack of competition, it is argued, produces inferior journalism. Papers become a bulletin-board for cheap wire service copy as expenditures on local reporting are curtailed. Without the push of competition to force coverage of community events and the investigation of local abuses or to break stories, papers deteriorate. Concern for high profits replaces social responsibility. In addition to the threat that may be posed to the development of expression and debate within a community, there is also the possibility that advertisers will be gouged. Local businesses that have to advertise have little choice but to accept the rates dictated by the monopoly.

Some analysts contend that the conventional wisdom is wrong and that monopolies are on the whole beneficial. They charge that, in contrast, competition produces hype and trivia as papers are goaded into reporting murder, mayhem, and movie stars in order to get the largest readership. Journalists are forced to break stories quickly to scoop the competition, and don't take the time or do the extra research that is often needed to provide a complete account. They also believe that only a profitable paper will spend money on editorial content, and that a newspaper belonging to a large chain is less likely to be intimidated by threats from local advertisers. Size and power, in other words, bring a measure of invulnerability. Often a chain paper also has access to costly wire services, syndicated columnists, and news bureaus that would be unavailable to a small or medium sized paper. Lastly, they make the point that "there is no such thing as a monopoly" in a multi-media society.[49] The flood of television, radio, video, and magazines, as well as access in most cases to national newspapers such as *The Globe and Mail* and *The Financial Post*, ensures a variety of perspectives.

Research on the effects of corporate concentration has produced mixed results. Dores Candussi and James Winter found that editorial content in *The Winnipeg Free Press*, a Thomson paper, deteriorated after *The Winnipeg Tribune* was closed in August 1980. The *Tribune*, a Southam paper, went under almost at the same time as *The Ottawa Journal*, a Thomson paper. There was wide suspicion that Thomson and Southam had exchanged monopolies—a Thomson monopoly in Winnipeg for a Southam monopoly in Ottawa created by Southam's ownership of *The Ottawa Citizen*. Candussi and Winter reported that by 1983 the *Free Press* had shorter stories, used fewer colour photos, and bought fewer stories by prestigious wire services such as *The New York Times* and *The Washington Post* than had been the case in 1979.[50] It is significant to note, however, that separate studies by Ronald Wagenberg and Walter Soderlund and by Wagenberg, Soderlund, Briggs, and Romanow concluded that chain ownership had not affected the editorial positions of newspapers during the 1974 and 1979 Canadian elections.[51]

That ownership has the potential to affect news decisions is a proposition widely accepted by media observers. The debate is over the extent of control and where the boundaries between corporate necessity and journalistic integrity lie. Peter Desbarats, a former television journalist who is now Dean of the University of Western Ontario's Graduate School of Journalism, drew the following analogy:

The social structure of the news industry perhaps lends itself to comparison with that of a feudal castle presided over by a baron. . . . The reporters would be the baron's knights, who, when they ride outside the castle to do battle with the enemy, are seen either as the admired protector or dreaded scourge of the peasants, depending which side they are on. Inside the castle, however, their position is far different—they are subservient to the baron, quarrelling among themselves and subsisting on scraps from his table.[52]

The Audience Model

In his book *Amusing Ourselves to Death,* Neil Postman contends that television has become primarily an entertainment medium because of its need to gain large audiences. According to Postman, "The problem is not that television presents us with entertaining subject matter but that all subject matter is presented as entertaining. . . ."[53] The need to appeal to audiences stems from the fact that advertisers don't buy programs so much as they buy the size and characteristics of the audiences that watch them. With audiences fragmented by the explosion in viewing choices— cable systems in Canada, for example, can accommodate thirty-six chan- nels or more—the financial survival of television stations depends on being able to secure and hold audiences. Linda Ellerbee, a former NBC reporter, has described what she sees as the life and death facts of television broadcasting: "In television the product is not the program, the product is the audience and the consumer of that product is the advertiser. The advertiser does not 'buy' a news program. He buys an audience. The manufacturer (network) that gets the highest price for its product is the one that produces the most product (audience). . . ."[54] Newspapers and radio are in a similar position: they need readers and listeners in order to attract advertising; consequently, they must amuse, shock, fascinate, and above all entertain.

The main hypothesis of this consumer model is the notion that news is selected and packaged according to audience demands and that enter- tainment values have come to predominate. Although individual jour- nalists may not be conscious of their audience—it may seem too amor- phous and distant—they still must work within news frames that have been constructed to appeal to it.

It has been argued, in fact, that news has been transformed by audience demands. Where journalists once told audiences what they thought audiences should know, they now tell audiences what they think the audience wants to see or hear. Moreover, gauging what the audience wants has become a top priority with news organizations, which spend enormous amounts of money on audience testing and monitoring. As one American radio news programmer described the process, "We do a lot of research when we decide how to target our newscasts. We select a core group of listeners and try to choose news that's appropriate, relevant and interesting to them and deliver it with an announcer who sounds like he fits in with the listeners."[55] The result is often slick packaging, stories that are punchy and dramatic, and journalists (at least television reporters) chosen for their good looks or home-spun appeal rather than their education or insights. Stories are short to fit the perceived attention spans of the audience and have heroes and villains, winners and losers, so that issues and events can be personalized and made more understandable to readers and viewers. Human interest stories; "news you can use" about investments, medical advice, or how to plant vegetables; and expanded weather and sports reporting are also part of the audience-grabbing formula. Mark Hertsgaard has described how a new president of CBS News, Van Gordon Sauter, fought the news ratings war in the early 1980s:

> Look, tone, pace, content—everything was up for grabs.... Washington stories in particular would be scaled back considerably, on the assumption that the average viewer did not much care what the average congressional committee or federal agency had done that day. The new *CBS Evening News* would boast feature after feature on wild animals, celebrities, natural disasters, medical breakthroughs, individual hard luck or good fortune stories, violent crime, the weather and various other topics that had traditionally been dismissed as too trivial to warrant coverage.[56]

The changing character of television news will be described in considerable detail in Chapter Four.

Defenders of the CBC often claim that it has remained an island of serious-purpose and high ideals because it is a crown corporation with a broad public mandate; indeed, Morris Wolfe's fine work about Canadian television is entitled *Jolts: The TV Wasteland and the Canadian Oasis.*[57] But even the CBC has had to bend to consumer demands. As former CBC president Pierre Juneau admitted, "... in its news and current affairs programs, the CBC must aim at the highest level of excellence ... a level of excellence that the constraints of the commercial markets make impossible."[58] Although advertising doesn't appear on CBC's *The National* or on CBC Radio, it does appear on *The Journal* and on *Newsworld.* As the network has had to endure a series of brutal cut-backs in its budget allocation from Parliament since 1984, advertising has become increasingly important. CBC executives see audience size as a barometer of success; there is a "ratings machismo" among senior producers who brag about their program's audience reach and how they've crushed the opposition. News directors whose shows do not attract large audiences, whose programs, for instance, are not first or second in their local markets, are likely to be reassigned.

The audience model suggests that news mirrors, either consciously or unconsciously, the demands of the audience. While some see the news process as debased and corrupted by the battle over audience ratings, others still see it as healthy and democratic; the appeal to audiences acts as a bulwark against the tyranny of owners. News that is pitched only to an elite audience would deprive the average citizen of the ability to be informed. Amid the clutter, vital information gets through. Whatever the pros and cons, news is distorted, however, because it reflects its audience's need for entertainment and not events and issues as they really are in a world where events are often ponderous and issues complex. As Todd Gitlin concluded in his study of the American media's coverage of the anti-war movement in the United States in the 1960s and early 1970s, "The media were far from mirrors passively reflecting facts found in the real world. The facts were out there in the real world, true: out there among others. The media reflection was more the active, patterned remaking performed by mirrors in a fun house."[59]

The Organizational Model

Another model that has been widely applied by scholars is the organizational mirror. Studies by Breed, Sigal, Epstein, and Gans found that the structure and purpose of the organizations within which journalists work condition how the news is produced.[60] Events and issues are like light being filtered through a prism, the prism being the news organization; how the light is reflected depends on the particular characteristics of the organization through which it passes. According to Edward Jay Epstein, ". . . certain consistent directions in selecting, covering and reformulating events over long-term periods are clearly related to organizational needs."[61] News, in short, is recontextualized to fit the product needs of the institution presenting it. As Reuven Frank, a former president of NBC News, has described the rigidities imposed by news organizations, "So many different people with so many different jobs and responsibilities have felt they wandered into the presence of a large blank canvas. . . . But the canvas is not blank. And none of us may fill it alone. The problem is given. The conditions for the most part are given."[62]

However much we might cherish the image of the reporter as a heroic individual, news reporting is a collective endeavour. TV reporters have to work with camera persons, and producers, editors, and writers can all have a hand in the story that finally emerges. As a senior producer at the CBC described the collective effort that exists among reporters, "It's a team effort. No one does it themselves. Some reporters do the leg work, get the quotes, while other reporters 'front the story,' presenting it on air."[63] Print reporters work within a hierarchical structure where the final authority about their assignments, whether their articles will run, and where they will appear are in the hands of superiors. Personal values are modified to fit the needs of the organization. The weight of bureaucracy constrains individual initiative and imposes the imperatives of the organizational culture.

The organizations themselves are shaped by a number of factors, among them the nature of the medium, markets, and competition, and whether they are public or private corporations. The constraints imposed by the nature of the medium is perhaps the most critical factor. For instance, the lengths of news stories vary depending on the medium that is used. Newspaper items usually run between 700 and 1,000 words and contain more information than in the highly condensed ninety seconds (150 to 250 words) of a typical television story, or in the stunted brevity of a twenty-second radio bite. Magazine articles, normally several thousand words in length, allow reporters to describe people and events in greater detail. The deadlines within which journalists work also vary according to the medium used. Time is an essential consideration in determining the shape that a news story will take. The sources that can be reached for interviews and whether facts can be checked, the issues researched, and conclusions drawn are all determined by the time that reporters have available to them. Deadlines impose closure. In a country spread across six time-zones, the location of the news organization and different times of publication or broadcast mean that reporters assigned to cover the same story may be working under very different conditions.

The texture and slant of a news story also depends on the audience that is being addressed. Newspapers tend to be stratified according to the education and income of their readerships. Upscale newspapers such as *The Financial Post, The Globe and Mail,* and *Le Devoir* use more sophisticated language, provide serious coverage of public policy issues, and carry ads that are aimed, to some degree, at a wealthier clientele. The influence of their readers gives their editorial content a certain imprimatur. Low brow newspapers such as the *Suns* or *Le Journal de Montréal* emphasize crime, celebrities, sports, pictures, and light breezy news, and are usually written for people with a high school education. All purpose newspapers such as *The Gazette, La Presse, The Toronto Star,* or *The Calgary Herald* are pitched to a wide readership and the full gamut of tastes. With a vast increase in the number of channels available, the television audience has also become increasingly fragmented. People interested in steady diets of news, weather, sports, business, or arts can now turn to specialty channels to find what interests them. While network news shows still appeal to a large general audience, there is evidence from the United States to suggest that the network news programs may be losing their once pre-eminent position as the prime conveyers of information. Don Hewitt, the executive producer of *60 Minutes*, once remarked that ". . . the CNNs and the Home Boxes and the Showtimes and the Hearst networks are to ABC, NBC, and CBS like Subaru, Toyota, Honda are to Chrysler, GM and Ford."[64] As discussed in Chapter Four, competition for audiences has made television news organizations change their formats and the pacing and content of news reports and turned leading journalists (especially anchors) into TV stars.

A distinction also has to be drawn between news organizations that have a national audience reach and those that cater to a local market. Although many local television news shows and, of course, newspapers offer national and international news, the local community is their bread and butter. Many a station manager or newspaper editor has paid the price for not reflecting the intense local concerns and tastes of their communities. National news organizations such as *Maclean's, The Globe and Mail,* or CBC News must reach into all the regions, some of which they can only thinly cover.

The dynamics within an organization are often created by a particular history and circumstances. *The Toronto Star,* under a series of strong publishers including Joseph Atkinson and Beland Honderich, has long been considered an editor's paper; that is, reporters are kept under tight editorial control. *The Globe and Mail,* on the other hand, has a tradition of being a writer's paper, where journalists maintain considerable discretion over their own work. At *Le Devoir,* which is run as a charitable foundation and not as a business, journalists tend to put much more of their own views into stories, a situation that might not be tolerated at many chain-owned papers where news is much more of a homogenized product.

The most fundamental demarcation line differentiating news is the gulf that separates publicly-owned media from media that is operated as a business venture by private individuals. The publicly-financed CBC has a mandate to provide comprehensive programming reflecting Canadian culture, the country's many regions, and the tastes and needs of a wide variety of audiences. Approximately 75 percent of the CBC's budget, which was $1.3 billion in 1988-89, comes through an annual grant from Parliament, with advertising revenue making up the remainder. The CBC's goal is to have Canadian content in over 80 percent of its programming. To be at the forefront of national stories and lead the national debate on issues of public policy is one of the imperatives of CBC journalism. As will be discussed in later chapters, the CBC has often been embroiled in controversy and enraged the politicians who control its destiny.

The private networks operate according to a different rhythm. Driven by the need to see a return on their investments, they are driven to a much greater degree by audience demand. CTV and Global TV have much smaller news departments than CBC and are bare bones operations by comparison. Ultimately, budgets dictate how stories are to be covered; it's often easier to buy stories from American networks, for instance, than to commit one's own reporters and resources.

Canadian journalism can therefore be compared to a quilt made up of many different organizational cloths, each distinct in size. Proponents of the organizational model argue that news is made to fit the shape of the cloth.

The Cultural Model

Many Canadians are deeply worried by the extent to which American values have penetrated Canadian life. Canadians often know more about the great events and important figures of American history, for example, than they do about their own legacy. One recent survey of Canadian university students found that a majority preferred the American political system to the Canadian and admired George Washington by a three-to-one margin over John A. Macdonald, and that most believed that Canada would join the United States within their lifetime.[65] The names of leading Canadian artists and writers are often unrecognizable to large numbers of university students. Many observers blame this loss of identity on the magnitude, force, and attraction of the American mass media. Less than 30 percent of the television programs and only 2 percent of television drama available to English Canadians are Canadian produced.[66] Over 70 percent of the magazines sold in Canada are foreign, as are over 95 percent of the films watched.[67] Even francophones, long nurtured by an intense cultural nationalism, appear to be turning to American cultural products instead of their own.[68] John Meisel, one of Canada's most distinguished scholars and a former chairman of the Canadian Radio-Television and Telecommunications Commission (CRTC), has observed that "inside every Canadian, whether she or he knows it or not, there is, in fact, an American. The magnitude and effect of this American presence in us all varies considerably from person to person, but it is ubiquitous and inescapable."[69]

To face this onslaught, Ottawa erected a series of cultural defences. CRTC regulations stipulate that over 60 percent of all programming has to be Canadian content, although the private networks are allowed to reduce the Canadian content level to 50 percent during prime time (6:00 p.m. to midnight). The CBC has to have 60 percent throughout its broadcast day. As buying a top-rated American program costs ten times less than producing one hour of Canadian drama (an hour-long episode of Dallas can be bought for $60,000) and is a lucrative advertising draw, the private networks sandwich American programs into the heart of their prime time schedules. Canadian programs are usually ghettoized into the supper hour and after 10:00 p.m. time slots. Supper hour and late night news shows are the centrepieces of Canadian programming for most local stations.

Bill C-58, introduced in 1975, bolstered Canadian radio and television revenues by taking away the ability to write off advertisements as a tax–deductible expense from Canadian advertisers who ran commercials on U.S. stations. Canadian advertisers could deduct the cost of advertising in magazines that were 75 percent owned and published in Canada. A policy of substitution allowed Canadian broadcasters to block out American advertising when the same program was shown at the same time by a U.S. station whose signals reached a Canadian market. Canadian television and film producers have also benefited from the Canadian Broadcast Production Development Fund, which, directed through Telefilm Canada, matches funds raised for specific projects by Canadian producers with government money.

Although Brian Mulroney assured Canadians that Canada's cultural sovereignty would not be affected by the Free Trade Agreement signed with the United States in 1988, there are powerful American interests that wish to undermine Canadian cultural protections. As European quotas on domestic television production squeeze American programs out of their once dominant position in European markets, the Canadian market has become increasingly important. Canadian TV networks are charged much more for American programs than are European networks.[70] The issue of what constitutes a subsidy has not yet been resolved by the two countries.

A cultural mirror is imposed to some degree on Canadian television news by legislation and regulation. The Broadcasting Act of 1968 directed the CBC to "contribute to the development of national unity and provide for a continuing expression of Canadian identity."[71] This is reflected in the extraordinary coverage given to national and state occasions. The opening of Parliament, the budget address by the Minister of Finance, First Ministers Conferences, state funerals, and federal elections are usually covered live and treated in news specials. When Prime Minister Mulroney visited the Soviet Union in the fall of 1989, CBC anchor Peter Mansbridge and a team of reporters covered virtually every aspect of the visit even though there was little actual news to report. This mission is also reflected in the large number of regional stories covered on *The National* and the *The Journal*. According to Mark Starowicz, the producer of *The Journal*, "In Canada it would be inconceivable not to do a P.E.I. election. CBS wouldn't do a Louisiana election."[72] In addition, the CBC has expanded its number of foreign bureaus so that on international stories, as producer David Nayman at *The National* described it, "We won't be prisoners of the American networks. We don't want an American slant. We try to minimize the use of American material."[73] If CBC is covering the same story as the American networks, there will often be a conscious decision to take a different angle, to do the story differently. The CBC rarely uses American reports or visuals.

Although newspapers do not have a cultural mandate similar to that of the CBC, it can be argued nonetheless that Canadian journalists are guided by distinct cultural norms. These norms are not only the product of specific traditions within news organizations but also, I will contend, of the circumstances surrounding the media's coverage of political events. As will be described in Chapters Two and Three, many of the values that underlie the culture of Canadian journalism stem from the conditions that prevail in the battleground between journalists and politicians, conditions that have a distinctly national focus.

The Political Model

The political model sees news as journalist-centred. Journalists are believed to have enough independence and discretion so that the primary digging for facts and focusing of a story is in their hands. In their daily battle for access and information, journalists are dependent on sources who are usually politicians, government officials, or the people close to those in power. Journalists craft their stories so that they speak or write through their sources; moreover, the use of sources confers legitimacy on what is being reported. News is largely the product of negotiations between journalists and their sources. Without sources to supply quotes or clips, put events in context, and provide background information, journalists would have great difficulty reporting the news. Or as Leon Sigal has summarized this perspective, "Sources make the news."[74]

For most journalists, however, routine reporting does not involve developing a relationship with sources. They work from press releases or reports that have been issued by governments, corporations, or interest groups; attend meetings, press conferences, or events staged for the media; and deal on a once-only basis with participants, onlookers, or victims in a particular situation. The reference here is to those reporters who work regularly with powerholders.

In their book *Negotiating Control*, Richard Ericson, Patricia Baranek, and Janet Chan describe how journalists navigate in a number of different environments: the crime beat, the courts, the Ontario Legislature, and the corporate world.[75] They describe an elaborate and well-defined process by which journalists are blocked, given only partial access, or allowed, in some situations, to enter the inner sanctuaries of established institutions. In this setting journalists and sources often form tacit alliances, for journalists need sources and sources need their stories—or their versions of stories—told. How stories are told usually involves a process of bargaining, sometimes explicit but usually implicit, about the ground rules governing the relationship. In a "free" marketplace, reporters "have multiple and varied sources of knowledge" and sources have a number of journalists and media outlets to choose from.[76] As the nature of events and interests constantly changes, relationships between journalists and their sources are often fleeting. The dance between them is described in considerable detail in Chapter Three.

Herbert Gans found in his pathbreaking study about the structure of news stories in the American media that "knowns," politicians and government officials, outnumbered "unknowns," ordinary people, by a ratio of four to one.[77] Ericson and his associates have argued that seeking out the knowns gives news reporting a conservative bias; for in so doing, journalists legitimize and celebrate the views of those at the apex of power. In their view, "news represents *who* are the authorized knowers and *what* are their authoritative versions of reality."[78] They also note that there is an emphasis in some quarters on "going to the people": doing interviews at streetcorners, profiling how particular events or policies will affect ordinary individuals.[79] In most circumstances, however, journalists seek out sources who have something tangible to offer—leads, confidences, background knowledge—precisely because of their powerful positions.

Table 1.2
Models of Newsmaking

Model	Main Influences	Priorities	Effects
Mirror	Event-Centred	Portray events accurately	News driven by events outside control of owners or journalists
Ownership	Owners	Interests of owners	Support legitimacy of social and economic order
Audience	Consumers	Market forces	"Infotainment," "News You Can Use"
Organizational	The News Organization	Socialization of news-room	Conformity, news fits organizational constraints
Cultural	Canadian Policymakers and Government Regulators	Canadian identity	Canadian content, enhancement of Canadian perspectives
Political	Journalists, Powerholders	Shaping public opinion	Critical reporting

The Many Faces of News

This book contends that, while the media and politicians each have different goals, each can only accomplish their goals with the help of the other. Even as they strike temporary accommodations and alliances, they are locked in an intensive struggle over which message, whose version of events will be conveyed to the public. It's a battle over who will control the public agenda and, ultimately, who will shape public opinion. The news that Canadians receive is dependent to a considerable degree on how this contest for power is conducted. This applies not only to news that one might label as being strictly "political" but also to a wide front of issues—from the environment to the economy, from defence to health care—where politicians want a particular perspective to prevail.

This book does not take the position that any single model is the correct one; in particular circumstances, one or more models may apply. Indeed, news can be seen as a kaleidoscope of shifting factors and situations, a complex mix of changing circumstances. Each model is a powerful but not total explanation of the nature of news. This study pays particular attention to the battle between journalists and politicians to determine the public agenda and shape public opinion. While the battle can sometimes reach epic proportions and amount to nothing less than a fight for survival for leaders and governments, there are other powerful forces that can determine what makes the news.

THEORIES ABOUT MEDIA EFFECTS

To understand the influence that news has on the values and perspectives of Canadians, it is necessary to address the question of media effects. An extensive literature now exists on the impact that the mass media have had in shaping political values and behaviour. The debate over media effects began during the inter-war period when it appeared that press jingoism had helped fuel the hysteria that led to the outbreak of the First World War; when Hollywood films became a primary source of entertainment, learning, and fantasy for tens of millions of people; and when vast populations were being manipulated and subjugated by the propaganda machines of Hitler and Stalin. It appeared that the new technologies of communication, radio and film, were powerful instruments of mass persuasion; there was an Orwellian aspect to these first impressions and considerable anxiety among scholars that new elemental forces were being unleashed on an unsuspecting public.

The first wave of research conducted in the 1920s and 1930s tended to support the view that the media were powerful, pervasive, and could dramatically alter the perceptions and beliefs of entire populations.

Sometimes called the "magic bullet theory," the hypothesis was that media images could directly penetrate people's conscious and unconscious thoughts.

The most persuasive studies during this period were the Payne Fund Studies conducted between 1929 and 1932. These studies examined the effects that movies had on children and adolescents in isolated rural communities in the mid-western United States, communities in which movies were the most significant outside influence. In one study of 1,800 children and adolescents, Herbert Blumer found that movies were a singularly powerful source for learning and imitation. The films strongly affected children's play and fantasies; boys would see themselves as gallant heroes and girls would pretend to be princesses in beautiful gowns.[80] Clothes, mannerisms, language, and ways of relating to the opposite sex were all imitated directly by the adolescents studied. Today, imitating behaviour seen in the media is known as modeling.

One of Blumer's important conclusions was that when his subjects saw experiences depicted in the movies that were beyond their own life experiences, images about the outside experience were shaped primarily by what had been seen at the movies. In one study, high school students who saw the film *Birth of a Nation*, a racist film filled with anti-black stereotypes, developed negative impressions about blacks even though the great majority of them had never actually met or, in many cases, ever seen a black person.[81] If we are to believe the Payne Fund Studies, what Walter Lippmann called the "pictures in our heads" are shaped by the media as much or more than by the real "world outside."[82]

During the 1950s, two scholars at the University of Toronto, Harold Innis and Marshall McLuhan, formulated what came to be called "medium" theories, the idea being that as a new medium becomes dominant, it influences virtually every aspect of human interaction. Innis's idea was that each medium of communication has a "bias" that affects the social and political order in society. The dominant medium of a culture, whether it be stone hieroglyphics or newspapers, determines how learning is diffused, and the extent to which governmental authority is centralized or decentralized.[83] McLuhan's hypothesis was that new forms of communication (oral, print, and electronic) alter people's nervous systems and sensory balance. Each new medium introduces its own mode of consciousness. McLuhan summarized the idea in a famous phrase, "the medium is the message."[84]

A recent book by Joshua Meyrowitz, *No Sense of Place*, has rekindled the debate about whether the media have the power to reshape human environments. Influenced by the ideas of sociologist Erving Goffman, Meyrowitz proposes a comprehensive theory about the impact that television has had on society. He contends that television has reordered the structure of learning, exposed people to "backstages" of life from which they have been excluded, and brought viewers a new range of experiences. Where there was once a strict segmentation of learning based on age—children would be given access to new knowledge only as they moved up the ladder through the school system—television has broken this process down. Meyrowitz claims that as children watched what adults watched, childhood itself was in danger of vanishing. The lives of children and adults became blurred. Similarly, where women were once largely confined to the home and denied entry to many jobs and careers and to the mystery-shrouded world of male exploits, television exposed women to male topics, deflated myths and fears, and gave women a sense of new possibilities. Meyrowitz also argues that television drastically altered the political environment. Once distant figures enveloped and protected by the trappings of power, politicians are now, because of television, mercilessly exposed to public scrutiny. As Meyrowitz writes, "Mystification and awe are supported by distance and limited access. Our new media reveal too much and too often for traditional notions of political leadership to prevail. The television camera invades politicians' personal spheres like a spy in back regions. It watches them sweat, sees them grimace at their own ill-phrased remarks. It cooly records them as they succumb to emotions. The camera minimizes the distance between audience and performer."[85] According to Meyrowitz, "the familiarity fostered by electronic media all too easily breeds contempt."[86] Television, in Meyrowitz's view, changed all of the rules.

A second body of research conducted during the immediate post-war period seemed to refute the magic bullet theory. The "minimal effects" theory that emerged out of this research held sway in the scholarly community well into the 1970s. Some studies found that people watch or read selectively and in accordance with their previous beliefs.[87] There is selective exposure and retention as the mask of pre-existing beliefs screen out uncomfortable or uncongenial views. The need to maintain cognitive balance is so enormous that people aggressively defend the integrity of the mental pictures that they already have; preconceptions are only hardened by exposure to the media. Doris Graber has developed an offshoot of this theory based on the presence of "schemata," which she defines as "a cognitive structure consisting of organized knowledge about situations and individuals that has been abstracted from prior experience."[88] Graber found that people erect cognitive structures in order to cope with the "flood-tides" of media information they face each day.[89] Schemata allow people to select, process, interpret, and assimilate new information based on their personal dispositions and interests. Where Graber's theory differs from previous ideas about cognitive balance is that she sees schemata as a flexible way for people to scan the horizon for information that meets their needs rather than as a rigid set of beliefs, an ideological fortress, that has to be defended.

Studies also showed that people are shaped by a series of formative relationships and experiences; through family, peers, educational institutions, and religious bonds.[90] Information from the mass media was mediated through these institutions: the magic bullets were blunted by heavy layers of social and psychological experience, moreover, their effect also depended on individual circumstances. Senior citizens were likely to be more attentive to news about pensions, and members of ethnic communities more alert to developments in their countries of origin. Research on "uses and gratifications" indicated that people use the media to fulfill basic needs. While one person may follow a particular news story or pick up a book or magazine because of their business interests, another person may just want to keep up with current events or the latest films so that they can chat with neighbours. Keeping on top of the latest developments may provide a sense of adequacy and fulfillment for others. Media effects depended on a complex interplay between audience, message, and society. As Bernard Berelson summarized the main current of thinking among the minimal effects theorists of the 1940s and 1950s, "Some kinds of communication on some kinds of issues, brought to the attention of some kinds of people under some kinds of conditions have some kinds of effects."[91]

Another body of literature dealt with the effects of television news. There was evidence to suggest that television was a passive experience, with viewers paying only scant attention as news stories flittered by one after another. In one study people could not "recall in any fashion" more than one or two items out of an entire newscast.[92] It was thought that television tended to put mental processes into second gear, sedating people so that they could relax and "veg" out. It was dead time. Others contended that television news was so devoid of substance, so light and breezy, that it couldn't have anything but the most limited impact. In a study of television coverage of the 1976 presidential election, Paterson and McClure concluded that "Since the nightly news is too brief to treat fully the complexity of modern politics, too visual to present effectively most events, and too entertainment-minded to tell viewers much worth knowing, most network newscasts are neither very educational nor very powerful communicators."[93] They argued that television news coverage had had no impact on voting behaviour during the presidential election.

Despite these studies, a new wave of concern about television's long-term effects swelled again in the 1970s. Previous studies were criticized for being too narrow and for measuring effects over relatively short time spans. Whether there was a cumulative impact over time had not been evaluated. Veteran teachers had begun to notice differences between the new TV generation and their previous students: the downward slide in Scholastic Aptitude scores, shorter attention spans, increased pessimism and cynicism. Jerzy Kosinski was among those who expressed worry. He gave the following alarming assessment: "Go into any high school and see how limited students' perceptions of themselves is [sic], how crippled their imaginations, how unable they are to tell a story, to read or concentrate, or even to describe an event accurately a moment after it happens. See how easily they are bored, how quickly they take up the familiar 'reclining' position in the classroom, how short their attention span is."[94] As a result of these concerns, the National Institute of Mental Health in the United States conducted a sweeping analysis of the existing scientific literature. One of their principal findings was that there was a consistent association between heavy TV viewing and an increase in aggressive behaviour. (Sociologist David Phillips has found recently that the number of homicides in the United States increases significantly after each nationally televised heavyweight championship match.[95]) Their review also found that exposure to the right kinds of television could produce co-operative behaviour, generosity and friendliness.[96] Television could be both saviour and villain.

A serious re-evaluation also took place among scholars interested in the political impact of media coverage. A third stream of research emerged in the 1970s and 1980s that took a middle position between the magic bullet theory and the minimal effects thesis. This conceptual breakthrough was tied to new ideas about agenda-setting and priming.

It was Walter Lippmann who first formulated the proposition that "the function of news is to signalize an event."[97] He meant by this that the mass media had the power to alert the public about which events were important and to set the context within which those events could be understood. Bernard Cohen, whose research was conducted during the 1960s, argued that, "The press is significantly more than a purveyor of information and opinion. It may not be successful much of the time in telling people what to think, but it is stunningly successful in telling its readers what to think about."[98] The term "agenda-setting" was first coined by Maxwell McCombs and Donald Shaw in a pathbreaking but limited research study on media coverage and voter responses during the 1968 U.S. presidential election. Their conclusion was that "the data suggest a very strong relationship between the emphasis placed on different campaign issues by the media (reflecting to a considerable degree the emphasis by the candidates) and the judgments of the voters as to the salience and importance of various campaign topics."[99] Thus a direct correlation seemed to exist between the issues given prominence by the media and the issues that were prominent in the minds of voters. Subsequent studies tended to support the agenda-setting hypothesis but suggested that the media's influence could be blunted under certain circumstances, for example, when the media source was not considered credible or reliable, an individual had personal experience that contradicted what had been described in media accounts, or a person had views so radically opposed to those reflected in the media that news reports were routinely discounted by that individual.[100]

Studies conducted by Shanto Iyengar and Donald Kinder, reported in their book *News That Matters*, have yielded rich insights. Network newscasts assembled from stories that had been previously broadcast were shown to a selected sample of participants. They found, as had other studies on agenda-setting, that lead stories were more influential than were stories at the middle or at the end of newscasts. They discovered, contrary to expectations, that news items that were visually powerful, revealing "flesh and blood" or the human dimension to problems, did not have a greater impact than stories that were less vivid or personal.[101] Iyengar and Kinder also identified a phenomenon that they called "priming." Priming the audience means that "By calling attention to some matters while ignoring others, television news influences the standards by which governments, presidents, policies, and candidates for public office are judged."[102] If stories about the environment are lead items in television news broadcasts for a significant time period, then environmental issues will become a litmus test for evaluating government and politicians. If the news focus should switch to economic issues, then the economy would soon become the bench-mark used by the public to evaluate their leaders.

Iyengar and Kinder also stress that there are limits to the media's agenda-setting and priming capacity. News organizations cannot sustain a story that flies in the face of objective reality, for instance, viewers cannot be convinced by news reports that the economy is buoyant if the realities of everyday life point to the opposite. Their position is that "the networks can neither create national problems where there are none nor conceal problems that actually exist."[103] They believe, however, that television has become "an imposing authority" whose power to alter the priorities of citizens is "virtually without peer."[104]

Some scholars have moved beyond the problems of agenda-setting to tackle the difficult question of agenda-building. The principal concern in agenda-building is to identify the forces and processes that have gone into the construction of the public agenda. Agenda-building is the product of the dynamic interaction of a large number of interests and conditions. In a study of agenda-building during the Watergate scandal, for example, Kurt and Gladys Lang found a "complex feedback" process whereby the Nixon administration, the news media, and public opinion each influenced the reactions of one another. This led to a chain reaction of causes and effects.[105] Everett Rogers and James Dearing have pointed out that nine possible relationships exist: "The media's influence upon itself, the public, and policymakers; the public's influence upon itself, the media, and policymakers; and policymakers' influence upon themselves, the media, and the public."[106] They argue that each relationship in this three-by-three matrix represents a gap in our knowledge that needs to be filled.

Table 1.3
Three-by-Three Matrix of Agenda-Building

Reactors	*Actors*		
	media	public	policymakers
media	media media	public media	policymakers media
public	media public	public public	policymakers public
policymakers	media policymakers	public policymakers	policymakers policymakers

Some would argue that the Rogers-Dearing model does not capture the interdependence of all of the parts or account for the social and economic forces that underlie each of the relationships. Neither does it portray the energy expended when the variables collide. The reality, in other words, is more than the sum of the parts shown in the matrix model. A systems model of agenda-building might better explain the interactive and highly charged nature of what actually takes place.

Table 1.4
Systems Model of Agenda-Building

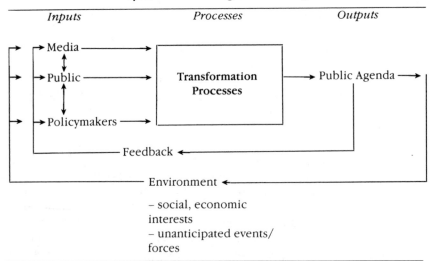

This book, in focusing on the relationship between the media and politicians, examines only one set of variables among many in a complex mosaic. Given the weight of scholarly evidence about media effects, it would be foolish to deny that the media play a role in shaping the public agenda and have, as a consequence, an effect on political outcomes. Scholars in Canada have for too long neglected the power that the media have to set the stage on which political drama is acted out, and the lengths to which political leaders have gone in adjusting themselves to the new technologies of power. This study will examine how the cut and thrust of this interaction has shaped the worlds of both journalism and politics.

NOTES

1. Mark Starowicz, "Open Skies: The Struggle For Canada's Airwaves," The Atkinson Lecture at Ryerson Polytechnical Institute, 12 March 1985, p. 3.
2. Ibid.
3. Ronald Rotenberg, *Advertising: A Canadian Perspective* (Toronto: Allyn and Bacon, 1986), p. 2.
4. Todd Gitlin, *The Whole World is Watching* (Berkeley: The University of California Press, 1980), p. 2.
5. Ancil Kashetsky, "Media Coverage of Gaza Disturbances Attacked," *Canadian Jewish News*, 4 February 1988, p. 22.
6. Ibid.
7. Quoted in Daniel Hallin, *The Uncensored War: The Media And Vietnam* (Berkeley: The University of California Press, 1986), p. 5.
8. Hallin, p. 9.
9. *Report of the Committee on Broadcasting* (Ottawa: Queen's Printer, 1965), p. 4.
10. Canadian Broadcasting Corporation, *Journalistic Policy* (Ottawa, 1982), p. 9.
11. Interview with Mark Starowicz, Toronto, 21 May 1986.
12. Theodore Peterson, "The Social Responsibility Theory," in Fred Siebert, Theodore Peterson, and Wilbur Schramm, *Four Theories Of The Press* (Chicago: University of Illinois Press, 1956), p. 87.
13. Quoted in Michael Parenti, *Inventing Reality: The Politics of the Mass Media* (New York: St. Martin's Press, 1986), p. 30.
14. Edward Herman and Noam Chomsky, *Manufacturing Consent: The Political Economy of the Mass Media* (New York: Pantheon, 1988), p. 14.
15. Parenti, p. 27. Perhaps the most significant study of the news process in Canada written from a political economy perspective is Robert Hackett's *Peace and the News* (forthcoming).

16. Patrick Parsons, John Finnegan, Jr., and William Benham, "Editors and Their Roles," in *Press Concentration and Monopoly*, Robert Picard et al., eds. (Norwood, New Jersey: Ablex Publishing, 1988), p. 97.

17. D'Arcy Jenish, "Media Wars," Maclean's, 17 July 1989, p. 29; Susan Goldenberg, *The Thomson Empire* (Toronto: Methuen, 1984), Ch. 1.

18. James Winter, "Interlocking Directorships and Economic Power," in Picard et al., p. 112.

19. Goldenberg, p. 12.

20. Fraser Michaels, "The Globe Wars," *Saturday Night*, December 1989, p. 44.

21. Jenish, p. 29.

22. Quoted in John Partridge, "Citizen Black," *The Globe and Mail*, 25 July 1987, p. D6.

23. John DeMont, "An Emerging Media Baron," *Maclean's*, 17 July 1989, p. 28.

24. Ibid.

25. Winter, p. 107.

26. Ibid, p. 111.

27. William Thorsell, "The Paper Chase," *Report On Business Magazine*, March 1989, pp. 25-27.

28. Lise Bissonnette, "Peladeau Unfurls Another Sheet," *The Globe and Mail*, 1 October 1988.

29. Harvey Enchin, "Bad Boy Made Good," *Report On Business Magazine*, September 1987, p. 32.

30. Bertrand Marcotte, "The Prince of Pulp," *Financial Times of Canada*, 6 November 1989, p. 22.

31. Enchin, p. 35.

32. Ibid.

33. Patricia Poirier, "Quebec Magazine Retracts Péladeau Article," *The Globe and Mail*, 7 April 1990, p. A3.

34. Enchin, p. 35.

35. Kevin Dougherty "Peladeau-Maxwell Match Unites Two Unpredictables," *The Financial Post*, 13 February 1989, p. 27.

36. Alexander Bruce, "Lords of the Atlantic," *The Globe and Mail*, 21 February 1987, p. D1.

37. John J. Pauly, "Rupert Murdoch and the Demonology of Professional Journalism," in *Media, Myths, and Narratives*, James Carey, ed. (Beverly Hills: Sage, 1988), p. 250. The extent of Murdoch's influence is questioned in W.H.N. Hull, "Public Policy and the Ownership of the Mass Media in Canada and Australia," a paper presented to the Canadian Political Science Association Meeting, Windsor, Ontario, June 1988, p. 20.

38. Quoted in Ted Magder, "Taking Culture Seriously: A Political Economy of Communications," in *The New Canadian Political Economy*, Wallace Clement and Glen Williams, eds. (Montreal: McGill-Queen's University Press, 1989), p. 283.
39. Ibid., p. 284.
40. Herbert Gans, *Deciding What's News* (New York: Vintage, 1980), pp. 9-13.
41. Richard Ericson, Patricia Baranek, and Janet Chan, *Visualizing Deviance: A Study of News Organization* (Toronto: University of Toronto Press, 1987).
42. Quoted in Ericson, Baranek, and Chan, pp. 7-8.
43. Quoted in Mark Hertsgaard, *On Bended Knee: The Press and the Reagan Presidency* (New York: Farrar, Straus, Giroux, 1988), p. 90.
44. Parenti, p. 36.
45. Peter Desbarats, *Guide to Canadian News Media* (Toronto: Harcourt, Brace, Jovanovich, 1989), p. 101.
46. F. Dennis Hale, "Editorial Diversity and Concentration," in Picard et al., p. 163.
47. *Royal Commission on Newspapers* (Ottawa: Supply and Services Canada, 1981), p. 1.
48. Quoted in Hale, p. 164.
49. Dores Candussi and James Winter, "Monopoly and Content in Winnipeg," in Picard et al., p. 139. For a wider discussion, see Fred Fletcher, *The Newspaper and Public Affairs*, vol. VII of the *Royal Commission on Newspapers* (Ottawa: Supply and Services Canada, 1981), Ch. 3.
50. Ibid., pp. 144-45.
51. Ronald Wagenberg and Walter Soderlund, "The Effects of Chain Ownership on Editorial Coverage: The Case of the 1974 Canadian General Election," *Canadian Journal of Political Science* (December 1976), pp. 682-689; see Ronald Wagenberg et al., *Media and Elections in Canada* (Toronto: Holt, Rinehart and Winston, 1984).
52. Desbarats, p. 95.
53. Neil Postman, *Amusing Ourselves to Death* (New York: Penguin, 1985), p. 87.
54. Quoted in W. Lance Bennett, *TV News: The Politics of Illusion* (New York: Longman, 1988), p. 3.
55. Bennett, p. 5.
56. Hertsgaard, pp. 173-74.
57. Morris Wolfe, *Jolts: The TV Wasteland and the Canadian Oasis* (Toronto: Lorimer, 1985).
58. Quoted in Peter Desbarats, "Radio and Television News: The Roles of Public and Private Broadcasters and Some Other Critical Issues," *Report for the Task Force on Broadcasting Policy*, February 1986, p. 18.

59. Gitlin, p. 29.
60. Warren Breed, "Social Control in the Newsroom," *Social Forces* (1955), pp. 326-35; Leon Sigal, *Reporters and Officials* (Lexington, Massachusetts: D.C. Heath, 1973); Edward Jay Epstein, *News From Nowhere* (New York: Vintage, 1973); and Herbert Gans, *Deciding What's News* (New York: Vintage, 1980).
61. Epstein, p. xviii.
62. Quoted in Epstein, p. 3.
63. Interview with CBC producer, Toronto, 15 July 1987.
64. Quoted in Ernest Leiser, "See It Now: The Decline of Network News," *Washington Journalism Review* (January/February 1988), p. 50.
65. J. Richard Finlay, "Uneasy on the Campus," *The Globe and Mail*, 14 July 1988, p. A7.
66. *Report of the Task Force on Broadcasting Policy* (Ottawa: Supply and Services Canada, 1986), pp. 691-93.
67. Magder, p. 288.
68. *Report of the Task Force on Broadcasting Policy*, Ch. 8.
69. John Meisel, "Escaping Extinction: Cultural Defence of an Undefended Border," in *Southern Exposure: Canadian Perspectives on the United States*, David Flaherty and William McKercher, eds. (Toronto: McGraw-Hill Ryerson, 1986), p. 152.
70. Colin Hoskins, Rolf Mirus, and William Rozeboom, "U.S. Television Programs in the International Market: Unfair Pricing?" *Journal of Communication* (Spring 1989), pp. 56-57.
71. *Journalistic Policy*, p. 3.
72. Interview with Mark Starowicz.
73. Interview with David Nayman. For an in-depth analysis of the differences between Canadian and American news broadcasts, see Stuart Surlin, Walter Romanow, and Walter Soderlund, "TV Network News: A Canadian–American Comparison," *American Review of Canadian Studies* (1988), pp.465-75.
74. Leon Sigal, "Who? Sources Make the News," in *Reading The News*, Robert Manoff and Michael Schudson, eds. (New York: Pantheon, 1986), p. 9.
75. Richard Ericson, Patricia Baranek, and Janet Chan, *Negotiating Control: A Study of News Sources* (Toronto: University of Toronto Press, 1989).
76. Ericson, Baranek, and Chan, *Visualizing Deviance*, p. 16.
77. Gans, pp. 9-13.
78. Ericson, Baranek, and Chan, *Visualizing Deviance*, p. 3.
79. Ibid, p. 15.
80. Shearon Lowery and Melvin Defleur, *Milestones in Mass Communications Research* (New York: Longman, 1988), pp. 44-46.
81. Ibid., pp. 40-41.

82. Walter Lippmann, *Public Opinion* (New York: Free Press, 1922).
83. Harold Innis, *The Bias of Communication* (Toronto: University of Toronto Press, 1951).
84. Marshall McLuhan, *Understanding Media* (Scarborough, Ontario: The New American Library of Canada, 1964).
85. Joshua Meyrowitz, *No Sense of Place* (New York: Oxford University Press, 1985), p. 271.
86. Ibid., p. 276.
87. Carl Hovland, Irving Janis, and Harold Kelley, *Communication and Persuasion* (New Haven: Yale University Press, 1953); Elihu Katz and Paul Lazarsfeld, *Personal Influence: The Part Played by People in the Flow of Mass Communication* (Glencoe, Illinois: The Free Press of Glencoe, 1955); and Joseph Klapper, *The Effects of the Mass Media* (Glencoe, Illinois: The Free Press of Glencoe, 1960).
88. Doris Graber, *Processing The News* (New York: Longman, 1988), p. 28.
89. Ibid., p. 29.
90. Paul Lazarsfeld, Bernard Berelson, and Hazel Gaudet, *The People's Choice* (New York: Columbia University Press, 1948).
91. Quoted in Edwin Diamond and Stephen Bates, *The Spot* (Cambridge: Massachusetts Institute of Technology, 1988), p. 351.
92. Graber, p. 250.
93. Thomas Patterson and Robert McClure, *The Unseeing Eye: The Myth of Television Power in National Elections* (New York: Putnam, 1976), p. 90.
94. "David Sohn Interviews Jerzy Kosinski: A Nation of Videots," in *Television: The Critical View*, Horace Newcomb, ed. (New York: Oxford University Press, 1982), p. 360.
95. "Ban Boxing," *The New Republic*, 8 and 15 August 1988, 7.
96. Lowery and Defleur, p. 372.
97. Lippmann.
98. Bernard Cohen, *The Press and Foreign Policy* (Princeton, N.J.: Princeton University Press, 1963), p. 13.
99. Quoted in Lowery and Defleur, p. 331.
100. Everett Rogers and James Dearing, "Agenda-Setting Research: Where Has It Been, Where Is It Going?" in *Communications Yearbook* II, James Anderson, ed. (Beverley Hills: Sage, 1988), p. 569.
101. Shanto Iyengar and Donald Kinder, *News That Matters* (Chicago: University of Chicago Press, 1987), Ch. 4.
102. Ibid., p. 63.
103. Ibid., p. 118.
104. Ibid., pp. 116, 133.
105. Rogers and Dearing, p. 577.
106. Ibid., p. 582.

PART 2
MEDIA

Robert Mankoff, the *Saturday Review*

"Dad, if a tree falls in the forest, and the media aren't there to cover it, has the tree really fallen?"

2

Canadian Journalists: From Servants to Power Brokers

The argument that the relationship between politicians and the media shapes much of our news must begin with an examination of how that often stormy relationship has changed in recent Canadian history. There is little question that journalists have, over time, gained considerable power both within the newsmaking process and in society. Once largely the servants of the organizations they worked for, following blindly the whims and dictates of their publishers, Canadian journalists have achieved significant professional status, considerable discretion over what they can say, write, and do and, with this, the ability at times to set the political agenda. From being the handmaidens of the political parties, journalists have gained at least an even hand and some would even say the upper hand in their relations with politicians. Prominent journalists enjoy recognition and prestige and can, on occasion, have significant influence. The journalistic elite has emerged in the 1990s as one of the most important groups in the country and one of the least studied.

The power of journalists is exercised in a number of ways. The most salient fact is that journalists, as a group, can prevent some aspects of a politician's or a government's message from reaching the public. They can do this by not covering events such as speeches or news conferences that are important to politicians, or covering them in such a way that political appeals are filtered, blunted, or discredited. Journalists determine which eight- or twelve-second visual clips or which quotations will be used in their stories. They also decide how much attention to give to the views of opponents, and to the political motives behind a particular proposal, appointment, or policy, and the flaws that may exist in it. They can screen out some messages while widely exposing others. They have the power to take events out of one context and recontextualize them so that they fit the media's requirements for a good story. Collectively, they have the power to be the gatekeeper of public information. Moreover, news organizations are "the arbiters" of the political system: they have the power to legitimize and delegitimize leaders, policies, and institutions.

This chapter will describe the evolution in the relationship between journalists and politicians by examining the attitudes and practices that prevailed in different eras. The partisan press, the culture of objective professionalism, and critical journalism will each be discussed. Aspects of each of these phases or models exist today, although critical journalism is now predominant. Through each phase, journalists have gained in power and prestige and in the ability to affect political agendas.

THE PARTY PRESS

Newspapers first developed in Canada in the eighteenth century as official gazettes. As the costs of printing presses and paper and the small readership in a society where education was not widespread made publishing uneconomical, government assistance was needed for presses to become established and survive. The colonial authorities, authoritarian and suspicious of subversion, maintained control of the press. The first newspapers announced the dates of ship arrivals and court hearings, published edicts and laws, and delivered some news from the home country. Editorial comment was highly restricted.

Dramatic changes occurred in the period from 1812 to Confederation as the press won considerable independence from government. The replacement of the hand printing press by the steam-powered cylinder press, the advent of the telegraph and railways, urbanization, and growing literacy brought the beginnings of the popular press and the daily newspaper. The colonial regime came under attack and a dynamic political life emerged, the major catalyst being the fight for responsible government and the turmoil of the Rebellions of 1837-38. William Lyon Mackenzie's *The Colonial Advocate*, Joseph Howe's *The Novascotian*, Étienne Parent's *Le Canadien*, and George Brown's *The Toronto Globe* were reform organs committed to sweeping away the privileges of the Family Compact and the Château Clique. In fact, the phrase "Family Compact" was first coined by Mackenzie.[1] The shackles placed on publishers by the colonial authorities were broken, although this did not occur without struggle and difficulties. During the 1820s and 1830s, publishers were quite often threatened, beaten, censored, put on trial, jailed, and bankrupted by the authorities. William Lyon Mackenzie and Joseph Howe fought and won important court battles that helped to ensure the right to publish freely. What was most important was that the economic ground had shifted: the growth of circulation and advertising made newspapers less dependent on government. Newspaper publishing had become a profit-making venture.

This was the era of firebrand journalism. Independent and strident, full of righteous indignation, the reform press could not be controlled even by the reform parties. Their anger and the vehemence with which they flayed their enemies was usually at a fever pitch. An often cited example of Mackenzie's style was a headline that appeared in *The Colonial Advocate* on 2 May 1833. It screamed:

Glorious Triumph!!!
Downfall of the Upper Canadian Oligarchy!
And Complete Success of Liberal Sentiments
   Over Tory Avarice!!!
Huzza for Reform!!! God Save the King!!![2]

Another example of the zealous approach to politics taken by newspapers during this period were the "famed and feared" editorials of *The Globe*.[3] They were, according to Paul Rutherford, "an inexhaustible well-spring of moral indignation. . . . The Globe in full frenzy was a marvellous engine of destruction."[4] Opponents were "torn to pieces."[5] An editorial that appeared on 5 November 1873 flaying John A. Macdonald was typical of the *Globe* approach:

> Sir John Macdonald has spoken. The Hector of corruption has come forward to defend his citadels, and he has discharged his task with his callous and repulsive valour, which yet challenges admiration, when we consider that he shook his spear not merely at the Achilles of the Opposition, but defied all the principles of right and justice, every dictate of morality, every sanction of conscience, every prescription of decency which belongs to the people of Canada. . . . We have heard of men who had the courage of their convictions. Sir John A. Macdonald surpasses these. He has the unique glory of having the courage of his corruption.[6]

The colonial regime was not without vigorous defenders of its own. William Pope's *Charlottetown Islander*, *Hamilton Spectator*, *Kingston Herald*, and *Montreal Gazette* and the ultramontane press in Quebec were among those that fought the reformers tooth and nail. Publishers also found that partisanship could have economic rewards. Strong political stances were one way of securing a loyal readership and also of attracting financial backers and advertisers. The newspaper market was soon segmented along political lines, with most major cities having at least two newspapers with differing political convictions.

The period from Confederation to the First World War was the heyday of the party press. As political parties formed—the consolidation of the Liberal and Conservative parties taking some time to occur in the post-Confederation period—newspapers were seized upon as the principal vehicle of propaganda, communication, and campaigning. Politicians were continually founding, financing, supporting, capturing, or deposing publishers and newspapers. The struggle for newspaper control was intense and brutal. In the mid- to late nineteenth century, Conservative backers founded the *Toronto Mail*, the *Toronto Empire*, and *La Presse*, although the Montreal paper was to change its allegiance. Sir Wilfrid Laurier had a hand in various schemes surrounding the emergence of *La Patrie*, *Le Soleil*, and *La Bataille*. His government also bailed out the failing *Montreal Herald* with a series of lucrative printing contracts.[7] Eventually each party had at least one representative newspaper in every major centre: in Toronto, the *Telegram* was Conservative, the *Star* was Liberal; in Vancouver, the *Sun* was Liberal while the *Province* was Conservative; and in Winnipeg, the *Free Press* flew the Liberal banner, the *Tribune* the Conservative. *The Regina Star* was established to back Conservative R.B. Bennett and combat the influence of the *Leader-Post*, which supported the Liberals.[8] The battle lines were well-defined. The glue holding the system in place was the promise of government printing contracts and advertising, loyal partisan readerships, and political parties dependent almost solely on newspapers as their primary means of reaching the public.

The relationship that existed between publishers and politicians during the era of the party press is one of the most interesting and critical interactions in Canadian political life. Clifford Sifton and J.W. Dafoe of the *Free Press*, Joseph Atkinson of *The Toronto Star*, Berthiaume of *La Presse*, and much later figures such as J.W. McConnell of *The Montreal Star*, John Bassett of the *Telegram*, and Jacob Nicol of *Le Soleil*, were like planets in their party's solar system. There was considerable friction in many of the relationships as strong disagreements sometimes overpowered mutual interests. Bruce Hutchison has offered this description of the influence of Dafoe's *Free Press* and its role within the Liberal party constellation:

> By Dafoe's method it moved like a turgid, relentless river, heavy with silt, slowly building up the alluvial delta of public opinion. It might bore the reader but it impressed him by its perpetual motion. . . . The newspaper had become almost a geographical fact on the Prairies. While it had long been linked organically with the Liberal Party, it was by no means a government organ. It was just the opposite—a critic, gadfly, and self-appointed conscience that the government feared, tried to mollify, and for the most part, hated.[9]

Still Laurier confided in Dafoe and the *Free Press* publisher was aware of cabinet discussions;[10] similarly, Mackenzie King would often phone Dafoe to discuss the latest government business. Joseph Atkinson, who battled King for years on many issues and maintained the *Star's* independence from the Liberal party, was still a frequent guest at King's home. When the publisher died in 1948, King was moved to write of his strong "lifelong bond" with Atkinson. He also made frequent pilgrimages to Mrs. Atkinson's grave.[11] Henri Bourassa's *Le Devoir* remained a robust critic of Liberal policies, even as Bourassa, himself, sat as a Liberal MP. *Le Devoir* would eventually leave the Liberal fold.

Yet certain things could be depended on. On most occasions, party newspapers were effusive in their enthusiasm for the party program and their coverage of the leader verged on idolatry. There was not even the veneer of objectivity: the party paper's mission was to glorify its friends and slay its enemies. As Paul Rutherford has described it, "In victory the organ gloated, telling all readers right had triumphed; in defeat the organ counselled courage and perseverance, sure evil would fail in the end."[12]

Reporters sent to cover Ottawa on behalf of party newspapers often enjoyed a special status as the "ambassadors" of their powerful bosses. When the *Toronto Globe* sent John Willison to report from the Press Gallery in 1887, he was given a year to contact Liberal party leaders and learn about the party's program before assuming his responsibilities.[13] On being invited for dinner by a Conservative cabinet minister, he had to seek his publisher's permission because even a polite dinner could be seen as indicating some disloyalty by his paper to the Liberal cause.[14] In his memoirs, Grattan O'Leary describes how he was sent by his paper, the Conservative *Ottawa Journal*, to accompany Prime Minister Arthur Meighen to London in 1921 both as a reporter and as the prime minister's aide.[15] Reporters' loyalties were so apparent that, until at least 1911, they sat in the Press Gallery according to party affiliation; journalists representing Conservative newspapers sat on one side of the Speaker, with journalists from Liberal papers seated on the other side.[16]

While the party press system went into sharp decline after the Second World War, some aspects of it remained visible well into the 1960s and traces of it can still be detected today. In his memoirs, Peter Dempson recalled the heat of partisan combat and the advice he received about how to cover the 1949 federal election for *The Toronto Telegram*, which supported the Conservative party led by George Drew: "If St. Laurent is speaking and one or two people boo, play up the interruption. Pay little attention to the applause. If he draws a big crowd, but fails to arouse them, write that up. If he attracts several thousand people to a meeting, but there are still some empty seats, play up the angle that St. Laurent failed to pack the hall."[17] Dempson explained that, "The *Telegram* would seize on every opportunity to attack St. Laurent and praise Drew. The *Star* did just the opposite. Journalistic scruples and ethics went out the window."[18] J. W. Pickersgill has commented that "Liberal propaganda during the 1949 election paled beside that of the *Star*."[19] Indeed, during that 1949 election the *Star* whipped itself into such a hysteria that at the close of the election campaign its banner headline, denouncing Drew and his Quebec lieutenant Camillien Houde, read:

Keep Canada British
Destroy Drew's Houde
God Save The King[20]

According to Robin Sears, the characterizations of socialist candidates that appeared during the 1940s and 1950s were so "staggering" that they would "shock *Toronto Sun* readers today."[21]

Political combat was not always waged at such a fever pitch; more often the tone of reporting was softer and more subtle. W.A. Wilson has described the attitude of *The Montreal Star's* powerful publisher, J.W. McConnell, in the 1940s and 1950s: "McConnell certainly called the shots especially with regard to provincial politics. He made the paper pro-Duplessis. Federally they weren't so much pro-Liberal as they took it for granted that the Liberals were the governing party."[22]

The heavy hand of political loyalty had not disappeared in the 1960s but it was less obvious. Dalton Camp, the Conservative Party's long-time election and advertising impresario, remembers how on the eve of the 1966 vote on whether John Diefenbaker should remain as Conservative Party leader, a reporter for *The Toronto Telegram* was uncertain about what to write because owner John Bassett appeared to be changing his mind about whom to support.[23] Veteran journalist Val Sears has told of being ordered to write puff-pieces about Conservative Party candidates, articles that were so flattering that they were used by the candidates in their election material.[24] Beland Honderich of *The Toronto Star*, perhaps the last of the titans, insisted in the early 1960s that Liberal Walter Gordon's national views about the economy be given wide coverage. According to one of the paper's editors, Gordon's statements were treated as if they were "an announcement of the second coming."[25]

As prime ministers and cabinet ministers maintained close links with reporters from newspapers sympathetic to their parties, journalists from the opposing camp were often frozen out. Sometimes relationships would form based on mutual sympathy rather than on the political allegiance of the newspapers that the journalists represented. The "in" reporters sometimes became the confidants of those in power; their advice would be sought, they were part of the party "brain trust," they would be tipped off about important new moves. While Prime Minister Diefenbaker usually met once a week with Richard Jackson of *The Ottawa Journal* and Peter Dempson of *The Toronto Telegram*, Patrick Nicholson of the Thomson chain, Jim Osler of *The Montreal Star* and Bob Needham of *The London Free Press* were also part of the inner circle. King, St. Laurent, and Lester B. Pearson each had their networks. In Pearson's day, Anthony Westell of *The Globe and Mail*, W.A. Wilson of *The Montreal Star*, and Blair Fraser of *Maclean's* were especially trusted. Reporters could benefit enormously from these close relationships. They were sometimes given important scoops or leads, they often enjoyed greater access to others in the government, and were read and became influential because they were known to have key connections and inside information. W.A. Wilson has commented on how Jim Osler reaped the benefits of being one of Diefenbaker's confidants: "Osler was freely given information that would have been denied to the rest of the press, often so that he could break stories. Even background information from a head of government can be very valuable."[26] On one occasion Osler was invited to Diefenbaker's home so that the prime minister could have his views about prospective cabinet appointments.[27] Their professional status, far from being diminished or tainted by their strong association with the government, seemed to be greatly enhanced.

The relationship between prime ministers and their journalistic allies was much like a chess game. Each side had its own agenda and employed a variety of strategies to get the most for themselves out of the relationship. Both sides maintained a wary eye for the maneuvers of the other. Peter Dempson has described the "cat and mouse" game that Diefenbaker played during his weekly get-togethers with Dempson and Richard Jackson. According to Dempson, "Diefenbaker enjoyed fencing with us, teasing us along. Jackson was always anxious to uncover a good civil service story, since there were close to fifty thousand government employees in the *Journal's* circulation area. Diefenbaker would seize on this . . . by dropping vague remarks about developments in this field. Sometimes the Prime Minister would have something for him; more times he did not."[28] Jackson, of course, had difficulty judging what was real and what wasn't and could be tugged along as Diefenbaker saw fit. Diefenbaker often wanted the reporters to "fly kites for him"[29] on new appointments or policy initiatives, so that public opinion could be tested before any moves were made. He also saw these contacts as a way for his version of events and his opinions to get through to the public. For Diefenbaker the meetings were a kind of catharsis, they allowed him to smolder and blow off steam and feel somehow that the truth, as he saw it, was being recorded. The danger for the reporters was that they were often used in ways that made them look foolish, and their credibility with bosses, colleagues, and readers was jeopardized as a result.

One of the most famous cases of a journalist being called on to aid a party leader was when Bruce Hutchison was called back to Ottawa from Washington in 1957 to conduct a television interview with Lester Pearson. Together they came up with the questions to be asked and rehearsed how the interview was to be conducted. Hutchison was treated as a loyal member of the Liberal team with little thought that he might betray secrets or write an exclusive story about what had taken place.[30]

In some places, the game was played less subtly. Under Quebec Premier Maurice Duplessis, many reporters accepted payments in exchange for writing positive stories about the Premier. He would literally dish out five and ten dollar bills to reporters who would attend one of his speeches or news conferences. Until 1960 members of the Quebec Press Gallery received an annual "stationary allowance."[31] In British Columbia similar rules seemed to apply. In 1981, the Royal Commission on Newspapers quoted a member of the British Columbia Press Gallery as saying that, "When I first came to the gallery (ten years ago) . . . half the gallery was on the government payroll, either directly or indirectly."[32]

From the vantage point of the 1990s, the intense partisanship, the intricate webs of personal loyalty and ideological conviction, seem part of a distant past. Although not nearly as obvious or as institutionalized as before, political biases, however, are certainly not absent from today's reporting. Political bias occurs on two levels. First, as described in Chapter One, publishers with strong partisan views can shape the outlook of their papers either by direct intervention in the editorial process, or because editors and reporters anticipate reactions and write stories that they know will please their publishers. According to Val Sears of *The Toronto Star*, for close to three decades, until Beland Honderich's retirement in 1988, reporters at that paper spent a good deal of their time in the "dusty" enterprise of trying to determine how their publisher, a man with firm views on many issues, would react to their work.[33] Walter Stewart recounts the following story from the 1970s about Honderich's (known at the paper as BHH) overpowering influence:

> The need to placate BHH is so strong that editors and writers often subvert their own judgment to what they think the boss will want. Anticipatory editing is the worst kind. One of the paper's best reporters during my time there proposed a series of stories on a major food company. She had gathered a great deal of information about the company, some of it damaging. She gave up the idea, however, not because her editors rejected the series, but because she was sure it would only lead to trouble. "BHH won't like it," she said. He was never given the chance to find out.[34]

A news-room culture can be created: publishers can hire and promote reporters who fit their image and hold their views and beliefs. It can also be created by more subtle means: the pecking order for important assignments, the degree of editorial supervision, the likelihood of advancement or promotion, the type of atmosphere hanging over the news-room that signals a way of looking at the world and the parameters of what is acceptable. A right-wing shift at the senior levels of *The Globe and Mail* in 1989 has reverberated throughout the newspaper. Reporters conceivably are reluctant to push stories on some topics in particular to a management that has signaled its preference for other kinds of stories.[35]

A distinction has to be made between the partisanship of news organizations and the partisanship of journalists as individuals or as a group. That reporters themselves may have beliefs that colour their reporting is the second level on which political bias operates. In a well-known study conducted in 1979 and 1980, Robert Lichter and his associates found that journalists working for leading American news organizations tended to be far more liberal than other members of their society, for example, they overwhelmingly supported the Democratic Party.[36] In a

1982 survey of the Ottawa Press Gallery done by Peter Snow, 37 percent of those responding said that they felt closest to the New Democratic Party, while only 17 percent said the Liberals and 11 percent the Conservatives.[37] A survey of Canadian newspaper journalists undertaken by Bob Bergen in 1986 also found considerable sympathy for the NDP, and a distinct lack of sympathy for the Conservatives. When Bergen asked respondents whether they would describe themselves as left or right of centre, 78 percent answered left and only 22 percent chose to describe themselves as being on the right. Almost all of those who replied to his questionnaire believed that their newspapers had a political ideology which was either "moderate left or right." Some journalists, 13 percent of Bergen's sample, admitted that they allowed their political views to shape their reporting. Significantly, perhaps, most of those who responded in this way were older journalists.[38]

In a 1986 study based on a content analysis of several programs, Barry Cooper charged CBC Radio with having a left-wing ideological bias. According to Cooper, "The conclusion we would make to account for the data that indicate a left-wing critical stance with respect to salient and important political stories is that over the last decade or so the CBC has recruited persons with left-wing views. They have now achieved positions of influence within the organization as hosts and producers and naturally enough seek the 'expertise' of those whom they know."[39] The CBC vehemently denied Cooper's accusations, and the methodology used in the study has been criticized in some quarters. Cooper arrived at similar conclusions in a follow-up study of news and current affairs shows on CBC television conducted from June 1987 to June 1988. Cooper contends that reporting about Alberta, for instance, was distorted to an extraordinary degree:

> Alberta's deviants are trigger-happy vigilantes and racists: victimizers of Indians, anti-Semites and anti-French. Businessmen have the eat-em-raw attitude of capitalism incarnate, which has even infected wholesome young women skiers from Banff. Capitalism was also, no doubt, responsible for all the innocent people who were hurt in the failure of the Principal Group and it lay behind the nurses strike. Not surprisingly, with capitalism calling the shots on the Olympics, it was plagued with problems. Whether or not this visualization simply reflects the non-capitalist nature of CBC or is the result of a deliberate and conscious attempt at agenda-setting, the conjunction of Alberta and capitalism does not, in the eyes of CBC, enhance the respectability of either.[40]

Certainly not everyone will agree with how Cooper interpreted the stories and reports that he analysed.

While the party press system has been largely washed away by the tides of change, pockets of it no doubt remain. Political convictions are an inevitable ingredient in news reporting. Journalists may deny that their political views or those of their organizations affect the way they report events, and their professional prestige depends on such denials, but as Bernard Cohen has observed, "Participant journalism, 'like illicit liquor . . . is found everywhere,' but it is rarely acknowledged."[41]

THE OBJECTIVE PRESS

As the party press was in full bloom, changes were underway that would lead to a much different kind of journalism, a journalism that had to be politically neutral in order to have mass appeal. Increased urbanization and education, advances in technology, and the emergence of a mass consumer market were behind the making of the popular press. The invention of the telegraph and wire services in particular contributed to a de-politicalization of reporting. The popular press would eschew a fixation with politics in favour of reflecting popular tastes, grabbing its reader's attention, and appealing mainly to human interest. Instead of attracting readers of only one party stripe, it would mirror a wide variety of opinions and interests. The move to more objective reporting was also the result of an emerging consciousness within journalism and among journalists. Frustrated with being used by political parties, journalists themselves demanded new professional standards based on ethical responsibility to their publics.

Among the most significant changes was that the family-owned newspaper gave way to newspaper chains owned by large business organizations. The much vaunted owner-publisher, for whom the newspaper was a vehicle for his own views and prejudices, was replaced by publishers who were more and more likely to be hired employees, albeit powerful ones, than owners themselves. Profits, not politics, became the measure of success, and newspapers had become an increasingly profitable enterprise. Industrialization and the advent of a consumer society brought other changes. Sharp increases in the level of education coupled with a reduction in the cost of producing newspapers (especially developments in making newsprint) greatly extended circulation. Where at the turn of the nineteenth century newspapers were relatively expensive and available only to a small elite, by the 1870s and 1880s the "penny" press was within the reach of ordinary people. The rise of department stores such as Eaton's and of brand name products brought a massive increase, indeed a revolution, in advertising; and newspapers were to be the chief beneficiary. Buoyed by circulation and advertising revenues, newspapers became less dependent on governments and parties. The new economics of the newspaper industry allowed for some severing of the old political ties. Newspapers went from being a cause to being a business.

Canadian newspapers were strongly influenced by American trends. James Gordon Bennett's *New York Herald* and Benjamin Day's *New York Sun* of the 1830s and 1840s, and Joseph Pulitzer's *The New York World* of the 1870s to the 1890s, brought new approaches to journalism. Using sensationalism, simple language, cartoons, and photographs, and stressing human interest stories, these newspapers symbolized a new popular journalism. Stripped of grandiloquent language and pretentious editorializing, the new mode of journalism attempted to portray human experiences as vividly and dramatically as possible. As Michael Schudson has put it, in the popular press "life was a spectacle."[42] *The Montreal Star, The Toronto Star, La Presse,* and *The Ottawa Journal* were among the newspapers that adopted at least some aspects of the new style in the late nineteenth century. They all used "black, flaring headlines,"[43] gloried in stories of crime and disaster, and developed separate sections on business, sports, and the home. These newspapers led crusades on local issues, engaged in stunts, and schemed endlessly to find ways to promote sales. In 1898, for instance, Montreal's *La Presse* reported the "mental visions" of the murderess Cordelia Viau and featured Tom Nulty's life of crime and an illustration of his scaffold on its front page. The newspaper later sent a reporter around the world in sixty-six days and a ship through the St. Lawrence to prove that the river could be navigated during winter.[44] Both stunts were milked for maximum publicity.

The development of a popular press created a stratification among newspapers based on the readership they appealed to. Some newspapers such as the *Globe* and *Montreal Gazette* remained "highbrow" in their style and readership; they were aimed at the business and governmental elite rather than at the masses. In the period from 1890 to 1940 many newspapers, unable to adjust to changing trends and conditions, find the right formula, or the desired niche in the market, fell by the wayside.

The strategy of popular newspapers was to gain as large a circulation as possible to attract advertising. Since partisan reporting and editorials would alienate large blocs of readers, newspapers were forced to become more objective in their approach or, at least, more subtle. The strategy, as W.H. Kesterton has described it, was "to make newspapers unprovocative, impartial, standardized and 'public service' in their approach."[45] Newspapers were to become community organs, open to everyone and appealing to everyone. Some newspapers like *The Toronto Star* continued to espouse causes even as they shifted to a public service role. For others, political crusades were not good business.

There were other developments that had an important impact on journalistic practices during the nineteenth century. As mentioned earlier, the invention of the telegraph, and from it the creation of news wire services, were of critical importance. They not only vastly accelerated communications and allowed newspapers to extend their newsgathering reach, but they brought a new objective style of reporting. The telegraph altered the rhythms and flow of language and imposed uniformity. As James Carey has written, "The telegraph . . . led to the disappearance of forms of speech and styles of journalism and storytelling—the tall story, the hoax, much humor, irony and satire—that depended on a more traditional use of language. The origins of objectivity, then, lie in the necessity of stretching language in space over the long lines of Western Union."[46] This process was reinforced by the emergence of wire services. In order to share the costs of using the telegraph, American newspapers founded the Associated Press (AP) in 1848. AP gathered, packaged, and delivered news stories using the new technology. Many Canadian newspapers became subscribers. In 1903 the Canadian Associated Press was established, only to be supplanted in 1917 by the Canadian Press (CP). Almost all Canadian newspapers became members of CP, which at first was heavily subsidized by an annual grant from the Canadian government. CP and its electronic outlet, Broadcast News (BN), remain a basic "building block" for news. They funnel stories collected by their own reporters and many members to members and subscribers across Canada. Robert Fulford has argued that CP's role as a news clearinghouse altered Canadian journalism: "CP took in the news from its member newspapers, processed it, and then transmitted it to all of them. The result could not exhibit partisan bias: one style had to fit all. . . . CP could not transmit material that offended the prejudices of its member newspapers. . . . This approach helped make the distinction between unopinionated news columns and opinionated editorials both evident and real."[47] The effect, as with the telegraph, was to flatten language, smooth out its wrinkles and bumps and diminish, if not quite extinguish, the fires of partisan reporting; in fact, the worst message that a CP reporter could receive from Gil Purcell, the CP general manager during the 1940s and 1950s, was "Tendentious as stands. Re Lead immediately."[48] The CP "sausage machine" relentlessly stripped away local flavour, colourful language, and political rhetoric. News was becoming centralized and made into a product.

Frederick Fletcher, one of Canada's leading media experts, has pointed out that the growth of newspaper chains also imposed a standardization of language and approach.[49] As chains owned newspapers in different regions, stories had to be "nationalized" to appeal to readers across the country and across different spectrums of opinion.

Another political leveler was public broadcasting. With the establishment of the Canadian Broadcasting Corporation (CBC) in 1936, radio journalism came under the scrutiny of government regulators. During the 1935 election the Conservatives, in an effort to tarnish Liberal Leader Mackenzie King, sponsored a series of hard-hitting political broadcasts. Mr. Sage, a fictitious country philosopher, accused King of wide scale corruption and said that among other things, "Mr. King's henchmen used to call up the farmers and their wives in the early hours of the morning and tell them their sons would be conscripted for war if they voted against King."[50] Listeners were never informed that the Conservatives had sponsored "Mr. Sage." In the housecleaning that took place as a result of these broadcasts, the airwaves became subject to a strict code of impartiality. The CBC's guidelines for news reporting published in 1941 stated simply, "Domestic political news must be treated with absolute impartiality. In controversial stories, both sides of the issue must be given equal emphasis."[51] Indeed, some would argue that the CBC went overboard in its adherence to political objectivity, that its offerings became bland and vacant. For instance, early CBC newsreaders developed an articulate authoritative style but one that eschewed any traces of emotion. Romeo Leblanc has complained that prior to 1960, CBC reporting "was objective to the point of being virginal."[52]

Together with these sweeping changes, a movement towards greater professionalism was gaining ground among journalists. The main tenets of a new professional awareness were that journalists had to develop ethical standards and guidelines, rigourous methods of reporting, and greater independence from publishers and owners. Walter Lippmann, perhaps the pre-eminent journalist of his time, was at the forefront in pressing for a new consciousness. Critical of the "muckraking" that was so much a part of American political reporting, the jingoism and propaganda that characterized newspapers during the First World War, and the inability of journalists to cover the Russian Revolution objectively, Lippmann wanted better educated and more independent journalists. Reporters had to become aware of the effects that newspapers had on readers' opinions, and they had a moral obligation to remain "clear and free of . . . irrational . . . unexamined . . . and unacknowledged prejudgements."[53] He called for a journalism of "facts"; the goal was for reporters to maintain "the disinterested realism" of the scientist.[54] This movement within journalism ultimately led to the founding of schools of journalism, codes of professional conduct and behaviour, and enhanced status and prestige. The claim to professionalism was predicated on journalists taking responsibility for the fairness and accuracy of their work, having both education and training, and feeling some loyalty to the profession as a whole. Identification with fellow professionals, and adherence to the standards of the profession, was to become as important in certain settings as the identity gained from working for a particular newspaper or a particular publisher. The ethics of the profession were juxtaposed against the ethics of the organization. Objectivity, rather than subjectivity, became the new ideal.

CRITICAL JOURNALISM

The culture of objective journalism made decisive inroads in Canada after the First World War and to an even greater degree after the Second World

War when schools of journalism were established. This new movement in journalism did much to eliminate the party press, although some vestiges remained. A third journalistic ethic, critical journalism, began to emerge in the 1960s. The premise behind critical journalism is that journalists, as professionals and as delegates of the audience, have an obligation to comment on as well as report the news. Its roots are twofold: in the dilemmas experienced by journalists covering the political turmoil in the United States of the 1960s and 1970s (although events in Canada produced some of the same difficulties for Canadian journalists); and in the impact of television on newspapers and how newspapers adapted to the television age. Critical journalism has usually meant criticizing politicians and government. By the 1970s "a culture of disparagement,"[55] a pervasive cynicism towards politicians, had become deeply embedded in Canadian journalism. Journalists had moved from being the handmaidens of politicians to being their harshest critics.

Although it is difficult to pinpoint the exact beginnings of critical journalism, some of the seeds were planted in the reaction of journalists to Senator Joseph McCarthy's anti-communist crusade in the 1950s. McCarthy received enormous media attention after a series of startling allegations that a number of important government officials were members of the Communist Party, and that communists had found their way into the U.S. State Department. The senator seemed to have an instinctive feel for how to get the most play from the media; he knew about the pressure of deadlines, how to make stories appealing, how to curry favour. Under the norms that existed at the time, reporters were unable to challenge the validity of McCarthy's charges and were thus unwitting accomplices in the web of fear and falsehood that he had sewn. Some journalists became concerned that they were actively aiding McCarthy by reporting charges they knew were unsubstantiated. Edward R. Murrow, probably the most distinguished and powerful broadcast journalist in the 1940s and 1950s and then the host of CBS' popular *See It Now* series, felt compelled to challenge McCarthy directly. As he told his audience, "This is no time for men who oppose Senator McCarthy's methods to keep silent, or for those who approve. We can deny our heritage and our history, but we cannot escape responsibility for the result."[56] Murrow's broadcast was by most accounts the beginning of McCarthy's downfall.

Some observers believe that critical journalism in Canada began with the pipeline debate of 1956. After introducing a controversial bill that would offer government financial support for the building of the Trans-Canada pipeline, the St. Laurent government invoked closure to prevent debate at every stage of the bill's passage; in fact, closure was moved immediately upon the bill's introduction by C.D. Howe. Emotions were at a fever pitch on all sides of the House, and journalists were caught in the swirl of controversy and partisanship. The Press Gallery felt itself in a peculiar moral dilemma. Since the opposition's voice was being stifled, many in the press now felt that it was their obligation to do the work of the opposition and criticize government policy. As J.W. Pickersgill has described it, "The newspapers considered themselves the opposition. They gave the Tories the first taste of blood they had had for years. Mr. St. Laurent's overwhelming majority created a kind of David and Goliath situation."[57]

By far the most important catalysts of change, however, were the Vietnam War and the Watergate scandal of 1973-74. While during the first years of American involvement in Vietnam the American press tended to report the war favourably, accepting the American and South Vietnamese governments' version of events, the more experienced reporters became and the more time they spent "in-country" with the troops in battle, the more it became clear to them that military spokesmen were giving them misleading and overly optimistic accounts of what was taking place. No one has written more movingly about the experiences of journalists in Vietnam than David Halberstam. As Halberstam described the situation:

> The reporters were young. . . . They were not connected to the military from other, happier wars, and they were too young to have seen friends' careers crushed by the McCarthy era. In that sense they came to the story remarkably clean. . . . What obsessed them was the story. They had no other motivation, no other distraction. Almost all of them were single. They worked seven days a week and eighteen hours a day and they knew above all else that they were riding a great story. . . . Given a government of monumental incompetence and an American mission that dutifully parroted every mindless statement of the government, many of the military's best-informed people, the most passionate and most knowledgeable, turned to the reporters as outlets.[58]

The Tet offensive launched by the Viet Cong in 1968 against the major cities of South Vietnam, something the American military said could never happen, was the turning-point in media-military relations. As Osborn Elliot recalled about journalists' response to the Tet offensive, after Tet "common ground began to form among us."[59] The press began to question the believability of military spokesmen; discovered cover-ups of massacres such as My Lai; and chronicled the secret bombing of Cambodia, a campaign that was undertaken without congressional knowledge. Many reporters found themselves waging a war of truth against their government, a government that, to use Richard Rovere's famous phrase, was "awash with lies."[60] Even the journalistic establishment turned against the government. Walter Cronkite, the dean of American journalists and the most popular television anchorman of the time, summed up the situation this way: "And perhaps that is our big lesson from Vietnam: the necessity for candor. We the American people, the world's admired democracy, cannot ever again allow ourselves to be misinformed, manipulated, and misled into disastrous foreign adventure. The government must share with the people the making of policy, the big decisions."[61] In contrast to the legacy of distrust and suspicion of government that resulted from the war, journalists emerged with enhanced status. It has been said that in Vietnam, journalists made their reputations while generals lost theirs. Journalists such as Halberstam and Seymour Hersh, who questioned and probed and exposed lies, became cultural heroes in some quarters. A new folklore was born that glamourized the role played by those who had exposed the truth about the war.

The Vietnam War was still being fought when the Watergate scandal enveloped the Nixon presidency. The White House had ordered a break-in at Democratic Party headquarters in the Watergate complex, then later attempted to cover up evidence that could implicate the administration. Although the FBI, federal prosecutors, and congressional committees ultimately unraveled the White House shroud over the scandal, the press was at the forefront in publicizing and to some extent pursuing the investigation. The television networks covered much of the congressional hearings live, reporters maintained their own vigils outside government offices and at the homes of leading officials, there was extensive analysis and detailed reporting of almost all aspects of the story. Bob Woodward and Carl Bernstein of *The Washington Post* were "lionized" in particular for their superb investigative work, later recounted in their bestselling book *All the President's Men*, which was later made into a movie starring Robert Redford and Dustin Hoffman. As with Vietnam, many in the media saw themselves in a struggle with government, that is, "the bad guys of the government strenuously guarding their nefarious doings from view, versus the good guys of the press, the investigative journalists, who were stripping away the veils of secrecy."[62] Journalists had become part of the drama, in fact, the heroes of the play.

Vietnam and Watergate opened deep schisms in the relationship between the press and government. Alienation from and suspicion of government and politicians also grew out of the wider "adversary culture" of the 1960s. A new generation of journalists, the product to some degree of the radical influences that were sweeping university campuses, were trained to question and even defy authority. Better educated than their predecessors and coming more from middle rather than working class backgrounds, they entered the profession at a time when journalists enjoyed enormous power and prestige; and many were attracted to journalism precisely because of its halo of power. (It might be added that the experiences of the turbulent sixties and seventies became embedded in the institutional memory of media organizations as those hired during that period rose to become leading media decision-makers in the 1980s and 1990s.) The prevailing sentiment among the Vietnam and Watergate generation of journalists was that politicians were to be looked upon with suspicion; approval of government policies or statements was a sign of weakness, and careers could be made by exposing incompetence and corruption at the top. As Edward Jay Epstein wrote in the early 1970s:

> The working hypothesis almost universally shared among correspondents is that politicians are suspect; their public images probably false, their public statements disingenuous, their moral pronouncements hypocritical, their motives self-serving, and their promises ephemeral. Correspondents thus see their jobs to be to expose politicians by unmasking their disguises, debunking their claims and piercing their rhetoric. In short, until proven otherwise, political figures of any party or persuasion are presumed to be deceptive opponents.[63]

Whatever the validity of Epstein's description of the prevailing attitude among American journalists, Canadian media organizations were deeply influenced by this new machismo. In fact, Pierre Trudeau used the term "Watergate envy" to describe the cynicism of the Canadian media and its desire to bring politicians down.[64]

The penchant for investigating government, however, took a slightly different course in Canada. There was, to be sure, a frenzy of scandal hunting. Anthony Westell recalls that "There was a time in the 1970s when we tried to replicate Watergate every day of the week. If you couldn't find a real scandal then an imitation one would do. Even papers as reputable as *The Globe and Mail* and *Montreal Gazette* were becoming scandal sheets; trying to expose the clay feet of every government."[65] Eventually there was a cooling off. Media organizations discovered that Canadians were less than enthusiastic about some of their most valued institutions coming under attack. The investigations of RCMP wrong-doing during the 1970s apparently won few admirers.[66] On several occasions, newspapers simply got the story wrong and faced legal action from angry politicians. Perhaps the most noteworthy case was the successful suit by a federal cabinet minister, John Munro, against the *Toronto Sun* in 1982. As time went on journalists became increasingly dissatisfied with their role. Elly Alboim of CBC television news describes the exhaustion and disillusionment that set in: "There was the sense that people had heard enough. Reporters themselves started to develop a distaste for these kinds of stories. Their self image is that they are there to analyze policy, not to do police stories, to become muck reporters. X became known as the guy who was trying to do in the Tories. Here was this excellent political reporter meeting people at street corners. It became a case of diminishing returns."[67]

Taking groups of reporters away from their regular assignments to pursue long investigations that might prove fruitless was also quite costly. While disgruntled officials and the losers in political in-fighting will inevitably approach the media with leaks, most organizations now exercise great caution in pursuing stories. A recent illustration is the attitude of news organizations towards the Mulroney government, which was shaken continually by scandals revealed by the media during its first term in office. *The Globe and Mail's* Hugh Winsor has remarked that "newspapers are becoming gun-shy about reporting scandals because we think people don't like reading about them. As it happens, most of the scandal news (about the Mulroney government) has come out of Quebec and so we're concerned about being perceived as being anti-Quebec."[68] The dangers are seen as being at least as great as the rewards.

Television also played a critical role in bringing about a transformation in professional values. When television arrived in Canada in 1952, newspapers were displaced as the basic news source of most Canadians. Television brought the news more quickly—regular programs could be interrupted at any time if there was an important news story—and presented it in a more immediate and entertaining fashion. Seeing films of events taking place and the faces of correspondents made television news more intimate, more inviting, and more powerful. Newspapers adapted to the new medium in two ways. One strategy was to imitate television by becoming increasingly visual. The trend was for newspapers to become a kind of "frozen television"[69] with larger photographs, a greater number of headlines, shorter and punchier articles, and whiter pages. The newspaper *USA Today*, for example, is sold in coin-operated boxes made to look like television sets.[70] The other strategy was that newspapers could do some things that television couldn't such as provide greater detail and much more opinion and commentary. The columnist became a more important feature in newspapers. Today, newspapers are laced with columns and columnists often give newspapers their character and flavour.

Magazines also had to adjust to the changes television brought. Most became specialized, tailoring themselves to specific audiences and interests: business, sports, cars, celebrities, or fashion, or to specific cities or provinces. Current affairs and news magazines began to stress reports and stories in which the authors expressed feelings and opinions and told about first-hand experiences. Articles were written in the first rather than the third person. Influential magazines such as *The New Republic, Commentary, Village Voice, The New Yorker*, and *Rolling Stone* all reflected to some degree the style that Pete Hamill called "New Journalism."[71] Tom Wolfe, the notorious Hunter S. Thompson and his "gonzo" brand of journalism, and Timothy Crouse were among those identified with this more personal style of writing.

Ironically, television journalism itself would be affected by the freedoms for expression in other mediums that television had itself spawned. Television reporters wanted to inject their own assessments about the motivations and strategies of politicians into their reports. As is discussed in Chapter Six, situations arose, particularly during elections, where it was felt that to report politicians' statements without supplying a context, providing criticism, or seeking out opposing positions would allow politicians to cynically manipulate the public. Today, television journalists have considerable latitude for shaping their stories, and the actions of politicians are rarely described without a personal assessment, some "edge," to the report.

Doug Fisher has described how in his view the "conventional wisdom" in Canadian journalism changed remarkably in the 1960s. What he describes as a left-liberal constellation made up of CBC public affairs, *The Toronto Star*, and *Maclean's* was in the ascendancy. According to Fisher, "What penetrated and has triumphed is a new conventional wisdom which is left-wing and liberal and steeped with a bit of nationalism. But even more it is steeped with emotions of helping the other guy, of everybody pulling together, of creating a kind of Eden here. The enemy, quite often, are those ruthless people who cut down trees and pollute streams and who won't give the poor and the sick and the badgered their share. The real revolution that has taken place is very substantial and it's one in outlook."[72] An ideological tilt was even more evident in Quebec journalism, as many journalists were drawn into the maelstrom of the Quiet Revolution and the rise of Quebec separatism. Journalists were at the forefront in urging political reform and in focusing attention on Quebec's position and power within Canada. Union activism within the news-room was almost a permanent feature of Quebec journalism during the 1960s and 1970s. René Lévesque, Pierre Laporte, Claude Ryan, and Gérard Pelletier, among others, would eventually leave journalism to play leading roles in Quebec's political life.

One of the most important landmarks on the map of journalistic change was CBC television's controversial public affairs program *This Hour Has Seven Days*. From its first show in October 1964 to its final program in May 1966, "Seven Days" captivated English Canada. Audiences sometimes reached over three million, almost half of the potential viewing audience on Sunday nights. Hosted by Dinah Christie, Laurier La Pierre, and Patrick Watson, the program featured interviews with celebrities and newsmakers and sensational reports and exposés. The intention was to shock, to experiment, and to entertain. The show's producer, Doug Leiterman, believed that "on television truth is revealed when men and women are shown under pressure,"[73] so interviews had to be hard-hitting and politicians made to squirm and sweat. Warner Troyer has described how the "Seven Days" crew sought to embarrass Mitchell Sharp, then a senior Liberal cabinet minister whom they thought was plotting to become prime minister:

> Sharp was gunning for [then-Prime Minister] Mike Pearson's job, lobbying behind the scenes for an anticipated leadership convention. We decided to give him a hard time. We argued extensively over what that first question

should be. We agreed we should open with a tight close-up, what we call an ECU, where you would probably see his hairline and most of his chin but that was all. The screen would be filled with Mitch Sharp's face. And that picture would hang up there for all of the first question and the first response.

As soon as the red light came on I smiled and said very softly, "Mr. Sharp, how long have you been working to take Mike Pearson's job away from him?" And Sharp hesitated for about a double beat, he was so shocked. It was about two seconds. And what his face did and his eyes did in that two seconds were incredible. His eyes went "flick-flick-flick" from side to side and then up and down. You could hear the wheels turn and you could hear the synapses dropping in. Then he said that was a preposterous question, that he was completely loyal to his leader and all the appropriate things. And slowly, slowly the camera pulled back. But it was too late. In those two seconds he had done himself in.[74]

The technique was typical of the "Seven Days" style. Television was there to open up the political process and, in Finley Peter Donne's famous phrase, "comfort the afflicted and afflict the comfortable."[75] The show was finally "canned" by CBC after numerous complaints from politicians and amid the controversy that was its *raison d'être*. Although it lost its battle for survival, "Seven Days" left an indelible mark on Canadian journalism.

Another factor that made the new critical journalism possible was the greater physical and social distance between politicians and the Press Gallery in Ottawa. Both the explosion in the Gallery's size in the 1960s and 1970s and the move by many media organizations out of the Parliament buildings to the press building across from Parliament Hill had important effects. Politicians and journalists no longer shared the same social world. Where there were once so few journalists that almost every reporter was known to the leading politicians, with much eating and drinking together and enjoying each other's company, especially as they waited for the evening sessions to begin, there was now little shared experience. Consequently, attacking politicians became easier. Journalists were unlikely to see the politician that they had written about the next day, or meet him or her in an uncomfortable social situation. Politicians became depersonalized figures easy to lampoon or be nasty to.

Some observers believe that negative reporting is now so pervasive that it has become the dominant mode in Canadian journalism. Critical stories are easier to write, inherently entertaining, and seem to have a greater impact. Anthony Westell has argued that it's much more flattering to oneself to be bravely taking on the prime minister or the government than merely commenting about policies in a judicious manner.[76] The accepted logic among many reporters is that "bad news is good news," and that the best stories are about the government being in trouble. Veteran journalist Charles Lynch has described the pervasiveness of negative reporting:

We are the most adversarial press corps I've ever seen. . . . It's sloppy. I don't think anybody can deny that it's easier to write a destructive piece than a positive piece. I can't say that I've never supported policy, but the minute you do, they're on you. Fotheringham sticks his head in the door, you go to the press club, or up to the House—"I see you sold out."

And this is ridiculous, it's crazy. But it does happen and it influences you. To the extent that it's easier to be negative than positive, then the whole pack—without consulting each other—say "what are these bastards up to now," meaning the elected government.

It's the same for Mulroney; it was the same when Trudeau was in; it was the same when Pearson was in. I'd sit down many a time and say to myself, "it's be kind to Pearson week"—I loved the guy. Half-way through the piece the monkey on my back would get there and the piece would end up another critique. I was almost incapable of writing a sustained positive piece about policy.[77]

Ken Colby, a former parliamentary correspondent for CBC television, complained that "everybody wants to write like Allan Fotheringham. Journalists have been reduced to a bunch of smart-alecks. Can't a prime minister ever be right? Can't a policy ever be good?"[78] According to Michel Gratton, a former press secretary to Prime Minister Mulroney, "The camaraderie, the nonchalance, the kind of cynical *joie de vivre* affected by journalists whose power to pontificate about anything that moves—without suffering any noticeable consequences for their errors and omissions—have outgrown rational bounds."[79] An appropriate joke is that walking on water would be described by the Ottawa Press Gallery as fear of land. Others have described reporting from Ottawa as a national "blood sport."

American television critic Jeff Greenfield has identified a sub-species of reporter that he calls the "killer" journalist, journalists who seek to enhance their own reputations by beating up on politicians. He advises politicians never to appear on television or give interviews to journalists if the sole purpose is to set them up. Greenfield has described how "Washington is littered with the bones of people who believed they could survive a profile by Sally Quinn, *The Washington Post's* premier feature writer. Time after time, Ms. Quinn has examined the lives of the powerful people of that city, and time after time has painted merciless portraits. Yet there are always those who believe they can charm or stonewall Ms. Quinn into painting a sympathetic picture."[80] In Canada, Peter C. Newman, Claire Hoy, and Allan Fotheringham are journalists who inspire a similar fear among politicians. Hoy has stated that he takes the H.L. Mencken view that "the relationship between a journalist and a politician should be as a dog to a pole."[81] Doug Fisher, a veteran of the Ottawa Press Gallery, has commented on Claire Hoy's brand of journalism: "Here's a man who says that you can't trust a politician and that all politicians are dishonest and that you can't believe any of them. None of them in the final analysis has any courage or honesty. Now, if you have someone running loose with that kind of view it's a prescription for hell."[82] Fotheringham's weapon is ridicule through cruel satire, and his flaying of Conservative Party leader Joe Clark in 1978 and 1979 was particularly venomous.

Many politicians are afraid to appear on radio talk shows or be interviewed on television. The hosts or interviewers sometimes have a prosecutorial style, constantly interrupt answers with new questions, and seem intent on pushing the interviewee into corners and "winning" the interview. Mark Starowicz, the executive producer of CBC's *The Journal*, deplores interviewers who batter and cajole their guests or lead them into unexpected traps. He does believe, however, that it is frequently necessary for interviews to be challenging. As he has written:

> This is desirable in situations of public accountability, when the interviewer is the surrogate of the viewer in examining the actions or views of an official, a politician, perhaps a journalist, any advocate—someone who is proselytizing a view or a course of action. . . . An interview is not a free-time political broadcast in question and answer form. It is not a soapbox. To agree to an interview is to consent to a dialogue. A dialogue should have a dynamic. A Finance Minister should have the principal objections expressed by the critics put to him in an interview; Jim Bakker should have the principal objections stated against him put to him. Someone expressing the view that Gorbachev will succeed in his reform should have the observations of those who believe he might be overthrown placed before him.[83]

Starowicz thinks that "glorified public-relations puff-piece interviews" are a danger to democracy.[84] While few can disagree with his interview philosophy, the line between what is challenging and what is confrontational is often a fine one. More than a few journalists see interviews as a way to promote themselves or their shows. The tougher the interview, the greater their prestige and notoriety. In one famous incident Dan Rather, the anchor of the CBS Evening News, found himself locked in a heated exchange with George Bush that degenerated into accusations and recriminations. The interview had become a contest.

Most journalists are aware that negative reporting has its limits and that at some level a relationship of co-operation with politicians has to be maintained. Conflict is tempered by a symbiotic relationship that sustains both groups. As is discussed in Chapter Three, journalists need access and sources and fear the consequences of being frozen out. Each side derives prestige through contact with the other. Some journalists know that pushing criticism too far, allowing the relationship to become too corrosive, is destructive to both sides. For other journalists caught in the frenzy of competition, swept along by the instincts of the "pack," or wishing to make a name for themselves, negative reporting will prove irresistible.

Ultimately, of course, respect for authority, the effectiveness of elected officials, and the credibility of institutions cannot be sustained in the face of persistent undermining and a carnival of cynicism fostered by the media. Perhaps the most thorough critique has come from Anthony Westell. Westell believes that the American adversarial style of journalism has been grafted onto a political system where it is not appropriate. In Canada, opposition to the government is institutionalized within the parliamentary system—there is no need to have the press usurp a role that the opposition parties are elected to carry out. As Westell has put it, "The mirror had become the message, a co-equal branch of government. This was the height of media arrogance."[85] Moreover, as government and public service fell in esteem, the ideological momentum shifted to a belief in private enterprise solutions. Journalists were, by their unrelenting attacks against politicians, bringing about the very opposite of what many of them as social democrats really intended to achieve. By imposing unrealistic expectations on government, journalists helped to enlarge the private sector and the values that went along with it.[86] The private sector, of course, was not subject to the same scrutiny by the press.

It can also be argued that negative reporting has created a kind of self-fulfilling prophecy. Many good people are discouraged from entering public life because they don't want themselves or their families exposed to the harsh, unflattering glare of the spotlight. As better people stay away, the quality of public life is diminished. As Hugh Segal has argued:

> It may lead . . . people . . . when they are asked to enter public life, to say 'Thank you very much, but I would really rather practice medicine or I'd rather run the family business.' And then that becomes a self-fulfilling prophesy. I mean the press' game is to destroy any politician, if not for his chin then for his first mistake. If it's not for his first mistake, then it's for his excessive candor or for his lack of candor. Then politicians who aren't overly well paid will decide there are other things they can do with their lives. Then we all begin to comment on the low quality of politician we have in the system and what are we going to do about that.[87]

One wonders how many people would go into journalism if journalists had to endure the same intense scrutiny that they put politicians under, where their financial affairs, medical history, and sexual relationships could become public knowledge, their physical characteristics and mannerisms open to ridicule and where every mistake is likely to be pounced upon. People with a sense of dignity and need for privacy would go elsewhere. The "chilling" effect of negative reporting may well have had an important impact on Canadian political life.

Another aspect of critical journalism is that the details of policies or statements made by politicians are now rarely reported fully. As journalists have gained more discretion and have been allowed to weigh in with their own evaluations and comments, the amount of space or time devoted to neutral descriptions of fact or to statements made by politicians has been drastically reduced. Newspapers, in particular, no longer see their role as that of recording events, maintaining the record of what has taken place. According to W.A. Wilson, during the 1940s and 1950s, "Any serious newspaper reported the debates and proceedings of the House of Commons everyday. *The Montreal Star* had two or three pages of parliamentary news; news about the debates going on in the House. It automatically printed the whole text of the budget speech."[88] As Charles Lynch has observed, "They'll often publish my critique of a policy and never publish the policy."[89] On television, little remains but commentary and colour; after the Meech Lake constitutional agreement of 1987, for example, CBC television news gave only a brief summary of what was in the Accord, leaving out many important details.[90] Moreover, television audiences rarely hear newsmakers speak for longer than eight to twelve seconds. The words that are chosen are usually disjointed, taken out of context, and fitted into what the journalist—not necessarily the person being quoted or the audience—considers important. Sometimes the major figures being reported on are not even heard. Geoffrey Stevens, a former managing editor of *The Globe and Mail,* made this observation about television coverage of the 1979 and 1980 elections:

> I don't know how many times in the election campaign I turned on the television set and what I saw was Pierre Trudeau or Joe Clark or Ed Broadbent standing on a platform, his lips moving and no sound coming out, while in the foreground there was one of the people from CTV talking into a microphone telling what the leader was saying, reading into the camera a script which he had written hours before, before the leader even stood up to speak, summarizing the leader's day, and you didn't actually hear in most cases, or not for any length of time, what the leader was really saying.[91]

Journalists are the central figures, the stars, of television reporting. As the latitude available to journalists has increased, the politician's ability to get his or her message to the public has decreased.

It is too early to predict whether the 1990s will see a new era in press-government relations. In the last decade politicians developed more sophisticated strategies for dealing with the media, and there was generally a more conservative mood in the country. Media organizations, struggling to survive in a changing business environment amid takeovers, new regulations, and increased audience fragmentation, may not have political reporting high on their agendas. Social and environmental issues rather than fierce political storms may dominate the headlines. The power and prestige achieved by journalists in the 1970s and 1980s may be eroded as media organizations change their priorities and the public its expectations. Journalists as a community, however, are unlikely to give up easily the significant role that they now play on the political stage.

THE POWER OF JOURNALISTS: A SUMMARY

All three models of journalism – party, objective, and critical—can be found in the press today. Although the party press has all but vanished, and with it the old regime of rival media organizations squaring off against each other in cities across the country, owners and journalists sometimes still act on partisan feelings and beliefs. This can be seen both in editorial opinions and in the treatment given to stories: partisanship is based on idiosyncratic variables, likes and dislikes, and reactions to individual personalities, issues, and events. The ideology of objective journalism, however, is deeply embedded. The beliefs that high ethical standards should prevail and that journalists are skilled practitioners precisely because they have been trained how to frame the news according to objective criteria are the backbone of journalism's claim to professional status. Meeting the needs of a mass audience, with diverse views and sensibilities, also imposes an adherence to objective reporting. Lastly, the rise of critical journalism has been the most dramatic development in the profession since the Second World War. In recent years, the relationship between journalists and politicians has been deeply adversarial, with no quarter given or expected. Journalists have come to see themselves cloaked in gallantry, vigilant against government wrongdoings, and capable of toppling or at least humbling those in power. These changing relationships within journalism and with politicians have had a great impact on political life, as will be discussed in Chapter Five.

The shifting patterns of media-political relations have also been critical to the news process. Journalistic practices are a principal element in how news is selected, written, and presented. News has been the product to some degree of how journalists have seen their role, and they have gone from being the servants of those in power to being critics and power brokers.

NOTES

1. Paul Rutherford, *The Making of the Canadian Media* (Toronto: McGraw-Hill Ryerson, 1978), p. 31.
2. Victor Mackie, "The Press and Partisanship," *Parliamentary Government*, vol. 7, no. 1-2 (1987), 23.
3. Paul Rutherford, *A Victorian Authority: The Daily Press in Late Nineteenth-Century Canada* (Toronto: University of Toronto Press, 1982), p. 41.

4. Ibid., pp. 41-2.
5. Ibid.
6. W.H. Kesterton, *A History of Journalism in Canada* (Ottawa: Carleton University Press, 1984), p. 43.
7. Rutherford, *A Victorian Authority*, pp. 41-2.
8. Kesterton, p. 75.
9. Bruce Hutchison, *The Far Side of the Street* (Toronto: Macmillan of Canada, 1976), p. 193.
10. Lloyd Tataryn, *Power, Politics and the Press* (Toronto: Deneau, 1985), p. 141.
11. Ross Harkness, *J.E. Atkinson of The Star* (Toronto: University of Toronto Press, 1963), pp. 16-19.
12. Rutherford, *A Victorian Authority*, p. 220.
13. Colin Seymour-Ure, "The Parliamentary Press Gallery in Ottawa," *Parliamentary Affairs* (1962), p. 36.
14. Anthony Westell and Carman Cumming, "Canadian Media and the National Imperative," in *Government and the News Media*, Dan Nimmo and Michael Mansfield, eds. (Waco, Texas: Baylor University Press, 1982), p. 163.
15. Ibid., pp. 164-5.
16. Ibid., p. 164.
17. Peter Dempson, *Assignment Ottawa: Seventeen Years in the Press Gallery* (Toronto: General Publishing Company, 1968), p. 62.
18. Ibid., p. 63.
19. Interview with J.W. Pickersgill, Ottawa, 8 December 1988.
20. Rutherford, *The Making of the Canadian Media*, p. 106. The headline appeared in the first edition but was dropped from later editions.
21. Interview with Robin Sears, Toronto, 4 June 1987.
22. Interview with W.A. Wilson, Ottawa, 18 April 1989.
23. Interview with Dalton Camp, Ottawa, 7 July 1987.
24. Interview with Val Sears, Ottawa, 26 May 1987.
25. Christina McCall-Newman, *Grits: An Intimate Portrait of the Liberal Party* (Toronto: Macmillan, 1982), p. 111.
26. Interview with W.A. Wilson.
27. Ibid.
28. Dempson, p. 101.
29. Ibid., p. 103.
30. Hutchison, pp. 245-53.
31. Peter Desbarats, *Guide to Canadian News Media* (Toronto: Harcourt, Brace, Jovanovich, 1989), p. 84.
32. Frederick Fletcher, *The Newspaper and Public Affairs*, Vol. VII of the *Royal Commission on Newspapers* (Ottawa: Supply and Services Canada, 1981), p. 61.
33. Interview with Val Sears.

34. Walter Stewart, "The Toronto Star: The Crazy Rat Syndrome," in *Canadian Newspapers: The Inside Story*, Walter Stewart, ed. (Edmonton: Hurtig, 1980), p. 118.
35. Murray Goldblatt, "Globe Tremors," *Content* (March/April 1989), pp. 19-20.
36. S. Robert Lichter, Stanley Rothman, and Linda Lichter, *The Media Elite* (Bethesda, Maryland: Adler and Adler, 1986).
37. Cited in Peter Desbarats, "Eye on the Media," *The Financial Post*, 13 July 1985, p. 7.
38. Bob Bergen, "A Profile of Canada's Major Daily Newspaper Men and Women," Masters project, The University of Calgary, April 1987.
39. Barry Cooper, Lydia Miljan, and Maria Vigilante, "Bias On The CBC? A Study of Network A.M. Radio," paper presented to the Canadian Communications Association's Annual Conference, Winnipeg, 1986.
40. Barry Cooper, *Sins of Omission: A Study of CBC Television News*, p. 456 (forthcoming).
41. Quoted in Michael Schudson, *Discovering the News* (New York: Basic Books, 1978), p. 186.
42. Ibid., p. 119.
43. Rutherford, *The Making of the Canadian Media*, p. 53.
44. Rutherford, *A Victorian Authority*, p. 69.
45. Kesterton, p. 83.
46. James Carey, "The Dark Continent of American Journalism," in *Reading The News*, Robert Manoff and Michael Schudson, eds. (New York: Pantheon Books, 1986), pp. 164-65.
47. Robert Fulford, " 'A Sort of Reckless Courage'," in *The Journalists*, Vol. II of the *Royal Commission on Newspapers*, (Ottawa: Supply and Services Canada, 1981), pp. 12-13.
48. Interview with W.A. Wilson.
49. Fletcher, p. 11.
50. Quoted in Frank Peers, *The Politics of Canadian Broadcasting 1920-1951* (Toronto: University of Toronto Press, 1969), p. 166.
51. Warner Troyer, *The Sound and The Fury* (Toronto: Personal Library, 1980), p. 91.
52. Interview with Romeo Leblanc, Ottawa, 26 May 1987; interview with Dalton Camp.
53. Schudson, p. 155.
54. Ibid.
55. Frederick Fletcher, "The Prime Minister as Public Persuader," in *Apex of Power*, 2nd ed., Thomas Hockin, ed. (Scarborough, Ontario: Prentice-Hall, 1977), pp. 99-100.
56. Peter Stoler, *The War Against The Press* (New York: Dodd, Mead and Company, 1986), p. 47.
57. Interview with J.W. Pickersgill, Ottawa, 8 December 1988.

58. David Halberstam, *The Powers That Be* (New York: Alfred A. Knopf, 1979), p. 451.
59. James Boylan, "Declarations of Independence," *Columbia Journalism Review* (November/December 1986), p. 36.
60. Daniel P. Moynihan, "The Presidency and the Press," *Commentary* (March 1971), p. 42.
61. Robert Entman and David Paletz, "The War in Southeast Asia: Tunnel Vision on Television," in *Television Coverage of International Affairs*, William C. Adams, ed. (Norwood, N.J.: Ablex Publishing, 1982), p. 195.
62. Tom Bethell, "The Myth of an Adversary Press," *Harper's*, January 1977, p. 35.
63. Edward J. Epstein, *News from Nowhere* (New York: Vintage, 1973), p. 215.
64. Patrick Gossage, *Close To The Charisma* (Toronto: McClelland and Stewart, 1986), p. 154.
65. Interview with Anthony Westell, Ottawa, 28 January 1988.
66. Fulford, p. 16.
67. Interview with Elly Alboim, Ottawa, 21 April 1989.
68. Interview with Hugh Winsor, Ottawa, 19 April 1989.
69. Fletcher, p. 11.
70. W. Lance Bennett, *News: The Politics of Illusion* (New York: Longman, 1988), p. 7; and Neil Postman, *Amusing Ourselves to Death* (New York: Penguin, 1986), p. 111.
71. Boylan, p. 34.
72. Interview with Doug Fisher, Ottawa, 27 January 1988.
73. Eric Koch, *Inside Seven Days* (Scarborough, Ontario: Prentice-Hall, 1986), p. 69.
74. From Paul McLaughlin, *How to Interview* (North Vancouver: International Self-Counsel Press, 1990), pp. 126-27. Reproduced courtesy of the publisher.
75. Bennett, p. 13.
76. Anthony Westell, "Reporting the Nation's Business," in *Journalism Communication and The Law*, Stuart Adam, ed. (Scarborough, Ontario: Prentice-Hall, 1976), p. 67.
77. Tataryn, p. 162.
78. Interview with Ken Colby, Calgary, 29 November 1986.
79. Michel Gratton, *"So What Are The Boys Saying?"* (Toronto: McGraw-Hill Ryerson, 1987), pp. x-xi.
80. Jeff Greenfield, *Playing to Win* (New York: Simon and Schuster, 1980), p. 67.
81. "The Parliamentary Press Gallery," *The Media File*, CBC Radio (1987), transcript.
82. Interview with Doug Fisher.

83. Correspondence from Mark Starowicz to author, 8 December 1989, p. 2.

84. Ibid., p. 4.

85. Interview with Anthony Westell; see also Anthony Westell "The Press: Adversary or Channel of Communication?" in *Parliament, Policy and Representation*, Harold Clarke et al, eds. (Toronto: Methuen, 1980), pp. 25-34.

86. Interview with Anthony Westell.

87. Hugh Segal, "Prospects and Proposals," in *Politics and the Media* (Toronto: Erindale College and The Reader's Digest Foundation of Canada, 1981), p. 110.

88. Interview with W.A. Wilson.

89. Tataryn, p. 161.

90. David Taras, "Television and Public Policy: The CBC's Coverage of the Meech Lake Accord," vol. 15, no. 3, *Canadian Public Policy*, September 1989, pp. 322-34.

91. Geoffrey Stevens, "Prospects and Proposals," in *Politics and the Media*, p. 101.

3

News Through the Ottawa Looking Glass[1]

Canadian political reporting is affected by the special conditions that prevail in the Ottawa Press Gallery. While overarching journalistic ideologies have a considerable bearing on how journalists perceive their role, daily routines, peer pressures, career ambitions, the part played by different media organizations in setting the reporting agenda, the competition and co-operation between journalists and among organizations are the grist from which much of the news is made. This chapter will examine the politics of the Press Gallery: the career paths of reporters sent to Ottawa, differences in outlook between English and French-speaking journalists, the most powerful agenda-setting institutions, the rules of the game in the "back channel" between reporters and their sources in political parties and government, and the legendary influence of "pack" journalism. These are the forces that drive much of political reporting in Ottawa.

What is commonly referred to as the Press Gallery encompasses two distinct entities. Literally, it is the gallery of seats overlooking the Speaker's chair in the House of Commons and the Senate that is set aside for the press. A large room on the third floor of the Centre Block of the Parliament building also constitutes part of the gallery and, until the 1960s, most reporters did their work there. The Parliamentary Press Gallery is, on the other hand, a self-governing association made up of the journalists assigned to cover Parliament. The Gallery comes under the administrative authority of the Speaker of the House of Commons and members are granted certain privileges: free stationery and the use of telephones, access to the Library of Parliament and to restaurants and lounges in the Parliament Buildings and, for some journalists the most valued prize of all—a parking pass. Although admission to the Gallery is virtually automatic for journalists from recognized media institutions, radio and television journalists were denied entry until 1959 and some applicants, i.e., freelancers and those from marginal organizations, still have difficulty gaining admission. In a generic sense, the Gallery refers to the corps of journalists who report from Ottawa about political affairs.

THE CHANGING OTTAWA GALLERY

It is difficult to trace the early history of the Gallery because a fire that ravaged the Centre Block in 1916 destroyed its records. We do know that the gallery predates Confederation but that prior to the First World War it had but a handful of members.[2] During the inter-war period there were usually two to three dozen journalists at any given time, with the number blossoming to over sixty after the Second World War.[3] Peter Dempson, who arrived in the gallery in the early 1950s, has left a magnificent but hardly uplifting portrait of the seedy and stifling atmosphere in what is now called the "hot room" on the third floor of the Centre Block. As Dempson described it:

> The floors creak. The garish tiles pop up periodically. The desks—big awkward wooden ones, some metal—are scarred with cigarette butts. The floor tiles are also pockmarked from cigar or cigarette ashes. Fluorescent lights beat down harshly; they are seldom extinguished. . . .
>
> The Gallery abounds in squalor and filth. It cries for fresh air. Just as quickly as the char staff cleans up the premises, the place becomes a shambles. Dust films the piles of newspapers, the yellowed pages of Hansard that lean grotesquely on desks.
>
> Empty beer bottles are to be found everywhere. Empty glasses, with the remains of scotch, rye or gin, clutter up the room. Pop bottles clog portable ash trays. . . . Electric fans whir on hot days bringing little relief to the congested quarters and newsmen cramped over their desks. . . . Typewriters clack. The loud-speaker system on the front desk squawks out the names of newsmen wanted on the telephone. There is the smell of human sweat. The air is rank. The Gallery bustles.[4]

The image of the disheveled, crusty, hard-drinking, and hard-living journalist is certainly brought to life by Dempson. It's no wonder that during the prohibition era the Gallery's "Blind Pig" was one of the country's better known bootlegging operations. As its clientele included some of Ottawa's most powerful politicians, it was never raided.[5]

Journalists working in the Gallery in the 1990s would barely recognize the world that Dempson described. In the 1940s and 1950s, the Gallery was made up entirely of print journalists; today, it is dominated by the electronic media. Tape recorders, micro-computers, fax machines, mini-cams, portable video cassette recorders, microwave sending and receiving units, and satellites have transformed journalism. Technology has brought greater speed and efficiency, a cleaner and sharper look. The Oasis cable system which links offices and buildings on Parliament Hill means that reporters need not attend the House or press conferences themselves; they can watch proceedings from the comfort of their offices or tape them for later viewing. A press clipping service called Quorum, produced by the Library of Parliament, is available each day before noon. The size of the Gallery has mushroomed to close to 400 members—more journalists cover Ottawa today for the CBC alone than were in the entire Gallery in 1946. Where small numbers of journalists could once hold casual conversations with cabinet ministers or party leaders, today politicians are swamped by dozens of reporters. Scrums, a not unfitting term borrowed from rugby, often involve over sixty people, including as many as fifteen camera crews, all trying to record the words of a surrounded politician. Many journalists are left at the edges of the circle, unable to fight their way in. Questions come in four or five at a time. The "hot room" still exists, but most media organizations have moved to offices in the National Press Building across from Parliament Hill. The press building has itself become overcrowded, and the flood of journalists will eventually need either an additional or a larger building. What was once clubby and intimate, where everyone knew everyone else, is now much more amorphous, indistinct, and unwieldy.

The most critical changes to the Gallery came with the arrival of the electronic media. Radio was the first intruder. From the 1920s to the 1950s, radio was among the most potent instruments of political communication. The 1925 federal election was the first to be covered by radio, and the first coast-to-coast radio transmission originated from Parliament Hill on 1 July 1927. In 1941, proceedings of the House of Commons were broadcast for the first time when Winston Churchill, at the height of the Battle of Britain, gave a moving speech to parliamentarians. Churchill mocked the prediction made by a French military strategist that Britain was about to have its neck wrung like a chicken by Hitler, saying "Some Chicken. Some Neck." In the United States, President Franklin Roosevelt soothed fears during the depression with his "fireside chats" over radio; the secret of his success was to speak with great assurance on only a single topic in each broadcast so that his message would not be diluted, and to speak infrequently so that what he said was considered important and he could gain a wide audience and attention. In Canada, William Aberhart used radio to storm to power in Alberta. It was also one of the tools used effectively by Duplessis in Quebec. Ironically, it was precisely radio's potency and appeal that led to the Gallery's refusal to admit broadcast journalists until 1959. Print journalists made extra income then by appearing as radio commentators; they feared that the Gallery's acceptance of radio journalists would deprive them of this role. They also feared that radio could get stories out faster and thus beat them to scoops. For years print reporters fought any advance by broadcasters and even stooped to sabotaging their work. They would stand close to microphones and disrupt interviews by interjecting loud noises or coarse language. On one occasion, print reporters surrounded Tom Earle of the CBC and clicked toy crickets to prevent him from conducting interviews.[6] For years broadcasters "skulked around the perimeter of the House" amid uncertainty over their status.[7]

When television arrived in 1952, the print establishment panicked. They immediately recognized that this new medium would dominate and change their own, and sought to delay its acceptance on Parliament

Hill for as long as possible. But as politicians demanded access to television, print reporters could no longer hold back the floodgates. In 1959, radio journalists Tom Earle of the CBC and Sam Ross, a private broadcaster, were finally admitted. The CBC's Norman DePoe was the first television journalist accepted for membership. By 1964, there were sixteen electronic journalists out of a total Gallery membership of 110;[8] and by 1985 broadcast journalists had become the majority, with 159 out of 319 members (although the number is bloated to some degree by the fact that camera crews, arguably more technicians than journalists, were allowed to join).[9] DePoe, CBC television's Ottawa correspondent during the 1960s and noted for his scratchy voice and tough demeanour, quickly overshadowed the leading print journalists in terms of public recognition. Politicians gravitated towards the television cameras, often bypassing or ignoring print journalists.

There have been other important changes in the Gallery. An Ottawa assignment was once considered "the jewel in the crown" for Canadian journalists. Many would arrive there at the pinnacle of their careers and could expect to stay for a long time. In the days of the party press they were treated as ambassadors of their newspapers, an important political as well as journalistic function that was often a stepping-stone to an editorship. This pattern changed with the advent of television. Television journalists tended to be moved more rapidly from place to place, to be younger and their careers shorter. In this respect, newspapers seemed to follow television's lead and there was soon a rapid turnover among print reporters as well. Colin Seymour-Ure found that two-thirds of the members of the Gallery in 1961 were not there in 1956.[10] Doug Fisher counted only 103 reporters remaining in 1986 out of 259 who had been in the Gallery in 1981.[11] CBC television's Ottawa Bureau Chief, Elly Alboim, estimates that the turn of the wheel following the 1984 federal election brought a 60 percent changeover.[12] There was less movement following the 1988 election largely because the previous turnover had been so great.[13]

A number of factors explain the high rate of attrition, though evaporation might be a better word. First, the explosion in international affairs reporting has opened up possibilities that were unavailable to journalists a generation ago. This is particularly the case at *The Globe and Mail*, Southam, CP, and the CBC. Assignments in Washington, London, or Tokyo are more desirable and at least as much a testing ground as is Ottawa. Second, many leading reporters have been attracted to business journalism. The creation of *The Globe and Mail's* "Report on Business," *The Financial Post's* move to a daily edition, the upgrading of *The Financial Times*, and the launching of numerous business magazines and newsletters, all of which has taken place since the 1960s, presented many opportunities for journalists. Many see this as a more prestigious route than being in the hurly-burly of the Press Gallery. Third, some "bench strength" has been lost to the United States, where television journalists in particular can expect to receive substantially higher salaries.[14] Although they were not all associated with the Gallery, over the years Morley Safer (CBS), John Blackstone (CBS), Mark Phillips (CBS), Don McNeill (CBS), Peter Jennings (ABC), Henry Champ (NBC), Robert MacNeil (PBS), and Keith Morrison (KNBC in Los Angeles) were drawn away from Canadian journalism. Canadians are sought because of their flat accents, slower speech, and more authoritative delivery. Recruitment firms routinely send tapes of Canadian TV reporters and newsreaders to the major American networks. Together, these factors mean that the pool of talent available for political reporting from Ottawa is substantially diminished.

Reporters also use the Gallery as a springboard to government or the private sector. Some reporters "cross the street" to work as chiefs of staff in the public affairs or communications bureaus of government departments where salaries are comparable but there is more security and less stress. Others migrate to public relations or advertising firms, or find positions in lobbying or public affairs for banks, corporations, or interest groups. Service in the Gallery is no longer seen as a place to end one's career, but rather a place to gain experience and build bridges that may be valuable in future. There also seems to be an inevitable exhaustion that sets in after journalists have stayed through more than one election cycle. While no studies have been done, it is generally believed that rates of divorce and burnout are higher than average because reporters often work long hours under great stress. One veteran Ottawa journalist described the divorce rate as "astronomic."[15] Moreover, salaries for many Gallery members are not particularly lucrative. News organizations can take advantage of the steady stream of graduates from journalism schools who are willing to work for relatively low salaries in order to gain experience. "The real tragedy of journalism in Canada," according to Doug Fisher, "is that employers have been able to get people so cheaply."[16] Peter Desbarats, Dean of the Graduate School of Journalism at the University of Western Ontario, has pointedly observed that, "When experienced journalists on major newspapers and national periodicals are paid in the range of $30,000 to $50,000 annually, it is appropriate to ask whether their salaries adequately reflect the influence and responsibility inherent in journalism and the ability of the newspaper industry to pay for a high quality of performance."[17]

Of course, some Gallery members become stars; and for those who make it covering Ottawa, the rewards in terms of salary, recognition, and influence can be substantial. David Halton, Pamela Wallin, Jeffrey Simpson, Richard Gwyn, Allan Fotheringham, Michel Vastel, and Charles Lynch are among those who have gained almost celebrity status. One journalist described how he found it difficult to leave Ottawa even though, in professional terms, the time to leave had come: "There's a sense of being where history is being made. I've seen every bit of history. It's hard to walk away from the excitement and from being at the centre of the action."[18] To leave the spotlight that inevitably shines on national politics is painful for some reporters. The Gallery has become their world.

The inevitable consequence of such persistent hemorrhaging of the Gallery's talent is that, at any given time, most Gallery reporters are relatively inexperienced. Robert Fulford has written about Gallery reporters that, "I don't believe there is one who could be called an expert on, say, foreign policy. There isn't a single man or woman who could speak with independent authority on defence, on welfare policy, or constitutional law. A politician or civil servant speaking to a reporter usually—not always, but usually—expects to encounter profound ignorance of whatever subject is on the agenda. After a while, he comes to both fear that ignorance and depend on it."[19] Geoffrey Stevens reached a similar conclusion based on his experience in the Gallery in the late 1970s and early 1980s: "Most of the people who report on the legislative process are poorly trained (if they are trained at all), lack comprehension of many of the subjects that they must report on, and (as a general indictment) not only know less than the civil servants who develop policy, and the politicians who announce it but, in many cases, the journalist knows less than his readers or listeners."[20] Elly Alboim of CBC has argued with regard to television reporters that it's difficult "to sustain interest or expertise when you don't have the space."[21] Not only the brevity of news reports but the emphasis on personalities and conflict discourages the gaining of any in-depth knowledge about the policy process. A cynic might point out that control by editors and producers is strengthened by the lack of expertise among reporters. The continued flood of new faces ensures that reporters will have to rely on the knowledge and experience of media managers.

An important change in the Gallery is the presence of women reporters. In 1946, there were only two women reporters out of sixty-two Gallery members.[22] The first woman member was Genevieve Lipsett-Skinner of *The Vancouver Sun*, who joined the Gallery in 1923.[23] By 1985, there were fifty-five women in a Gallery with 319 members.[24] Although women are still significantly underrepresented and many still complain that the top stories and better assignments go to men, a number of women journalists are influential in Ottawa. The CBC's Judy Morrison is a past president of the Gallery, and Pamela Wallin was CTV's Ottawa bureau chief. Wendy Mesley and AnnaMaria Tremonti of CBC television, Carol Goar of *The Toronto Star*, and Marjorie Nichols of *The Ottawa Citizen* have achieved positions of some prominence and are widely respected.

There are also persistent complaints that women have largely been shut out of managerial positions in media organizations, and that the profession still exudes a macho image. A survey of daily newspapers in Canada conducted by the *Ryerson Review of Journalism* in 1988 found only two women in positions above the rank of city editor.[25] Although Joan Donaldson has risen to be head of *CBC Newsworld* and Trina McQueen is CBC's Director of News and Current Affairs, an inquiry into the CBC's hiring practices with regard to women and visible minorities was initiated by the Canadian Human Rights Commission in 1989. Women presently occupy only 14.1 percent of the CBC's middle management positions.[26] As one woman commentator expressed the frustration felt by many women in the media, "we've come a short way and don't call me baby."[27]

TWO WORLDS OF CANADIAN JOURNALISM

Hugh MacLennan's description of Canada as consisting of "two solitudes" can be applied in some degree to the Press Gallery, as, indeed, can all of the well-worn analogies about French-English relations: Atwood's portrait of the two cultures as Siamese twins; Brossard's image of two women standing back-to-back; Aquin's description of two warriors locked in battle but each needing the other to justify his own existence, his own struggle. Francophone reporters have different outlooks and agendas, take different angles on stories, and must appeal to a different audience. Approximately one in six Gallery members is French speaking, less than the percentage of francophones in the general population. English-speaking journalists, because of the force of numbers, set the atmosphere and tone of the Gallery. There is little interchange between the English majority and the members of "la presse québecoise à Ottawa," as they prefer to call themselves.[28] Some reporters, a minority, move between and are comfortable in both milieux. The Prime Minister's Press Office has usually had a press secretary from one language group assisted by a deputy press secretary from the other. There was considerable resentment on the occasions when the press secretary was unable to speak French. One journalist, Don Braid, spent a brief period in the Gallery, and concluded that the amount of antagonism between the two groups was "astounding."[29]

Most francophone reporters are products in some way of the intense political struggles of the Quiet Revolution. Quebec journalists remain preoccupied by constitutional and language issues. The francophone media, unlike its English counterpart, "never tired of the constitutional debate."[30] Quebec's powers and its place in Canada and the activities of francophones in Ottawa—these are the lenses through which francophone journalists tend to see the Ottawa political world. Moreover, the major focus of news is Quebec City, not Ottawa. Being in the Ottawa Gallery is not considered a prestige assignment, and most news organizations have two or three reporters in Quebec City for every one they have in Ottawa. In addition, there is still not a single correspondent representing a French-language newspaper anywhere in English Canada (except in Ottawa).[31] Arthur Siegel found in his 1977 study that about half of all news stories on French-language television were about events in Quebec, with "Canadian national" items accounting for less than 30 percent of all stories.[32] Even Ottawa stories tended to be reported from the perspective of how they would affect Quebec. The exploits of Quebec's political leaders and Quebec politicians in Ottawa dominated the news.

Another important difference is the tendency of French-language journalists to analyse issues and events more deeply or, as Louis Plamondon put it, "They don't report the news in Quebec, they critique the news."[33] The great journalists in Quebec's history—Henri Bourassa, André Laurendeau, and Claude Ryan, among others—have been editorialists; and there is a firmly established tradition of journalists carrying out a dialogue and influencing political, intellectual, and business leaders via editorial and opinion pages. This is especially evident in the op-ed pages of *Le Devoir*, which have been described as the "village square" of Quebec society. The editorial tradition grows out of the fact that journalists in Quebec were, with lawyers and priests, part of the educated elite; and they tended to see themselves as playing a critical role in Quebec life, some would even say an exalted role. There has also been a great deal of crossover between journalism and politics. Henri Bourassa, René Lévesque, Claude Ryan, Gérard Pelletier, Pierre Laporte, Romeo Leblanc, and Gérard Godin are among many who have distinguished themselves in both fields. Journalists were expected to be activists; the editorial was part of the commitment to a *journalisme engagé*. Even though Quebec newspapers have largely adopted the formula journalism of visuals, lifestyles, and sensationalism that is found in most Canadian and American newspapers, the editorial tradition remains intact. As Lysiane Gagnon has observed, French-language journalism has been characterized by " . . . the predominance of analysis, as opposed to simple reporting of events; the tendency to treat matters conceptually rather than in terms of people and events; the very Cartesian need to rationalize . . . ; the greater personalization of articles (a French-language daily has more bylines and editorials are always signed, even when they must reflect newspaper policy); and the priority given to theory."[34]

This analytical style has carried over to television. According to Patrick Gossage, a former press secretary to Prime Minister Trudeau, French-language television is " . . . less captured by pictures and visual incidents. *Le Point* can spend 15 minutes dissecting an issue, while *The*

Journal feels it needs action and pictures in every show."[35] The view of Michel Vastel of *La Presse* is that "Radio-Canada is much less aggressive, less pushy, less violent. If you listen you hear a different tone of voice."[36] Vince Carlin, the chief correspondent for CBC Radio News, remembers that when mobile video cameras were first introduced to the CBC in the mid-1970s, the Radio-Canada station in Montreal set up the camera on a tripod in the studio rather than taking the camera out to cover news events. Given the same camera equipment, the English-language station in Montreal brought it into the field almost immediately. As Carlin recalls, "We were more attuned to getting news and putting it on the air. They were more interested in reflecting on events. Facts were not as important as analysis."[37]

Following the victory of the Parti Québécois in November 1976, there were charges that the French-language media in general, and Radio-Canada in particular, had a pro-separatist bias. In response to these allegations, the Canadian Radio-Television and Telecommunications Commission (CRTC) set up the Boyle Committee to conduct an inquiry. The Boyle Committee strongly criticized both the CBC and Radio-Canada for not working hard enough to promote Canadian unity. The report's chilling conclusion was that, "As presented by the (broadcast) media, Canada is in a state of deep schizophrenia: if English and French Canadians were on different planets there could hardly be a greater contrast of views and information."[38] Romeo Leblanc, a former Radio-Canada correspondent and federal cabinet minister under Pierre Trudeau, remembers that, at the time, francophone journalists were "shaken by inner tensions."[39] Undoubtedly some journalists had affection for René Lévesque, a former journalist, and were strong believers in the Parti Québecois' national and social vision. The explanation given by Marcel Pepin of *Le Soleil* is that "the French press has a natural tendency to side with the Quebec government when this government is under attack from outside. This has been the case for the Lévesque government. . . . So, a sort of family reaction occurs in the French press, when the feds and all the other provinces fire bullets on Quebec City."[40] The same family reaction occurred when it appeared to French-language reporters that Pierre Trudeau was being attacked for having increased "French power" in Ottawa. There was a similar response when Suzanne Blais-Grenier was forced to resign from the Mulroney cabinet. Some francophone reporters accused English journalists of singling out a Quebec minister for unfair criticism. On the other hand, the Quebec media will not shy away from attacking one of their favourites if they feel that it is warranted. Towards the end of its tenure, the Lévesque government was under intense scrutiny by the press as it was besieged by alleged scandals and torn by dissent.

Another significant difference is that French-language journalists have more editorial control than their English counterparts. Quebec media organizations were rocked continually by strikes and union militancy for over two decades. *La Presse* endured strikes in 1958, 1964, and 1977 and a lockout in 1971. *Le Soleil* in Quebec City weathered a long and tumultuous strike in 1977-78. Radio-Canada was hit by strikes in 1959 and for nine months in 1981-82. In almost every case, journalists demanded greater control over their assignments and story content. As a result, editorial supervision over journalists' work is all but non-existent in some news-rooms. The argument that journalists shape the news is truer in Quebec and among French-language reporters in Ottawa than it is in English-speaking news organizations.

A number of observers have noted that francophone reporters are not as interested in politicians' private lives or in their sexual foibles as their English counterparts. While U.S. presidential candidate Gary Hart's involvement with model Donna Rice received rapt attention from the English media in 1987-88, the French media did not give the controversy the same attention. The same was true of Margaret Trudeau's escapades: while the English press gave them intensive coverage, the view of French-speaking reporters seemed to be that this was an unsavoury voyeurism unworthy of prolonged attention. Some English journalists claim that French-language reporters are more tolerant of scandal generally. For their part, francophone journalists are dismayed by the relative lack of interest shown by their English counterparts in what they consider the main dividing lines of Canadian politics: language, the constitution, and the conflict over Quebec's place in Canada.

A continuing problem is that many of the Gallery's English-language reporters are unilingual and thus unable to understand pronouncements made in French by politicians and officials. Some stories are missed entirely, while in other cases nuances are not picked up on. In addition, the French-language media is rarely read, watched, or listened to so that the Quebec response to politics and issues is not appreciated fully. It is as if the unilingual reporters were attending a doubles tennis match but could follow the play of only three of the players. The other player remains shrouded in mist and misconception.

SOURCES AND LEAKS

If journalists are to have influence they need to have sources: insiders who can give them background on what is taking place or information that they could not otherwise obtain, and confirm or deny rumours or suspicions. Although much of day-to-day reporting consists of covering set piece events such as news conferences, question period, official engagements and ceremonies, speeches, or the release of government reports, journalists have to find out what is taking place behind the scenes—the real strategies, ambitions, and manoeuvres. Journalists with better access get stories that their rivals don't. Background knowledge is particulary important to columnists, who are expected to take their readers "inside" Ottawa. Ultimately, journalists have to cultivate reliable sources within political parties and in the government who will talk candidly about what is taking place. The courtship between reporters and sources can involve intricate steps. Each has a different agenda, and the rules in each relationship are different. Reporters need sources in order ultimately to break major stories covering set piece events. Journalists have to have a grip on events beyond the daily chase if they are to be successful and beat the competition. The competition is as much from reporters within one's own organization with whom one has to contend for choice assignments and promotions as from reporters in rival organizations. Sources want to influence events and policies. By contacting journalists, they hope to attract attention for a particular policy option or argument, affect the timing of events, or send signals to a particular policy community. Many seek to sabotage or embarrass political opponents. The news story becomes a political bullet fired by sources at their intended targets.

Reporters take years to develop their network of sources. Sources will often approach journalists, especially if they are from major news organizations. It is the size and influence of the news organization that the reporter represents that attracts sources rather than the reporter's intelligence or skills. As Elly Alboim, the Ottawa bureau chief of CBC television news, has described it, "The longer you're there the more respected and important you get. Events start gravitating to you. The sources come to you. Mansbridge, Duffy—they have dozens of sources."[41] Jason Moscovitz of CBC Radio put it simply, "when you're with the CBC they call you."[42] Reporters have to know their sources thoroughly. Their reliability, intentions, and ambitions have to be checked on and understood. The network of sources must be constantly massaged. Entire days may be spent touching base with sources, meeting them for lunch or over drinks, and putting in hours on the phone. As phone calls in some government offices are logged, reporters sometimes have to wait until after regular working hours to make their connections.

Reporters often establish a close working relationship with opposition MPs. *The Globe and Mail's* Stevie Cameron has described the politics of the relationship this way: "A reporter wants the story, the MP wants good publicity and to make the government look incompetent, sleazy or stupid and preferably all three. When an MP gets a hot tip on a good story, he or she will often pass it on to a favourite reporter; the deal is that no other reporter will get it and the two will share information as the story is nailed down. If the story looks as if it will work, the two must come to an agreement on how it will be handled."[43]

Moreover, reporters must have tangible assets or goods to offer their sources in exchange for information. They have to be willing to trade information and act "as sources to their sources."[44] Sources may also be given special coverage and accorded preferred treatment. In their study of reporters covering the Ontario Legislature, Richard Ericson and his associates discovered that "Beat reporters often give coverage to news conferences or ceremonials not because they see them as intrinsically important or even interesting, but as a favour to sources. Reporters also maintain a sense of their sources' dignity and decorum by omitting potentially embarrassing material or retaking broadcast interview clips."[45] The news stories that emerge really involve two sets of negotiations: negotiations between reporters and sources, and negotiations between reporters and their editors and producers. These are the two arenas in which the "pulling and hauling" of the newsmaking process occur.

John F. Kennedy once remarked that "the Ship of State is the only ship that leaks at the top."[46] Almost all government and political leaders have been frustrated by their inability to prevent leaks to the media. Some have seen leaks as a direct threat to their ability to govern, as plans cannot be made in confidence or secrets kept. Hunting down the guilty parties was an obsession in the Nixon and Carter White Houses. Lester Pearson gave a stern lecture to his Cabinet about leaks only to have a story about his warnings to the Cabinet appear a few hours later in *The Toronto Telegram*. Trudeau's rule was that while one indiscretion could be forgiven, a second would not be tolerated.[47] According to Michel Gratton, Brian Mulroney was also deeply affected:

> To be fair, it has to be said that the Prime Minister had some reason to keep his own counsel, to be wary of his own personnel. His office was a veritable sieve. His closest advisors would regularly leak information to the media. Sometimes, we knew who the culprits were, sometimes we only guessed, but we had only to read the newspapers to know there were culprits. But, for one reason or another, they were kept on once the anger of the moment had passed. Every time he was betrayed, the Prime Minister would be bowled over by the idea that he couldn't count on even his closest associates.[48]

Yet the backchannel game, the tango between politicians and officials and reporters, is probably inevitable and unstoppable. Even when American presidents resorted to censorship and logging phone calls, the tide could not be stemmed.

For some politicians and officials the need to leak is almost compulsive. One senior CBC editor has told of officials wanting to leave "markers" with reporters whether through conversations or documents so that the roles they played and the positions they took could be chronicled. Bureaucratic and political battles are often so fierce that politicians and officials inevitably seek the advantages to be gained by going to the media with their version of events. There are numerous examples from recent years. It was a source within the Nixon White House, the famous "Deep Throat," that led *Washington Post* reporters Woodward and Bernstein through the many tricks and turns of the Watergate cover-up. An important memorandum on federal strategy towards constitutional talks with the provinces was leaked to the press by someone in the Trudeau government in 1980. The memo infuriated the provinces and embarrassed Trudeau. Leaking details about budgets has become an accepted ritual of Canadian political life. Governments invariably use leaks to test public reaction to budget measures that are being contemplated, with stories about one proposal or another "kited" in the days or weeks before a budget is presented. Opponents of budgets have on occasion gone to the extreme of leaking their contents in order to embarrass the governments concerned. In 1988, a reporter received a copy of the Quebec budget a day before it was to be released and quickly revealed its contents.[49] A copy of Finance Minister Michael Wilson's 1989 budget was given to Global Television's Ottawa bureau chief Doug Small the day before it was to be brought down. Small reported details of the budget on television that night and subsequently faced court charges.

In the years when Brian Mulroney was waiting to make another run at the Conservative Party leadership, he was apparently one of the best sources for insider information on Tory politics and for stories about leader Joe Clark. As Doug Fisher put it, "He raised the leaking of information . . . into an art . . . he sponsored a clever operation on Parliament Hill that fed a regular stream of anti-Clark tales to reporters through two men on the staffs of pro-Mulroney MPs."[50] Those who wished to depose John Turner as Liberal Party leader mounted a similar campaign for years.

A survey of former U.S. government officials conducted by the Institute of Politics at Harvard's John F. Kennedy School of Government found that over 40 percent were sources at one time or another. Eighty percent of those who acted as sources said that they did so primarily to counter false or misleading information, three-quarters wanted to publicize a particular policy option, and 64 percent saw it as a means of boosting support for an on-going initiative.[51] One suspects that the incidence of leaking in Ottawa is at least as great.

In his book *The Government/Press Connection*, Stephen Hess listed the motivations that politicians and officials have for planting stories with reporters. His typology of leaks includes:

1. *The Ego Leak*

Politicians and officials leak to journalists to bolster their own importance and trumpet their achievements. Ego and ambition being the fuel of politics, there is no shortage of those enticed to play the media game. The benefits can be real. To be described in the media as powerful or persuasive, a key strategist or mover of policy, can add luster to one's career and image.

2. *The Goodwill Leak*

An insider will try to build "credit" with a reporter by giving him or her a valuable tip about a forthcoming event or policy. Later the leaker can call on the reporter to have the favour returned.

3. *The Policy Leak*

The motivation is to advance the case for one policy over another. Key documents might be slipped to a reporter and the reporter's ear bent by politicians or officials putting forward the pros and cons of a particular policy. Negative publicity can affect public perceptions and alter the timing of policy initiatives.

4. *The Animus Leak*

This is an attempt to damage or embarrass opponents. Rivalry, jealousy, vendettas, or simple dislike can lead to information being leaked to a reporter. Evidence about a politician's business improprieties, drinking, sexual escapades, mismanagement, declining support, or other sordid dealings can be given to reporters by implacable enemies.

5. *The Trial Balloon*

Reporters will be told about the possibility of a new appointment or policy in the hope that it will receive wide play. If the story provokes an outcry from the public, the government can deny that such a development was ever being contemplated. The government has not sacrificed popularity or prestige and retains flexibility.

6. *The Whistle Blower*

A disenchanted official who has discovered scandal or wrongdoing and wishes to go public with the information. Whistle blowing is not usually based on personal animosity; it is usually the last resort taken after all else has failed and all other channels have been closed off.

There are two additional categories that could be added to Hess' list. Hess doesn't mention the need to correct false information. In many cases, leaks are used to counter rumours or misleading statements. It's a defensive action meant only to set the record straight. Another category is what can be called the "therapeutic leak." Politicians or officials weighed down by heavy responsibilities and socially isolated, far from friends or family, may need someone to confide in. They need to be able to talk openly about their problems with someone who seems concerned and interested. This is, of course, a dangerous game. But this is exactly the kind of relationship that seemed to develop between David Stockman, Ronald Reagan's first Director of Management and Budget, and William Greider of *The Washington Post*. Stockman had apparently turned to Greider to unload his frustrations and disappointments, for understanding and friendship, not realizing that all his confidences would be revealed. The relationship nearly led to Stockman's downfall, as Greider published Stockman's candid admissions in an article entitled "The Education of David Stockman," which appeared in *The Atlantic* in 1981. As Nora Ephron has written, "The world is full of people who honestly don't know that journalists are not their friends."[52]

Perhaps the greatest difficulty in the murky subterranean world of journalists and sources is defining the rules that govern the relationship: what is on and what is off the record, when and how information can be used. The basic understanding is that sources are shielded by anonymity; without this guarantee it would be unlikely that anyone would come forward. Each media organization then has its own rules. Most news organizations will agree to mask their sources in some way, describing them only as an official, a spokesperson, a senior advisor, etc. Some organizations require that a story be confirmed by at least two independent sources before they will publish or broadcast the item. Others are content to run with the information that they've received from a single source and seek no other confirmation.

The critical problem is whether conversations are considered on or off the record. Government officials usually use the following system to set the conditions under which an interview will be granted and serious information exchanged:[53]

on the record:	the official can be quoted directly and identified by name.
on background:	the information can be used, but the source cannot be identified in the story other than by a vague cloak that protects the source such as "an official said," "a source close to the Prime Minister," etc.
deep background:	the information can be used, but no attribution is permitted.
off the record:	the information cannot be used and the source cannot be identified.

Media organizations have also established guidelines to protect their own interests and many do not accept the rules laid down by governments, in fact, this is one of the important ways in which the Gallery has changed. During the tenures of prime ministers from Macdonald through to Pearson, confidences were kept and the rules well understood. Statements that were intended to be off the record were kept off the record. As Romeo Leblanc described the situation that prevailed during Pearson's time, "Agreements stuck in those days. We could give advance copies of policy documents to senior journalists twenty-four hours before they were released. You could organize briefing sessions and have everyone agree on the groundrules. But with the volume, the increased size of the Gallery, the competition became so great that the system broke down."[54]

Jim Coutts' experience when he was principal secretary to Prime Minister Trudeau in the late 1970s was that "some reporters instinctively support and keep agreements. Others would be against you and would break the informal agreement. After that you didn't see them a lot."[55] When John Turner returned to politics in 1984 after an absence of almost a decade, he was apparently quite startled by the extent to which the old understandings had dissolved. Among his first blunders on returning to the political wars was to tell reporters about his cool relationship with Pierre Trudeau, believing that his remarks about Trudeau were off the record. The next day his comments were the leading story in the news. Brian Mulroney was stung in a similar way when he spoke to reporters on a flight to his riding during the 1984 election about his feelings regarding the appointment of Bryce Mackasey to a diplomatic post by John Turner. The following day he was quoted in *The Ottawa Citizen* as having said, "There's no whore like an old whore. If I'd been in Bryce's place, I would have been the first with my nose in the trough, just like all the rest of them."[56] The rules governing that conversation were blurry, to say the least. Soon after that, Mulroney imposed a tight-fisted policy limiting the access that reporters had enjoyed.

The rules vary from news organization to news organization, and reporters often work out their own private deals with sources. Val Sears of *The Toronto Star* has what he calls "Sears rule": "Everything is on the record unless he agrees that it's not."[57] Charles Lynch's view is that "We are in the business of disclosing and everything is on-the-record."[58] *The Globe and Mail* warns its reporters in its 1987 "Policy Guide for Globe and Mail Reporters" that they should:

> Be careful about how you use off-the-record conversations. In the first place, don't go off the record unless you have to and, if you do, make sure both parties understand where the agreement starts and where it stops. Never allow anyone to make a statement and then say, "Of course, that's off the record." You might sometimes have to make allowance for people making their first contact with a newspaper reporter (but who have watched Lou Grant) but be merciless with those accustomed to dealing with reporters.
>
> If you do go off the record, make clear what exactly this means. There are different types of off-the-record agreements and it's not always true that the information can't be used. For example, can we use the information to try to get it on the record elsewhere? Can we use the material without named attribution?

The understanding at *The Ottawa Citizen* is that stories must have full attribution "in all cases unless there are extremely good reasons not to do it."[59] Most news organizations insist that information received from a source be verified by a second independent source before they proceed with the story. The CBC's guidebook entitled *Journalistic Policy* states that:

> Information from sources who do not wish to be publicly identified may be used if the source is known to the journalist and has a prima facie credibility. However, to avoid the possibility of being manipulated to advance inaccurate or biased information, the journalist must carefully check the reliability of the source and must obtain corroborative evidence from other pertinent sources.[60]

Ericson and his associates found that if a story was important enough, reporters would break the rules and violate previous understandings. On a hot story news executives would "play hard ball" and go with the information, regardless of how it was obtained.[61]

Some journalists find ways to use the information they've obtained so that it "surfaces" in some way. A favourite tactic is for reporters to try to legitimize the story by circulating the information, although not the source, to third parties who are willing to make the matter public. Information can be passed to MPs, government officials, or other journalists who are willing to ask questions, release corroborating evidence, or speculate on "current rumours." Once the matter is in the public realm, the journalist is then free to comment on new developments. The basic rule is that leaks of statements by sources are a form of political currency and, like real money, they are circulated, spent, gain interest for long-term investment, and used to pay off debts—but inevitably they are used. The old confidences, the old relationships based on knowing trust have been eroded. Today, politicians have to be more careful, distant, and secretive, constantly patching up holes in their leaking ships and aware that everything they say can be on the record. One is reminded both of John F. Kennedy's comment that in politics, "one has no friends," and his warning that "If there is more than one person (yourself) in a room, consider anything said to be on the record and a probable headline in the morning paper."[62]

SETTING THE MEDIA'S AGENDA

The media's agenda is set by the leading news organizations and to some degree by leading columnists and commentators. Identifying which news organizations are the leaders is always a dangerous game, given the diverse audiences that are reached by the different media institutions and the difficulty of establishing appropriate criteria. In his study of "the inner ring" of American news organizations, Stephen Hess used four criteria for evaluating influence. These were scope, the extent to which an organization reaches a national audience; resources, the size of the organization in terms of number of personnel, budget, and amount of money spent on investigation and travel; audience, the size and prestige of the audience; and purpose, which Hess defines as "seriousness of function."[63] Using these criteria, there are relatively few big players that have the power to set the agenda among the Canadian media. They are *The Globe and Mail, The Toronto Star, Le Devoir, La Presse, The Financial Post, Maclean's,* CBC television's *The National* and *The Journal,* CBC English Radio News, CTV's *National News,* Radio-Canada's *Télé-journal* and *Le Point,* and Canadian Press/Broadcast News and the Southam News wire services. Each of these organizations is read, watched, or listened to by sizeable populations, reports in a national context, and has some prestige. They are at the top of the pecking order.

In 1989 CBC's *The National* had a complement of about thirty reporters, eight in Ottawa and six overseas. CTV's *National News* had fifteen reporters scattered through seven domestic and four foreign bureaus, and it had four reporters in Ottawa.[64]

Excluded from the first tier are newspapers such as *The Ottawa Citizen, The Montreal Gazette, The Calgary Herald, The Winnipeg Free Press,* and *Le Soleil* of Quebec City, which are important to their regions but do not have a national voice. *The Ottawa Citizen,* which has pretentions to being *The Washington Post* of Canada, is read widely by Ottawa politicians and civil servants and by members of the Press Gallery, but its claim to national stature seems premature based on its lack of presence outside the capital region. *The Toronto Star,* on the other hand, which services Metropolitan Toronto and its satellite communities, has the largest circulation of any newspaper in Canada. It reaches the top rung by the sheer weight of its circulation and resources. *The Financial Post, Le Devoir,* and *La Presse* have relatively small readerships, but *The Financial Post* and *Le Devoir* reach an elite audience and *La Presse* is, if you wish, *The Toronto Star* of Canada's largest French-speaking city. The Canadian Press wire service (CP) and its radio arm, Broadcast News, are the clearinghouses for much of the news consumed by media organizations across Canada. CP not only supplies news to its subscribers, it is also a critical reference point for editors and producers about the priorities and play that stories should receive. The Southam News Service, which has a dozen or so journalists in Ottawa, provides background and commentary to supplement reporting by the Southam papers across the country.

By all accounts, *The Globe and Mail* has a unique role among media institutions in setting the public's as well as the media's agenda. The present paper evolved out of an amalgamation of three newspapers, the *Globe,* the *Mail,* and the *Empire;* however, it still retains the motto chosen by George Brown for the masthead of the original *Globe,* "The subject who is truly loyal to the Chief Magistrate will neither advise nor submit to arbitrary measures." *The Globe and Mail* does a number of things that no other newspaper does in quite the same way. Since 1980, the paper has had a national edition that is printed in centres across Canada and appears in all major cities and communities. Its "Report on Business," which dates from 1962, has a wide circulation among the business elite. *The Globe and Mail* has also made an extraordinary commitment to international coverage, with approximately a dozen correspondents posted outside Canada. Yet the paper's real influence is its role in shaping political developments in Ottawa, largely because it is the paper read by most members of the political and bureaucratic elite. A study of over 600 leading decision makers interviewed by the Institute of Behavioral Research in the late 1970s found that 89 percent of business leaders, 98 percent of high-ranking civil servants, and 91 percent of media managers in the sample were regular readers of *The Globe and Mail*.[65] In a survey of members of Parliament conducted in 1983 by David Dewitt and John Kirton, 65 percent of the MPs who responded said that they read the paper daily, and 94 percent read it at least once a week.[66]

The Globe and Mail's influence reaches beyond its circulation. Stories that appear in the paper are often the trigger for questions that opposition politicians will ask during Question Period. Reporting by other media is also affected, as many news organizations use the paper as a reference point for their own news line-ups and will generally feature stories or issues that the paper has prominently reported. According to *The Globe and Mail's* national political editor, Hugh Winsor, "Other papers often get the story faster but when the Globe picks it up, the story gains an imprimatur that it wouldn't ordinarily have. We are everywhere in the morning and we have that good gray respectability."[67] Moreover, Don Newman, now with CBC television but formerly with *The Globe and Mail*, remembers that "When you were writing your story you knew that you were writing Question Period the next day."[68] As Hugh Winsor explains, "The opposition parties, instead of doing their own research, take their questions for Question Period from *The Globe and Mail*. This makes everything very predictable because the Government reads the Globe too so they know what questions to anticipate."[69] Peter Stockland of *The Calgary Sun* and *The Edmonton Sun* contends that *The Globe and Mail* is the linchpin in a circular process whereby what's in the paper influences Question Period and Question Period, in turn, affects what is shown on television news. As Stockland has described it:

> Everybody acknowledges that *The Globe and Mail* sets the agenda for the day
> . . . the opposition is going to take their first two swings at the cat with what
> *The Globe* has set as the agenda. And then they'll come out after Question
> Period . . . and repeat what they just said in the House, which everybody's just
> read in *The Globe and Mail* that morning, and they'll all give it to the waiting

hordes (of reporters) and they'll all run off and file it. It seems like it's almost a self-perpetuating circle. It's like those games with the silver balls on the strings. You pull one out at this end and it hits the ball and the other ball comes out at the other end and they just rock back and forth until all the motion ceases. Which is summer recess.[70]

Others don't credit *The Globe and Mail* with such singular power. They see the process as much more complicated and amorphous, with the *Globe* being only one of a number of potential agenda setters. Michel Vastel of *La Presse*, for example, believes that the media feeds off itself. Stories often originate with sources who have leaked information to a leading newspaper, then "the opposition raises that with all the theatrics and the drama they can put in it."[71] Having made it onto television that night, the story emerges again in the newspapers the following morning.

There is, however, nothing automatic or spontaneous about the chain reaction that Vastel has described. The chain can be broken at various points. Opposition MPs may have their own agenda, television editors and producers can choose not to run the highlights of Question Period, or the story can be smothered by other events or issues. According to Elly Alboim, "Everybody has the power to affect the agenda negatively more than positively if they choose not to cover a story—not to keep it going. There are competitive pressures and there's a tendency not to go with other people's stories. It's disheartening and pernicious. Some stories are too big and you have to cover them. Other times a consensus doesn't develop."[72] There have been many occasions when a leading news organization has broken what it considers a major story only to have it drop like a stone into water without so much as a ripple being created. There is little that is inevitable or predictable about the process.

Some observers believe that there is a collective mentality among journalists that largely sets the media's agenda, a mentality that is rooted in "pack journalism." Pack journalism was perhaps best described by Timothy Crouse in his highly readable book *The Boys on the Bus.* Crouse, at the time a writer for *Rolling Stone* magazine, followed the press as it reported the 1972 U.S. presidential race. He found that covering a major event, especially an election, meant that one had to join a pack of other journalists. Trapped in the same situation, hearing the same speeches, reading the same press releases, mining the same sources, eating and drinking together, and spending long periods of time in each other's company, they eventually came "to believe the same rumors, subscribe to the same theories, and write the same stories."[73] A cast of mind developed among the pack as a whole, a herd instinct that had all the members of the press stampeding in the same direction. While the pack phenomenon has been most apparent during election coverage or other events where reporters are isolated together for significant periods of time, some argue that the pack forms even in ordinary, everyday circumstances.

Peter Dempson recalls in his memoirs that sharing and borrowing stories among "syndicates" of reporters was routine in the Press Gallery during his day; the same stories, slightly altered, would often appear in several newspapers at the same time.[74] Today the system is more subtle, but no less pervasive. According to George Radwanski, the pack instinct (which he describes as "tremendous") emerges out of both social needs and competitive pressures.[75] There is, on the one hand, the strong human need to be accepted by one's peers and colleagues and in Ottawa this also means being included in a social scene that revolves around the National Press Club, private parties, and key professional contacts and exchanges. The view of Graham Parley of *The Ottawa Citizen* is that "It's a cliché, but a lot of opinions are formed in the press club bar. If someone has a logical argument then it has an impact. Stories along that line will appear. There's a cross-fertilization."[76] Reporters are also driven by the necessity of "matching" what their competitors are doing. If they do not have the same story, they have to justify their choice to their editors and the logic of most journalists is that it's better to be safe—and match their competitor's story—than sorry. There is also a good deal of direct exchange and sharing. Journalists will often give their notes to other journalists to allow them to catch up; some will even borrow quotes or use phrases passed on by colleagues, particularly those who work for news organizations whose product does not appear in the same market.

Reporters try not only to match competitors but also to find new facts or a different angle that will advance the story. Don Newman explains it this way: "The pack doesn't exist in any formal way but a good story is a good story is a good story. When a story breaks, on a daily basis, others will try to advance the story and that's the way the pack works. The pack also works on impressions. Politicians tend to be hot and cold with the Gallery. It's more a mentality of personalities than it is of ideology."[77] So the Gallery seems to fixate on the same story, with the same point of view, at the same time. Perhaps the best metaphor was applied by Lloyd Tataryn when he compared Ottawa commentators to crows sitting on a power line. When one leaves to station himself somewhere else, the others follow. When one flies back to the power line, all the others move as well.[78] While this analogy stretches the point, a collective feeding does seem to take place. Jeff Sallot of *The Globe and Mail* believes that group think can be a problem when "a mind set takes over that Joe Clark is a wimp, that Trudeau is arrogant, that Mulroney is baloney or whatever the consensus seems to be."[79] Maintaining an independent view in the face of social and professional pressures can be difficult, if not impossible. During the famous "wimp watch" of 1978-79, when the Gallery was producing story after story about Joe Clark's mistakes, editors sought stories about Clark's bungling from their reporters, who were trying to outdo each other in finding gaffes and errors to report. A story about what a good job Clark was doing would not have fit what was expected, would probably have not made it into news stories, and would have been lost amid the tide of anti-Clark ridicule.

The Gallery is certainly one of the most influential institutions in Canadian life. While it continues to undergo great changes, it remains an institution with long traditions, distinct habits and outlooks, and pervasive power. It's the looking glass through which Canadians view the unfolding drama of national politics.

NOTES

1. The idea for the title comes from Kim Richard Nossal "Allison Through the (Ottawa) Looking Glass: Bureaucratic Politics and Foreign Policy in a Parliamentary System," *Canadian Public Administration* (Winter 1979), pp. 610-26.
2. Colin Seymour-Ure, "The Parliamentary Press Gallery in Ottawa," *Parliamentary Affairs* (1962), p. 36.
3. Alex Shprintsen, "The Gallery: History and Evolution," *Parliamentary Government*, vol. 7, nos. 1-2 (1987), 14-15.
4. Peter Dempson, *Assignment Ottawa: Seventeen Years in the Press Gallery* (Toronto: General Publishing, 1968), pp. 2-3.
5. Ibid., p. 7.
6. Judy Morrison, "The House On The Hill," *Radio Guide*, September 1987, p. 5.
7. Ibid., p. 6.
8. Ibid.
9. Shprintsen, p. 15.
10. Seymour-Ure, p. 40.
11. Shprintsen, p. 14.
12. Elly Alboim, "Inside the News Story: Meech Lake As Viewed By An Ottawa Bureau Chief," in *Meech Lake and Canada: Perspectives from the West*, Roger Gibbins et al., eds. (Edmonton: Academic Printing and Publishing, 1988), pp. 238-39.
13. Ibid.
14. Interview with Elly Alboim, Ottawa, 6 July 1988.
15. Ibid.
16. "The Fourth Estate: The Parliamentary Press Gallery," *Parliamentary Government*, vol. 3, no. 1 (Winter 1982), 11.
17. Peter Desbarats, *Guide to Canadian News Media* (Toronto: Harcourt, Brace, Jovanovich, 1989), p. 94.
18. Interview with Elly Alboim.
19. Quoted in Lloyd Tataryn, *Power, Politics and The Press* (Toronto: Deneau, 1985), p. 140.
20. Geoffrey Stevens, "The Influence of the Media in the Legislative Process," in *The Legislative Process in Canada*, W.A.W. Neilson and

J.C. MacPherson, eds., (Toronto: Institute for Research on Public Policy, 1978), p. 228.

21. Interview with Elly Alboim.
22. Shprintsen, p. 15.
23. W.H. Kesterton, *A History of Journalism in Canada* (Ottawa: Carleton University Press, 1984), p. 163.
24. Shprintsen, p. 15.
25. Quoted in Desbarats, p. 98.
26. "CBC, Bell Canada Face Discrimination Probe," *The Vancouver Sun*, 17 July 1989, p. A6.
27. Beverly Beyette, "Media Women's Glum Message," *Los Angeles Times*, 3 March 1988, p. VI.
28. Michel Gratton, *"So What Are The Boys Saying?"* (Toronto: McGraw-Hill Ryerson, 1987), p. 4.
29. Christopher Harris, "La Tribune De La Press," *Parliamentary Government*, vol. 7, nos. 1-2 (1987), 12.
30. Interview with Romeo Leblanc, Ottawa, 26 May 1987.
31. Jeffrey Simpson, "Drifting out of Touch," *The Globe and Mail*, 21 June 1989, p. 6.
32. Arthur Siegel, *Politics and the Media in Canada* (Toronto: McGraw-Hill Ryerson, 1983), pp. 222-27.
33. Harris, p. 11.
34. Lysiane Gagnon, "Journalism and Ideologies in Quebec," in *Royal Commission on Newspapers*, vol. II (Ottawa: Supply and Services Canada, 1981), p. 28.
35. Graham Fraser and Ross Howard, "Linguistic Solitude Often Present in French, English News Coverage," *The Globe and Mail*, 7 April 1988, p. A8.
36. Ibid.
37. Interview with Vince Carlin, Toronto, 5 June 1987.
38. Quoted in Arthur Siegel, *Politics and the Media in Canada* (Toronto: McGraw-Hill Ryerson, 1983), p. 222.
39. Interview with Romeo Leblanc.
40. Marcel Pepin, "Prospects and Proposals," in *Politics and the Media* (Toronto: Erindale College and Reader's Digest Foundation of Canada, 1981), p. 99.
41. Interview with Elly Alboim.
42. Interview with Jason Moscovitz, Ottawa, 6 July 1987.
43. Stevie Cameron, *Ottawa Inside Out* (Toronto: Key Porter Books, 1989), p. 226.
44. Richard Ericson, Patricia Baranek, and Janet Chan, *Negotiating Control: A Study of News Sources* (Toronto: University of Toronto Press, 1989), p. 203.
45. Ibid.

46. Elie Abel, *Leaking: Who Does It? Who Benefits? At What Cost?* (New York: Twentieth Century Fund/Priority Press, 1987), p. 17.
47. Correspondence with Anthony Westell, November 1989.
48. Gratton, p. xiii.
49. Mark Hertsgaard, *On Bended Knee: The Press and the Reagan Presidency* (New York: Farrar Straus Giroux, 1988), p. 147
50. Jeffrey Simpson, "Threat to Press Freedom," *The Globe and Mail*, 31 May 1989, p. 6.
50. Interview with Doug Fisher, Ottawa, 27 January 1988. See also Patrick Martin, Allan Gregg, and George Perlin, *Contenders: The Tory Quest For Power* (Scarborough: Prentice-Hall, 1983), p. 96.
51. Abel, p. 62.
52. Nora Ephron, "Dangerous Liaisons: Journalists and Their Sources," *Columbia Journalism Review* (July/August 1989), p. 22.
53. Michael Grossman and Martha Kumar, *Portraying The President: The White House and the News Media* (Baltimore: The Johns Hopkins University Press, 1981), p. 227.
54. Interview with Romeo Leblanc.
55. Interview with Jim Coutts, Toronto, 3 June 1987.
56. Quoted in Gratton, p. 27.
57. Interview with Val Sears, Ottawa, 26 May 1987.
58. Quoted in Paul McLaughlin, *How to Interview* (North Vancouver: International Self-Counsel Press, 1986), p. 222. Reproduced courtesy of the publisher.
59. Quote cited in Chethan Lakshman, " New Editor Bans Anonymous News Sources" *Content* (January/February 1990), p. 6.
60. Canadian Broadcasting Corporation, *Journalistic Policy* (Ottawa, 1982), p. 31.
61. Richard Ericson, Patricia Baranek, and Janet Chan, *Visualizing Deviance: A Study of News Organization* (Toronto: University of Toronto Press, 1987), p. 243-44.
62. Hugh Sidey, "Smile and Sharpen Your Knives," *Time*, 6 February 1989, p. 29.
63. Stephen Hess, *The Washington Reporters* (Washington, D.C.: The Brookings Institution, 1981), pp. 26-27.
64. John Haslett Cuff, "Differences in CBC and CTV Newscasts Not Always Subtle," *The Globe and Mail*, 15 June 1989, p. A15.
65. Frederick Fletcher, *The Newspaper and Public Affairs*, vol. VII of the *Royal Commission on Newspapers* (Ottawa: Supply and Services Canada, 1981), p. 20.
66. David Dewitt and John Kirton, "The Media and Canadian Policy During the 1982 War in Lebanon," *Middle East Focus*, vol. 9, no. 3 (Winter 1986-87), 13.
67. Interview with Hugh Winsor, Ottawa, 19 April 1989.

68. Interview with Don Newman, Ottawa, 26 January 1988.
69. Interview with Hugh Winsor.
70. "The Parliamentary Press Gallery," *The Media File*, CBC Radio (1987), transcript.
71. Ibid.
72. Interview with Elly Alboim.
73. Timothy Crouse, *The Boys On The Bus* (New York: Ballantine, 1973), pp. 7-8, 15.
74. Dempson, p. 21.
75. Interview with George Radwanski, Toronto, 23 May 1986.
76. Interview with Graham Parley.
77. Interview with Don Newman.
78. Tataryn, p. 165.
79. Interview with Jeff Sallot, Ottawa, 28 May 1987.

4

Television News: The Infotainment Agenda

The relationship between politicians and the public is conditioned to an extraordinary degree by the demands imposed by television. Television's routines, rituals, and ceremonies, and the fact that it is primarily an entertainment medium, have altered the ways that politicians perform their roles. Television is the stage upon which the political drama takes place.

The power of television to mould public opinion is one of the essential realities of Canadian political life. Canadians view the political world mostly through television: polls indicate that Canadians use television as their preferred source for "detailed report and analysis" of national and international events as well as for local news, once the preserve of newspapers.[1] The network news programs have an enormous reach. CBC's *The National*, which airs at 10:00 p.m., attracted an average of 1,799,000 viewers in 1989 with audiences that frequently surpassed two million viewers. The *CTV National News*, which is on at 11:00 p.m., has an average audience of 1,178,000.[2] CTV's news program attracts 32 percent of the viewers in the eleven o'clock time slot; *The National* gets 19 percent of the audience at ten o'clock.[3] In the CBC's submission to the Task Force on Broadcasting Policy, it described its own news and current affairs programs as "the informational spinal column for the nation,"[4] a claim that may seem pretentious but is not without some truth.

What gives television its magnetic power is the sense of intimacy, of direct experience, of "witnessing": television conveys the feeling to people that they are seeing things for themselves, firsthand. Political leaders are no longer distant, mysterious figures but "pseudo-intimate acquaintances,"[5] part of a nightly parade of people whom viewers feel they have come to know. As Reuven Frank wrote nearly a generation ago, "The highest power of television journalism is not in the transmission of information but in the transmission of experience."[6]

A significant scholarly literature now exists on television news reporting. There is widespread agreement in the scholarly community that television now operates according to a well-defined set of routines and formats. Journalistic decisions are made within the constraints of a highly structured news format and the format, in turn, largely dictates the nature of news. The driving force is entertainment—not journalism, public service, or political beliefs. Indeed, some would argue that the current formats are so rigid, and news shaped so much to appeal to and entertain the consumer, that journalists are forced to work under circumstances that drastically limit their discretion. As is discussed in Chapters Two and Three, however, journalists can still exercise considerable power.

THE AUDIENCE IMPERATIVE

The structure of television news is dictated by a series of harsh realities. The most basic external reality is that news shows must sell the size and characteristics of their audiences to advertisers in order to survive. Advertisers buy audiences, not programs. As the audience has increasingly splintered with the proliferation of new channels, services, and technologies, networks are locked in a desperate battle to capture and maintain audiences and, of course, to keep their advertisers. Where in the 1950s the CBC, for example, had only to compete against the main U.S. networks, it now has to contend with cable systems that carry at least thirty-six channels in most Canadian cities. A number of American systems already offer packages with more than 100 channels. By the mid-1990s most systems will offer more than fifty channels, and some expect that the number of channels will mushroom to as many as 200 by the turn of the century. Home satellite dishes will cause even greater diffusion when they become readily available at cheaper prices. Between 250,000 and 300,000 dishes have been sold in Canada so far. Viewers will literally be able to choose from a galaxy of channels. The advent of VCRs has also fragmented the audience by giving viewers the freedom to move beyond the constraints of channels, schedules, and, most importantly, commercials. Television advertisers have become increasingly nervous as viewers have gained the capacity to "zap" from channel to channel and "zip" through commercials, and have undertaken a series of new strategies to ensure that their messages get through. The advertising industry has fought back with shorter, sharper, funnier, and more entertaining commercials, commercials that hook the viewer immediately.

Another challenge is pay-TV. News afficionados in Canada now have access to the Cable News Network (CNN), based in Atlanta, which provides around the clock news. CNN now reaches 1,300,000 Canadian homes. But more important, perhaps to the CBC in particular, is that the specialty channels on pay-TV such as Arts and Entertainment and Business channels appeal to the same older, higher income audience that has been the backbone of CBC's news and current affairs viewership.[7] The CBC mounted its own all-news channel, *CBC NewsWorld*, in 1989 in concert with *The Globe and Mail's* "Report on Business," *The Financial Times*, and other private outlets. The goal is to give Canadians an ongoing window on events with in-depth coverage. It is too early to speculate on the effect that this channel will have on the nature of the news-watching audience, or whether the channel will be able to survive. The worst fear is that *CBC NewsWorld* will become background noise offering second-hand news served up cold.

The expanding horizon of local television news now poses an unexpected threat to network news programs. Local news programs, which are the flagships of their stations, increasingly carry national and international news segments that were traditionally the preserve of the network-wide broadcast, and have largely adopted the American big city news model with its diet of "happy news," attention-grabbing human interest stories, and lively chit-chat. As Ronald Berman has pointed out, "Local stations need to sell themselves and not the news."[8] During the 1960s and 1970s many local stations in the U.S. brought in "news doctors," consultants who advised them how to package their news in order to get the highest possible viewership. Part of the basic prescription, according to Barbara Matusow, was a faster pace with shorter reports; a turn towards tabloid-style sensationalism; greater emotional content in news items; advice on how to cope with the rigours of daily life, with service-oriented features on health care, money management, legal problems, etc.; and a friendly, "caring," anchor team. Audiences are now familiar with the "willards" who host local television news shows, folksy downhome types who embody civic spirit and are cheerleaders for civic pride and virtues. Surveys also showed that people wished to be reassured that their world, particularly their local neighbourhood, was safe and secure. There was also to be a new emphasis on portraying personalities and celebrities.[9] Some local stations in the United States now carry segments of the program *Lifestyles of the Rich and Famous*, not as filler but in response to what the audience apparently wants. The threat, as some see it, is that the definition of what constitutes news has changed from "the nation's business" to "how people live their lives" and "what people are doing."[10]

Even more disturbing to those who believe in serious journalism is the new world of tabloid television programs, called "trash TV" or "slime time television" by some observers, which have become popular in some American and Canadian markets. Shows such as *Inside Edition, This Evening,* and *A Current Affair* deal with crime, celebrities, odd-ball occurrences, and sensational events but use a news program format. According to writer Philip Weiss, "The untrustworthy family is the central narrative of much of this journalism. Whenever a piece begins with the image of a happy couple you can be sure someone is about to be betrayed, flayed, made a fool of, sprayed with gunshot, burned to a still-living crisp after a visit to Disneyland, or shot outside the hot tub while ┤ ~~ing several women."[11] "Samurai" journalists interview killers diences for an "inside look" at the latest in drugs, sex, or mon and trade freely in gossip, rumour, and innuendo. When a T⟨ accused of attempting to murder her parents by allegedly ⟨

rat poison, she was interviewed on two of the shows on the same evening.[12]

With audience fragmentation increasing and the advent of programs that masquerade as news, some of the old assumptions may be changing. Reuven Frank of NBC News has described the essential difference between meeting the demands of newspaper and television audiences, a difference that lies at the heart of how television news is now presented: "A newspaper . . . can easily afford to print an item of conceivable interest to only a small percentage of its readers. A television news program must be put together with the assumption that each item will be of some interest to everyone that watches. Every time a newspaper includes a feature which will attract a specialized group, it can assume it is adding at least a bit to its circulation. To the degree a television news program includes an item of this sort . . . it must assume its audience will diminish."[13] The presumption has always been that television news must appeal not to narrow segments of viewers, but to the entire market-place.

It might be argued, however, that "narrow-casting," the targeting of relatively small audience segments that have certain characteristics desired by advertisers (educated, white-collar audiences with discretionary income), may become a sanctuary for serious, contemplative, television journalism. The *MacNeil-Lehrer Report*, for example, which airs on the American educational Public Broadcasting System, explores news events in far greater depth and with fewer jolts than regular network newscasts, and has attracted a "small but loyal up-scale audience."[14]

Another factor are changes in production that have taken place, particularly the technique that Morris Wolfe calls "jolts per minute," although it is also known as "machine gunning." In the late 1960s, American television executives realized that ". . . if a long time goes by without a jolt of verbal or physical or emotional violence on the screen, or if the picture doesn't change quickly enough as a result of a jolt of rapid editing or camera movement, or movement by people or objects within the frame, or if the soundtrack doesn't have enough decibels, viewers will switch to a channel and a programme that gives them more of those things."[15] Jolts soon became a strong feature in American entertainment programming and also had an impact on news. News directors are now conscious that the news must also contain its share of jolts, usually through pacing, graphics, stings, etc.

While no advertising appears during CBC's *The National*, the network as a whole is increasingly dependent on advertising revenues since the government imposed several rounds of strenuous cut-backs beginning in 1984. Advertising does appear during *The Journal* and advertising on shows that appear before *The National* depends on audiences switching to CBC in anticipation of the news. The Crown corporation also has to satisfy the privately-owned affiliates that account for approximately 35 percent of the CBC's total audience. Most important is that CBC management is deeply committed to winning the battle for the newswatching audience because news is central to the CBC's mandate. In order to compete, the CBC has had to adopt some of the formats and values that have triumphed in North American television through economic and audience pressures. This has forced the CBC to change the character of its news reporting. Before going to the 10:00 p.m. time slot in 1982, *The National* used surveys and special viewings to test audience reactions. The program was completely overhauled to make the show more visually exciting, faster paced, and marked by a snappier delivery by the newsreader. According to producer Tony Burman, *The National* had to be "sharper, faster, tougher . . . first and best."[16]

Some of the pressures to maintain the current news format are internal. Reporters are in stiff competition over assignments, prestige, and promotion; to most, getting their reports on the news is the scorecard by which they measure daily success and, over a longer period of time, their status within the news organization. Having one's story not appear after much work and effort is discouraging, even painful, under the best of circumstances. To win the battle, reporters have to supply the kinds of stories that will appeal to their editors and producers, stories that fit the news format. One reporter in the CBC's Ottawa Bureau described the situation this way: "It's become more and more like a business. Before it was more creative, compassionate and caring. The war was lost when the news went to ten o'clock. There's a greater emphasis on entertainment, on interesting stories. There are fewer Ottawa stories and we have to make our stories more exciting. They now had to be more dramatic, more human, more visual. To get your story on the air you have to show that it isn't just another one of those Ottawa stories. You jazz it up so that it's more interesting, colourful and moves along. The desk's attitude is that nobody cares about policies. They want human interest— news that they can use."[17] David Halton, the CBC's chief political correspondent, expressed it this way:

> Any dramatic news will obviously make it a lot more easily than the drier and more difficult process stories about government. . . . If I did a series of exposés of government activity, my desk in Toronto would think this is tremendous stuff. Keep it up. If I did a series of stories on government policies that happened to be working out extremely well, they'd look askance and say what's happening to Halton . . .?[18]

Ed Joyce, a former president of CBS News, recounts in his memoirs how ABC reporter Ted Koppel set out to impress his superiors after falling into disfavour by using interesting graphics and a punchier style. Koppel's climb up the ladder was soon assured.[19]

When interviewed about their work, television reporters rarely talk about their audience. Perhaps it's too vast, distant, and indistinct. When at work, their main concern is a small, immediate audience of editors and producers. News stories are a group endeavour, with reporters' scripts approved in advance and usually well worked over by a team of editors, producers, and writers. When journalists step out of the confines of their own world, however, they are often surprised by the extent to which they are recognized, have developed a following, and have even become celebrities. And the hard fact is that the format within which their reports must fit and the organizational context within which they must fight to survive is determined largely by perceived audience demands—an audience imperative.

THE TELEVISION NEWS FORMAT

Todd Gitlin, whose book *The Whole World Is Watching* has become something of a modern classic for students of politics and communications, has argued that television is structured to fit precise "frames." To Gitlin, "Frames are principles of selection, emphasis and presentation composed of little tacit theories about what exists, what happens and what matters."[20] He believes the frame is based on ideological assumptions that are meant to preserve the power structure in society. The frame is "clamped over the event" being reported so that only stories or elements of stories that fit the frame are likely to be selected.[21] Stories that fall outside the frame, that do not have certain inherent characteristics, are dispensed with or downplayed. They simply do not become part of television's depiction of reality. Other scholars use different terms to describe similar phenomena; Altheide refers to the "news perspective," while Ranney uses the term "structural bias."[22]

Researchers have different views about the characteristics of news frames, of what the news formula actually consists of. For instance, Galtung and Ruge identify twenty characteristics in their well-known study.[23] For the purposes of this chapter, only some of the most obvious attributes will be discussed. The first and most essential attribute is that news has an "instant" quality: news is what is happening now or is about to happen, not what happened last week or even yesterday. Even if the story is a continuing one that takes place over a considerable length of time, such as an election or a court case, reporters have to find a new angle each day. News takes place in the "continuous present tense."[24] Like freshly-baked bread, it quickly grows stale; the events of last week or even yesterday, regardless of how important they may have been, can be displaced by almost any new development, regardless of how trivial. News is constantly turning over, and the speed of modern communications has ensured that the shelf-life of news stories is desperately short. For example, the Soviet-American agreement on reducing intermediate-range nuclear weapons negotiated in December 1987, arguably one of the most momentous events in the history of the post-war era, lasted for barely two days as a news story. Hurricanes, earthquakes, and plane crashes quickly become yesterday's news. The U.S. invasion of Panama in December 1989 was rapidly displaced as the lead news story by the fall of the Ceausescu regime in Romania during the same week.

Much of the work of editors and producers involves "winnowing" what they consider real news from the ocean of material that descends on them each day. At *The National*, thirty to forty hours of videotape and at least half a million words of wire service copy come in each day.[25] There are decision points, a series of ever narrowing gates, throughout the news day that eliminate most of the material that comes in. Journalists often claim that decisions are made on the basis of instinct, of having a nose for the story, and that news stories are easily recognized. Journalistic experience and training are seen as prerequisites for making these judgements. The way in which the newscast is structured, however, also conditions the decisions that can be made. News stories are usually grouped into subject areas or clusters so that the newscast as a whole is balanced in terms of the topics presented; in this respect television news resembles the format found in the front section of newspapers, where a number of pages are devoted to certain types of news. At the beginning of the newscast, two or three stories are given the lead. Canadian networks seek a balance among national, international, and regional stories, as well as reporting disaster or human interest stories. Stories out of Ottawa will be grouped together. A plane crash and an earthquake would likely be reported in the same cluster. There is usually room for between two and four items from each subject area, but a heavy news day in any one area can consume more than four stories. Normally, however, the space allocated for any one cluster, for instance, Ottawa news, does not intrude dramatically on the space available for others regardless of how heavy a news day it may have been on a particular topic. One producer has observed that the process is quite routine and mechanical, "a paint by numbers" system,[26] although others insist that senses and "feel" are still of prime importance in shaping the news.

Stories that fit the needs of television are ones that can be easily labelled and condensed. Stories are described using catch words such as "Iran Contra," "tunagate," or "free trade." This kind of shorthand not only helps simplify issues but also ensures that the story will not have to be re-explained to viewers with each new development. In most cases, a new event or situation is explained only once; after that, the presumption is that the audience is already aware of the details of the story and only the politics of the issue now need to be covered. In fact, complex policy initiatives such as free trade, the Meech Lake Constitutional Accord, or the Goods and Services Tax may need repeated explanation to be fully understood, something that the current television news format does not allow for. Small wonder, then, that surveys show that Canadians know little about the Meech Lake Accord even though it has been a major news story for over three years.[27] In a departure from previous practice, CBC's *The National* has re-explained the contents of the accord on several occasions during periods of heavy coverage in 1989 and 1990.

These examples highlight perhaps the most difficult problem in television news: how to telescope a complex event or issue into the time frame required by the format. The average news story is roughly ninety seconds long and contains no more than 150 to 250 words; in fact, a transcript of *The National* or the *CTV National News* would take up only about one-third of the front page of a newspaper. "Quick and dirty in a minute thirty" is an expression widely used among TV journalists. The ideal length of a clip of someone speaking or being interviewed is, according to one CBC producer, twelve seconds.[28] CTV's Craig Oliver remembers that in the mid-1970s clips were roughly forty seconds in length, but "now if they're 16 seconds, the desk is asking us why they're so long. There's a constant pressure for tighter clips and livelier items."[29] The trend is towards "ballistics," clips that are five or six second bursts. Walter Cronkite once described television news as "a headline service" and complained about the difficulty of "shoving a hundred pounds of news into a one-pound bag every evening."[30] The rationale for coverage being so brutally truncated is the perceived attention span of viewers and the need to grab and hold the audience with sharp, fast-paced, action-oriented stories.

Drama is the prime ingredient of most news stories. As NBC's Reuven Frank once put it in a much-quoted memo, "Every news story should, without sacrifice of probity or responsibility, display the attributes of fiction, of drama."[31] Van Gordon Sauter, former president of CBS News, put it this way: "The kind of thing we're looking for is something that evokes an emotional response. When I go back there to the Fishbowl, I tell them God-damnit, we've got to touch people. They've got to feel a relationship with us. A lot of stories have inherent drama, but others have to be done in a way that will bring out an emotional response."[32] Drama does require sensationalism, winners and losers, and an emotional human element, but most of all it requires conflict. As a CBC news editor observed about the CBC news process, "We look for conflict often to the exclusion of a story. It's overwhelmingly prevalent. It's the nature of journalism to be a storyteller. It needs drama."[33] In television news, conflict is structured in a certain way. Largely because of demands for objectivity and fairness that have come from government regulators, as well as the need not to take positions that might offend too many people in a mass audience, almost all news stories have a point-counterpoint format. As one CBC document has instructed, "CBC programs dealing with matters of public interest in which differing views are held must supplement the exposition of one point of view with an equitable treatment of other relevant points of view."[34]

From the perspective of media decision-makers, the best issues are those that neatly divide individuals or groups into two clearly opposing camps. The pro-con model is so rigidly adhered to, so ironclad, that items are routinely dropped if spokespersons for opposing positions cannot be found. Moreover, the process is often carried to absurd lengths. When the Surgeon-General in the United States recently announced more new and damning evidence against smoking, a spokesperson for the tobacco industry was given the opportunity to dismiss the findings as irrelevant. During the trial of hate propagandist Ernst Zundel in 1985, the testimony of concentration camp survivors was juxtaposed with claims by Zundel that the holocaust never occurred. This model can also lead to some peculiar generalizations. During a broadcast for CBC's *The Journal* in May 1987, Terence McKenna did a half-hour documentary on the Meech Lake Accord. While *The Journal* is supposed to digest, elaborate on, and delve more deeply into events and problems, it often continues with the same format and assumptions presented on *The National.* McKenna could not resist couching his report in the "there are only two positions" model. He argued that since Confederation there have been "two opposing visions of Canada," although they have appeared in different guises, "centralization versus decentralization, federal power versus provincial power, one Canada versus two nations and one Canada versus a community of communities."[35] McKenna had thus crudely taken a whole series of diverse issues and conflicts and created but two alternatives for the viewer.

Even more outrageous was a situation observed by Richard Ericson and his associates in their study of television news reporting at CBC's Toronto affiliate, CBLT. A news story featured two versions about what was contained in a police memo describing the conduct of a particular group. The reporter never bothered to obtain the memo, even though it was available to him, so that he could actually see what the memo contained. Having presented two sides to the story, he felt that he had done what was expected of him.[36]

To heighten the sense of conflict, persons espousing opposing viewpoints are often shot from different camera angles.[37] Extreme positions are given the most play. In his book *Deciding What's News* based on studies done during the 1960s and 1970s, Herbert Gans explained the particular logic at work: ". . . the news is more objective when there are two sides to a story, and it is often more dramatic as well. When the sides involved are not apt to protest, journalists are likely to select two extreme positions in order to achieve highlighting. A television reporter pointed out that 'at anti-war demonstrations, we shot the Viet Cong supporters and the Nazis because they were interesting, and because they are what sells. You always go after the extremes; the same in the South, where we shot the black militants and the Ku Klux Klan.'"[38] According to the former press secretary to President Carter, Jody Powell, the media has "an incurable tendency to hype any public comment by one side and then race to someone on the other side with the most provocative interpretation possible in hopes of eliciting a response that is as provocative as the question."[39]

The problem with the pro-con model is that many issues lend themselves to a variety of opinions and many shades of argument and cannot be readily collapsed into a choice between two sides. A given issue may have only a single defensible position; smoking is in fact dangerous to people's health and the holocaust did take place. Odd or extreme positions can be legitimized or given inordinate attention. In addition, this format tends to limit investigative journalism. Since journalists are there merely to present the two sides of any issue, there is no pressure on them to analyse further or discover the truth or, as witnessed by Ericson and his associates, even familiarize themselves with the basic facts.

The model may also affect political outcomes in that thinking in these terms may have become so habitual, so much the lens through which everything is seen, that events such as leadership races and even elections are inevitably telescoped into races between a front runner and a challenger. George McGovern, who ran for U.S. president in 1972 and 1984, was continually shocked by the press' tendency to make the presidential primaries into a two-person race despite the presence of a number of strong candidates.[40] Once the media had fixated on two individuals, none of the others received more than passing mention. During both the Conservative and Liberal Party leadership races held in 1983 and 1984, there were complaints that the media concentrated on only two candidates in each case—Clark and Mulroney, Turner and Chrétien—making it impossible for the other contenders to receive the attention that they needed in order to win.

Politicians and journalists often have different goals when it comes to drama and conflict. Where politicians tend to value caution and unity, the media look for the opposite: conflict, controversy, gaffes and mistakes, and spontaneous outbursts. The need for drama is so great that it is sometimes imposed on situations where it is not inherently there, or dramatic elements are highlighted even if they are not the most important aspects of a story. Knowlton Nash has recounted the lengths to which one CBC producer went to instill his broadcast with the necessary quotient of dramatic confrontation. Three politicians were being taped discussing economic and financial issues. Upset by their lack-lustre conversation, the producer startled the politicians by leaping from the control room and, in an apparent rage, began berating them for their poor performance. The politicians agreed to heat up their remarks so that the exchange would have more jolts.[41]

Another tenet of news reporting is what Tuchman calls "the spatial anchoring of the news net at centralized institutions."[42] When journalists cast their net for news, their catch is likely to be limited to political leaders or high-ranking government officials. Stationed as they are at fixed listening posts, such as the House of Commons, and under sharp budgetary constraints and deadlines, journalists usually turn to a small number of "knowns" for stories or comments.[43] It is tempting to argue that there is a kind of Ottawa "echo chamber" where the same people are always being interviewed, each reacting to statements made by others in the "echo chamber." The danger is that issues, events, or people that lie outside the net are unlikely to receive the same level of coverage or, in some cases, even be covered at all. A good example was CBC television's coverage of the Meech Lake Constitutional Accord in May and June 1987. Almost half of the stories in the five-week period between the first meeting of Prime Minister Brian Mulroney and the Premiers at Meech Lake and the negotiations at the Langevin Block that sealed the agreement were on in-fighting within the Liberal Party and the effect this would have on John Turner's leadership. The reactions of womens', aboriginal, and ethnic groups—the constituencies that were to emerge as the deal's principal opponents—received virtually no coverage.[44] These groups were positioned outside of the prime news locations. The length of the news net had largely determined who would be covered, which views would make news, and what would not be included. Thus, news generally occurs at certain locations and involves certain kinds of people and not others.

It is often argued, for example, that in Canada the news net covers the Ottawa-Toronto-Montreal corridor more extensively than any other region. In his study of CBC radio news and current affairs programs, Barry Cooper claimed that there was a central Canadian bias, and that events and issues important to western Canada in particular were under-reported. He asserted that news from the regions did not reverberate out with the same intensity as the news coming in.[45]

Budget is the key factor in deciding the span of the news net. If media managers have committed substantial resources to reporting a particular event or issue, it becomes their story and is likely to receive considerable coverage regardless of other stories that develop. For instance, when the CBC decided to cover the arrival of Sikh refugee claimants in Nova Scotia in July 1987 by flying in a reporter and a camera crew, renting transportation, putting their personnel in hotels and paying them overtime, the investment was such that CBC was locked into the story. Small wonder that it remained a lead item on *The National* for almost two weeks. When Brian Mulroney visited the Soviet Union in 1989, the CBC invested heavily in the story by bringing anchor Peter Mansbridge along with a host of other reporters, producers, and crew to the Soviet Union. Reports about the Mulroney visit dominated the news despite the fact that there was little real news to report.

Corporate executives and business leaders almost never appear regularly in the news. One can argue that this is because they are outside the net and not inherently newsworthy. Some scholars are convinced that private corporations and corporate leaders are almost never subject to the same scrutiny, under the same spotlight as politicians, because the powerful private interests that largely control the Canadian media will not, as Ericson and his associates have put it, "set the watchdogs loose on their friends."[46] Corporate scandals, mismanagement, and greed will remain hidden from public view. Shielded from scrutiny, some of the most powerful men and women in Canada are "unknowns" in terms of television news. Corporate behemoths such as Ken Thomson, Charles Bronfman, Paul Desmarais, or Galen Weston would be unrecognizable to most Canadians.

Another factor affecting the news net is what is termed the "Afghanistan Complex": the more foreign or distant the event, the less likely it is to make news unless it is particularly relevant, meaningful, or monumental. Several years ago, reporters at the British Broadcasting Corporation (BBC) devised a scale, intended to be humorous, that the deaths of 1,000 Arabs had the same newsworthiness as that of fifty Frenchmen, and the deaths of fifty Frenchmen the same newsworthiness as the death of one Briton. Cultural proximity and the need to touch the home audience is an element found in virtually all national broadcasting systems. Moreover, entire areas of the world—Africa, Asia, Latin America—are rarely reported on unless there are coups, disasters, or outbreaks of war.[47] They are outside the routine net of international news. The democratization of countries like Argentina and Brazil that took place in the 1980s, a slowly evolving but significant development, went largely unreported on Canadian television. Elections held in Israel or France, however, countries with which there is some cultural affinity, are almost certain to be well reported.

Coverage of foreign issues or events is sometimes influenced by working relationships that CTV has established with ABC and CBC with NBC. The arrangement usually involves the right to use each other's material (except if the story is exclusive), and a gentlemen's agreement when working overseas to share information, satellite time, and even camera crews. Reports from American networks will often be used in their entirety, or a Canadian reporter will do a voice-over when tape obtained from American sources is shown. The CBC, in particular, has attempted to expand foreign coverage in order to minimize the use of

American materials. With limited resources, however, these arrangements have proven valuable.

In most other aspects, television news thrives on personalities. Drama can be enhanced and issues simplified if the focus is on conflict between individuals. News shows have succumbed to the voyeuristic fascination with celebrities that the public has such an appetite for, a tendency that might be referred to as "People magazine journalism" or "Charles and Diana" news. According to Gitlin, "From the media point of view, news consists of events which can be recognized and interpreted as drama; and for the most part, news is what is made by individuals who are certifiably newsworthy. . . . In the mass-mediated version of reality, organizations, bureaucracies, movements—in fact, all larger and more enduring social formations—are reduced to personifications."[48] From the perspective of television, elections are not fought between parties—they are fought by individuals. The focus is on the party leaders almost to the exclusion of other forces, developments, or candidates. One study found that in television's coverage of international events, nations were "embodied fully in key leaders"; Sadat was Egypt, for example, and Khomeini was Iran.[49] The fact is that news analysis rarely goes beyond a discussion of the ambitions and motivations of individuals. Television journalists almost invariably want to know who is to blame, who has won or lost, who is doing what to whom. The social and economic forces that propel events are seldom credited with being as important as the actions of powerful individuals, in fact, social and economic forces are rarely touched upon at all. For instance, in a report on the summit meeting held between U.S. President Bush and Soviet leader Mikhail Gorbachev in Malta in December 1989, Brit Hume of ABC News observed that the two men had not yet become friends, as if friendship rather than national interests would decide the outcome of Soviet-American relations.

An offshoot of this is the tendency in journalism to tell a story through a person. The belief is that issues or events can be explained more poignantly if the description stresses how the average citizen would be affected. The story is thus humanized and made more understandable and graspable for the audience. As the CBC's Elly Alboim has observed, "Television . . . communicates . . . through personalization of issues, the ability to take complex thoughts and reduce them to the mouths of 47 year-old housewives in Halifax or farming couples in Manitoba. And where normal intellectual thought goes from the general to the specific, television has evolved a storytelling model that goes from the specific to the general. It's counterintuitive."[50] This level of analysis, technique if you will, is so much the accepted practice that experts are now rarely interviewed about complex issues. During the CBC's coverage of the negotiations that led to the Meech Lake Constitutional Accord, for example, constitutional experts appeared in only one of the thirty-nine reports.[51] The perspective of the man or woman in the street was considered more important—or at least more interesting.

A particular problem in covering Canadian politics is that drama, conflict, and personality all converge in the spectacle of Question Period in the House of Commons. Question Period, with its heated exchanges and jousting, charges and countercharges, and clashes between leaders, is made for television. As former MP John Reid has observed, "Question Period was a natural for television because it moves quickly. You never go into detail on a subject and, because of its nature, Question Period has always tended to push personalities to the fore as opposed to issues."[52] Alistair Fraser, a former Clerk of the House of Commons, believes that television has changed Question Period; questions became longer as MPs prefaced their questions with sharply-pointed accusing preambles, and answers were less answers than counterattacks meant to ridicule questioners and throw them off-balance. According to Fraser the advantage, as in war, is to the attacker.[53] Indeed, members of the opposition parties will often tip off television reporters about which questions will be asked so that the reporters can build their stories around the expected confrontation.

For television reporters, Question Period is a feast. It has everything required for a good story, usually in abundance. There is no shortage of ten-second clips containing the needed quotient of personal vitriol and conflict. Personalities are magnified and issues condensed. Mike Duffy has described the lure of Question Period for editors and producers: "Every night we have a phone call at six o'clock to Toronto and we fight to get in four or five pieces. They do want what's sexy and what's hot. They want those kinds of hot exchanges. They want George Baker talking about the French fishing agreement. 'Mr. Speaker we've been french fried!' If it isn't in the piece and they see it on the other network, they come back and say how come you didn't put in the colourful stuff?"[54] Radio-Canada correspondent Francine Bastien has admitted that few reporters "have the guts to say to our editors, 'Well, yes they did scream at each other but nothing of substance came out.' . . . It's a very comfortable way of working. Your assignment is there every day at 2:00 o'clock and at 4:00 o'clock you phone your editor with a neat, well-packaged job. "[55]

For the prime minister and opposition party leaders, the daily dramatics of Question Period can have a corrosive effect. Instead of being shown in a dignified setting where their authority is respected, they are seen hurling accusations at each other and in shouting matches. The glow of office and images of competence and even rationality can be quickly eradicated. Parliament itself, inasmuch as it seems to have the atmosphere of a prize-fight—at least as presented on television—has dropped considerably in public esteem in recent years.[56] Little attention is paid to Parliament's other activities and this, too, has its dangers. As

John Holtby has written about the work of parliamentary committees, "An unreported committee does not exist in the mind of the electorate . . . unless the media take increased note of the actual work done in the committees, much of it will become the private preserve of the special interest groups and the bureaucracy."[57] To this extent, the real workings of politics are misunderstood and misrepresented in television's depiction of Ottawa.

Another essential ingredient of a television news story is high impact visual material. Visuals account for some fourteen to seventeen minutes of *The National's* on-air time of twenty-two minutes and the *CTV National News'* twenty-four minutes (excluding commercials). A cynic would argue that the news process has become little more than packaging visuals. Story angles are often dictated by and wrapped around the available visual material; in fact, reporters invariably view the camera footage before writing their texts and then speak to the pictures. As Richard Ericson and his colleagues found during their intensive study of CBC station CBLT in Toronto, "The importance of visuals was revealed when there were problems in obtaining them. If particular visuals could not be obtained, or if obtained were deemed to be lacking in drama, immediacy or exclusivity, then the entire story was dropped."[58] On one occasion, they witnessed an editor dropping a story about a major fire because the camera crew had been unable to get shots "of the guy coming out in flames."[59] The same day a different camera crew happened to pass a car fire; with exciting visuals in hand, that item was included in the evening news. Other interesting examples can be drawn from international news. South Africa lost its place as a leading story almost as soon as the South African government imposed a ban on filming riots and demonstrations in 1986. Without visual material, the situation in South Africa could not be sustained as a television news story. When reporters were given access in late 1989 and in 1990, South Africa again became a leading news story. Indeed, the international media was in South Africa *en masse* to report the release of black nationalist leader Nelson Mandela in February 1990. Throughout the 1980s, Ethiopia was ravaged by famine; yet starvation in Ethiopia became a leading news story only when pictures were available. Without pictures, the tragedy of Ethiopia went unreported. The carnage of civil war continues in Lebanon even though, without visuals (Beirut has become too dangerous for western reporters), it is rarely in the news. It can also be argued that sometimes an important event will not be covered extensively if, by nature, it does not contain exciting visuals. Corporate takeovers, union decertifications, Canada's trade relations, and the problems of international debt are not stories that lend themselves to hot visuals. Critical meetings of OPEC, where the international oil price is established, are closed to cameras and therefore rarely become leading news items, although what is decided is of critical economic significance. The crude reality is that, as Albert Hunt of *The Wall Street Journal* has expressed it, "TV producers are like nymphomaniacs when it comes to visuals."[60]

The best visual material captures action or emotion or conflict. Stories are often shot and videotape edited so that these elements are highlighted. Each news story that contains visual material has undergone a series of technical changes—cuts, zooms, splicing, etc.—to create the maximum effect. Because visuals are so important, liberties are often taken to ensure the best footage; for example, interviews are often shot several times with an eye to the best lighting and effect, and some events are "staged" or recreated for the cameras. Stocks of old footage are often used with no indication to the audience that this is being done.[61]

Television reporters take special care to ensure that their appearance and presentation is the best possible. The "stand-ups" that have them speaking into the camera are routinely shot a half dozen times or more until the reporter or production team is satisfied with the result. In contrast, politicians are often shown in the worst possible light. Unlike television reporters they cannot do voice-overs, wear make-up (since they don't know if or when they're going to be on camera), rehearse their lines, or redo answers to questions. Offhand comments or jokes or even unpleasant physical characteristics or gestures cannot be erased. In editing visual material, reporters sometimes look for the least flattering shots. When cabinet minister Marcel Masse was under opposition attack for alleged infractions of the Canada Elections Act, the CBC reporter assigned to the story sought out clips of Masse that showed him under great strain as a way of enhancing the dramatic effects of the story. In a similar fashion, Joe Clark's nervous hands and John Turner's throat clearing became familiar to Canadians.

The most critical realization is that what is seen on television is far more potent, has a far greater impact on viewers, than the words that are spoken. An interesting illustration of this was the experience of CBS correspondent Leslie Stahl in covering the 1984 U.S. presidential election. At one point, she did a story that was quite critical of Ronald Reagan and, as a result, she expected a rough time from White House officials. To her surprise, Reagan's press people seemed delighted with her story. Rather than giving her a cold shoulder, they were profuse in their congratulations. On replaying the report, Stahl realized that her words were overshadowed by "a magnificent montage of Reagan in a series of wonderful, upbeat scenes, with flags, balloons, children, and adoring supporters—virtually an unpaid campaign commercial."[62] In Doris Graber's study of how people "process" the news, she found that visual themes were twice as memorable as verbal themes.[63] Research cited by Patrick Devlin concluded "that 80 to 85 percent of the information retained about television commercials is visual."[64] One is reminded of the old advertising adage that the eye will remember what the ear forgets.

RECONTEXTUALIZING REALITY

As currently constituted, then, the television news frame is predisposed towards covering certain kinds of stories and not others. Stories that do not involve conflict among political leaders or high drama or have interesting visuals are likely to be outside the news frame. The greatest difficulty is with stories that are complicated, diffuse, or legalistic: stories that run against the grain of what television wants. The collapse of a bridge is far more likely to make it onto the news than a collapse in the price of oil, even though the latter may have more far-reaching effects. As Jim Coutts has put it, "It's more interesting to cover a fire than new insurance legislation."[65] Covering the political process seems a particular anathema to television because it is time-consuming, cumbersome, difficult to explain, and involves meticulous detail.

Elly Alboim, the Ottawa bureau chief for CBC television news, has argued that there is now a new generation of television-only journalists who "accept the theology that television cannot deal with complex thoughts or issues and so stories are rejected because of their complexity."[66] This includes most stories about the political process. The attitude is that "all you have to do is staff the beginning and the end. We're too impatient to cover the middle, the ingredients of policy. The result is that we spring stories fully baked on the country."[67] One is tempted to use Edward Jay Epstein's description that news seems to come from "nowhere."[68] Vince Carlin, a former head of national television news for the CBC, believes that "the problem is that one is unable to signal along the way when a Meech Lake or drug bill is coming. The problem is also that we treat all items as being of equal importance all the time. We have to supply texture as opposed to serving things up hot and fast."[69] Thus, while television speeds up information and makes information easier to understand and digest, at the same time it undervalues the consequences of that information.

By its nature, television news "recontextualizes" events. Television journalists set out to cover a story already conscious of the requirements of the news frame. Stories will be cast according to the reporter's image of what is necessary. Camera angles and locations, the types of questions asked, the people chosen to be interviewed, the facts that are lifted from among so many other facts, etc., are the context imposed on the event by the reporter and his or her editors and producers. Journalists rarely "go bowling for news," looking for news without having predetermined the context. As a consequence, persons who are part of the news story almost always feel that they have been shown or taken out of context. The people who are the "material" for the news story often find it unsettling that a thirty-minute interview has been telescoped into an eight-second clip, or that a careful and detailed explanation is left out entirely or drastically simplified. According to Michael Novak, even seasoned observers are continually bewildered by the extent to which television imposes its own reality. As he describes it, "Anyone who has participated in a large-scale event comes to recognize vividly how straight and narrow is the gate between what has actually happened and what gets on television. For the millions who see the television story, of course, the story is the reality. For those who lived through a strenuous sixteen-hour day on the campaign trail, for example, it is always something of a surprise to see what 'made' the television screen, or, more accurately, what the television screen made real. . . ."[70]

In the world of television news, consumer demand overrides almost all other considerations. Walter Lippmann has compared the news process to a spotlight that scans the horizon, bringing some events out of darkness and into the light.[71] The image is an appealing one. The reality, however, is that the spotlight itself has become distorted, a half-light pitched at an angle that allows it to pick up only certain elements of a story. The reality, as Todd Gitlin aptly points out, is that ". . . news concerns the event, not the underlying condition; the person, not the group; conflict, not consensus; the fact that 'advances the story', not the one that explains it."[72] In the television frame, public affairs has merged with entertainment.

NOTES

1. Peter Desbarats, *Guide to Canadian News Media* (Toronto: Harcourt, Barce, Jovanovich, 1989), p. 28. See also Michael Adams and Jordan Levitin, "Media Bias as Viewed by the Canadian Public," in *Canadian Legislatures 1987-1988*, Robert Fleming, ed. (Ottawa: Ampersand Communications Services, 1988), pp. 3-12.
2. John Haslett Cuff, "Comedy Writers to Discuss How to Get Bucks for Yuks," *The Globe and Mail*, 15 June 1989, p. A15.
3. John Haslett Cuff, "Differences in CBC and CTV Newscasts Not Always Subtle," *The Globe and Mail*, 10 June 1989, p. C5.
4. Canadian Broadcasting Corporation, *Let's Do It* (Ottawa: December 1985), p. 19.
5. S. Robert Lichter, Stanley Rothman, and Linda Lichter, *The Media Elite* (Bethesda, Maryland: Adler and Adler, 1986), p. 10.
6. Quoted in Edward Jay Epstein, *News From Nowhere: Television and the News* (New York: Vintage, 1974), p. 39.
7. W. Brian Stewart, "Canadian Social System and Canadian Broadcasting Audiences," in *Communications in Canadian Society*, Benjamin Singer, ed. (Don Mills: Addison-Wesley, 1983), pp. 17-40.

8. Ronald Berman, *How Television Sees Its Audience* (Beverly Hills: Sage Publications, 1987), p. 31.

9. Barbara Matusow, *The Evening Stars* (New York: Ballantine, 1983), pp. 188-92.

10. Berman, p. 30.

11. Philip Weiss, "Bad Rap For TV Tabs," *Columbia Journalism Review* (May-June 1989), pp. 40.

12. Ibid.

13. Quoted in Epstein, p. 40.

14. I am grateful to Professor Gerald Sperling for bringing this point to my attention.

15. Morris Wolfe, *Jolts: The TV Wasteland and the Canadian Oasis* (Toronto: Lorimer, 1985), p. 13.

16. Knowlton Nash, *Prime Time At Ten* (Toronto: McClelland and Stewart, 1987), p. 238.

17. Interview with CBC Television reporter, Ottawa, 6 July 1987.

18. Quoted in "Interest Groups and the Media," Canadian government and politics film series, School of Public Administration, University of Victoria, 1984.

19. Ed Joyce, *Prime Times, Bad Times* (New York: Doubleday, 1988).

20. Todd Gitlin, *The Whole World is Watching* (Berkeley: University of California Press, 1980), p. 6.

21. Ibid., p. 7.

22. David Altheide, *Creating Reality: How TV News Distorts Events* (Beverly Hills: Sage, 1976); and Austin Ranney, *Channels of Power: The Impact of Television on American Politics* (New York: Basic Books, 1983).

23. Johan Galtung and Mari Ruge, "Structuring and Selecting News," in *The Manufacture of News*, Stanley Cohen and Jock Young, eds. (London: Constable and Beverly Hills: Sage, 1981).

24. Michael Schudson, "Deadlines, Datelines and History," in *Reading the News*, Karl Manoff and Michael Schudson, eds., (New York: Pantheon, 1986), p. 89.

25. Address by Elly Alboim, The University of Calgary, 19 November 1987.

26. Richard Ericson, Patricia Baranek, and Janet Chan, *Visualizing Deviance: A Study of News Organization* (Toronto: University of Toronto Press, 1987), p. 138.

27. "The Globe and Mail/CBC News Poll," *The Globe and Mail*, 12 February 1990, p. A10.

28. Ibid., p. 237.

29. Interview with Craig Oliver, Ottawa, 17 April 1989.

30. Quoted in William A. Henry III, "News as Entertainment: The Search for Dramatic Unity," in *What's News*, Elie Abel, ed. (San Francisco:

Institute for Contemporary Studies, 1981), p. 135; and Fraser Kelly, "Television: Does the Image Reflect Reality?" in *Politics and the Media* (Toronto: Reader's Digest Foundation of Canada and Erindale College, University of Toronto, 1981), p. 38.

31. Quoted in Epstein, p. 4.
32. Joyce, p. 177.
33. Interview with CBC producer, Toronto, 21 May 1986.
34. Cited in Ericson, Baranek, and Chan, p. 107.
35. See David Taras, "Television and Public Policy: The CBC's Coverage of the Meech Lake Accord," *Canadian Public Policy*, vol. 15, no. 3 (September 1989), 332.
36. Ericson, Baranek, and Chan, pp. 259-60.
37. Ibid., p. 273.
38. Herbert Gans, *Deciding What's News* (New York: Vintage, 1979) p. 176.
39. Jody Powell, *The Other Side of the Story* (New York: William Morrow and Co., 1984), p. 62.
40. George McGovern, "George McGovern: The Target Talks Back," *Columbia Journalism Review* (July/August 1984), pp. 27-28.
41. Nash, p. 182.
42. Gaye Tuchman, *Making News: A Study in the Construction of Reality* (New York: The Free Press, 1978), p. 23.
43. Gans, pp. 9-13.
44. See Taras. See also Debra Clarke's description of "the national news map" in Debra Clarke "Constraints of Television News Production: The Example of Story Geography," *The Canadian Journal of Communication*, vol. 15, no. 1 (February 1990), 67-94.
45. Barry Cooper, "Bias on the CBC? A Study of Network AM Radio," paper presented to the Canadian Communication Association Annual Meeting, Winnipeg, June 1986.
46. Ericson, Baranek, and Chan, p. 38. See also Edwin Black, *Politics and the News* (Toronto: Butterworths, 1982), Ch. 8.
47. Robert Hackett, "Coups, Earthquakes and Hostages? Foreign News on Canadian Television," *Canadian Journal of Political Science* (December 1989), 809-825. See also Stuart Surlin, Walter Romanow, and Walter Soderlund, "TV Network News: A Canadian–American Comparison," *American Review of Canadian Studies* (1988), pp. 465-75.
48. Gitlin, p. 146.
49. William Spragens, "Camp David and the Networks: Reflections on Coverage of the 1979 Summit," in *Television Coverage of International Affairs*, William C. Adams, ed. (Norwood, New Jersey: Ablex, 1982), p. 122.

50. Elly Alboim, "Television and the Democratic Process," Banff Television Festival, 6 June 1989.
51. See Taras.
52. "A Very Public Forum: The House on TV," *Parliamentary Government*, vol. 3, no. 1 (Winter 1982), 4.
53. Ibid.
54. Mike Duffy, "Questioning Question Period Coverage," Center For Investiga tive Journalism, Ottawa, Spring 1987, tape.
55. Quoted in Bob Miller, "Battle Before The Cameras," *Parliamentary Government*, vol. 5, no. 4, (1985), 16.
56. Jeff Sallot, "Poll Suggests House is Irrelevant to Majority of Canadian Public," *The Globe and Mail*, 10 September 1983, p. 1.
57. Christopher Harris, "When It Comes to Committees, Are the Media Doing Their Job," *Parliamentary Government*, vol. 7, nos. 1-2 (1987), 10.
58. Ericson, Baranek, and Chan, p. 280.
59. Ibid., p. 141.
60. Lawrence Zuckerman "The Made-for-TV Campaign," *Time*, 14 November 1988, p. 63.
61. Ericson, Baranek, and Chan, p. 278.
62. David Broder, *Behind the Front Page* (New York: Simon and Schuster, 1987), p. 182.
63. Doris Graber, *Processing the News* (New York: Longman, 1988), pp. 114-115.
64. L. Patrick Devlin, "Campaign Commercials," in *Television in Society*, Arthur Asa Berger, ed. (New Brunswick, New Jersey: Transaction Books, 1987), p. 22.
65. Interview with Jim Coutts, Toronto, 3 June 1987.
66. Interview with Elly Alboim, Ottawa, 27 May 1987.
67. Ibid.
68. See Epstein.
69. Interview with Vince Carlin, Toronto, 5 June 1987.
70. Quoted in Austin Ranney, *Channels of Power* (New York: Basic Books, 1983), p. 29.
71. Walter Lippmann, *Public Opinion* (New York: Free Press, 1965).
72. Gitlin, p. 28.

PART 3
POLITICS

5

Prime Ministers in Prime Time

In order to be successful, a prime minister must be first and foremost "a public persuader."[1] A prime minister cannot lead unless he (or she someday) is able to sell policies and a vision of the country to the public, for without support from the public even the best plans are doomed to failure. Yet the prime minister cannot build an agenda without using the media. He has to understand the media's interests and expectations and how these can be used to his advantage. As many journalists believe that their role is to criticize government policy and television's infotainment agenda twists and distorts how issues and events are presented, the prime minister must wage a constant struggle to have his actions conveyed in a positive light. Various analogies have been used to describe the relationship between prime ministers and the media. It has been described as a dance or a game. The bitter experiences of Joe Clark and John Turner, however, suggest a harsher reality. Prime ministers must survive in the "battleground" of media relations.

At first blush it seems that political leaders are at a disadvantage in dealing with the media. Journalists have the power to decide which politicians will be interviewed and to choose the words that will be quoted in newspaper articles or used in TV and radio clips. They provide the context within which the politicians' remarks are presented. They also have the last word: showing up contradictions, taking the politician to task for missed opportunities, or stressing what they—not the politician—consider important. Moreover, journalists and especially television journalists are surrounded by auras of authority and objectivity. As P.H. Weaver has written, "There is hardly an aspect of the scripting, casting, and staging of a television news program that is not designed to convey an impression of authority and omniscience. This can be seen most strikingly in the role of the anchorman . . . who is positively god-like: he summons forth men, events and images at will; he speaks in tones of utter certainty; he is the person with whom all things begin and end."[2] Indeed, political leaders are unlikely to look as good on television as the journalists who report on them. TV reporters are usually chosen for the ease and comfort of their on-camera presence; moreover, their words and delivery are often edited and lines repeated until they are perfect. In contrast, television cameras often catch politicians at awkward moments, with their unintended words, uncomfortable glances, and nervous mannerisms captured for all to see. Unlike TV journalists, they cannot do retakes, reformulate their words, or be made to seem as if they are towering authoritatively over events.

In addition, journalists, who do not have to bear the weight of office, often appear bolder and more decisive than government leaders. Journalists are free to fume or make witty remarks about people and events or argue for snap solutions and instant action. As Thomas Griffith observed about the attractiveness of popular American journalists, "Ted Koppel often seems more knowledgeable than the experts he questions, and George Will triumphantly bolder than Cabinet members who, unlike him, must bear responsibility for what they say."[3] In contrast, foreign governments, the financial community, or powerful interest groups will hold a prime minister or cabinet minister accountable for his or her words. For government leaders, cautious pronouncements rather than bold assertions are often the better part of valour.

Virtually all modern prime ministers have complained about their treatment by the media. The standard complaints are that their messages have been distorted by the media's need to personalize and sensationalize issues, and that important concerns are often overshadowed by the attention given to minor scandals, trivia, and gaffes. They are also surprised by the intense criticism that greets almost any action. Prime Minister Lester Pearson claimed in his day that "newspaper editors are always bleating about the refusal of politicians to produce mature and responsible discussion of the issues. The fact is, when we discuss policies seriously, we are not reported at all, or reported very inadequately. Reporters do not appear even to listen, until we say something controversial or personal, charged with what they regard as news value."[4] Two decades later Brian Mulroney made similar charges: "There's a cottage industry in this country that deals with facile and mostly pejorative references to what any prime minister is doing at a given time. . . . I'm not saying it with bitterness, I'm saying it calmly, as a matter of fact. The message has been distorted in going out."[5]

One can predict with virtual certainty that prime ministers will endure a "media crisis" at least once during their term of office. A media crisis occurs when the media seizes on an issue that embarrasses the government and makes it a leading news item for a considerable length of time.[6] The media, not the government, set the agenda. The prime minister is placed on the defensive and relations with the media deteriorate sharply amid antagonism and mistrust. During Brian Mulroney's first term in office, for instance, he often spoke about the country's improved economy and what he saw as a new harmony in federal-provincial relations; during the same period, the media focused relentlessly on scandals and broken campaign pledges. Mulroney's message was drowned out by a steady downpour of stories about cabinet ministers in trouble. Faced with a media crisis, Mulroney was forced to undertake new survival strategies to win back control of the agenda. Some politicians, Joe Clark and John Turner, for example, never fully recovered from the wounds inflicted by the media during similar crises. Mark Hertsgaard compares political leaders to lion tamers, with journalists being the lions, and claims that even with obedient lions, "they only had to pounce once in the space of four years to leave their masters bloodied if not buried."[7]

Yet prime ministers are not altogether defenceless. They have a number of formidable weapons that can be used in their battle with the media, weapons that allow them to affect the media's agenda and get their messages out to the public relatively unfiltered. This chapter will exam- ine how these weapons are used, will focus in particular on television performance as an important instrument of power, and will describe the stormy relationship that has often existed between prime ministers and the media.

TELEVISION AS AN INSTRUMENT OF POWER

Some observers believe that a politician's ability to perform on television is her or his most important political asset. Where political leaders were once distant figures seen firsthand by only small numbers of people, television's intimacy has now made them a familiar presence to the majority of Canadians. Audiences feel that they have a relationship with the politicians they see on television, that they have "met" and "know" them personally.[8] As Robert Lichter and his colleagues point out, "the stars of television, from anchormen, to rock performers, to politicians, have become pseudo-intimate acquaintances."[9]

There are two schools of thought about the influence of television performance on political success. One view is that television appearance carries enormous political weight. Joshua Meyrowitz, for instance, be- lieves that some of the great leaders of the past would not have made it in today's political world because they would not have projected well on television. George Washington's deep pockmarks and wooden teeth, Thomas Jefferson's speech impediment, and Abraham Lincoln's unattrac- tive face and thin, reedy-sounding voice would have disqualified them from seeking public office.[10] The fact that Franklin Roosevelt was "vir- tually a hopeless cripple," a man who "had to rely on heavy steel leg braces, canes, and more often, the support of someone's arm" might have been played prominently by television camera crews to the detriment of his buoyant personality and confidence, enormous determination, and political skill.[11] Some Canadian journalists argue that Robert Stanfield's gaunt looks and slow, deliberate speaking style, Joe Clark's weak chin and gawky body language, and John Turner's burning stare and overbear- ing "hotness" on television damaged their chances for political success. On the other hand, Pierre Trudeau's natural instinct for television may have helped him survive his many political wars. According to a former press secretary, Romeo Leblanc, Trudeau's face, voice, and gestures were just right for television. Trudeau lasted as long as he did because "he had strong control over every muscle" when he faced the "electronic cannons." On TV "every bead of sweat, every twitch becomes an editorial."[12]

Anthropologist Max Atkinson contends that only certain speaking styles are suitable for television. TV rewards those who appear "cool," low-key, and casual. A conversational speaking style and a relaxed delivery are the prerequisites of a convincing performance. Atkinson considers Ronald Reagan and François Mitterrand to be consummate TV performers, affecting a casual confidence on television and appearing relaxed, as if talking to neighbours across a picket fence. He also noted that Martin Luther King had learned the language of television. King omitted "expansive non-verbal actions from his oratory" and stood "almost motionless while delivering his speeches."[13] Some of history's greatest orators—Leon Trotsky, Adolf Hitler, Huey Long—might have looked foolish on television. Their dramatic gestures, flailing arms, and pounding fists would have looked overheated and frantic. As Atkinson advises:

> Practices which are visible, audible and impressive to those sitting in the back row of an auditorium are likely to seem exaggerated, unnatural and even oppressive when viewed on a small screen from a distance of a few feet.[14]

Moreover, television by nature coarsens and distorts reality. Virtually all mannerisms are exaggerated: imperfect chins look more imperfect, a hand seems to shake more than it actually does, sudden movements give someone a frenetic look. American media advisor Michael Sheehan warns his clients that "television takes facial expressions down. So if you look neutral or thoughtful in person, you look dead or embalmed on the air. That's why you have to smile."[15] For many, the greatest difficulty is having to express a complex idea in the ten or fifteen seconds allowed by television's time frames. There is often too little time to build an argument or discuss the history or background of an event or policy. Under these conditions, the glib politician may have an advantage over the thoughtful one.

There is also the argument that television uses or burns people up very quickly. Even the best entertainers and shows can last only a few seasons. The audience's demand for fresh faces, new formats, and a steady stream of jolts ensure a constant turnover. Only exceptional performers such as Johnny Carson or Larry Hagman (the star of the TV show Dallas), who are completely at home on television, are able to withstand prolonged exposure. With the exception of René Lévesque, Canada has not produced a national political leader completely comfortable with the medium.

Some believe that success on television can be easily translated into political success and can overcome or reverse failures suffered in other political arenas. Scholars have noted that after the fiasco of the Bay of Pigs invasion in 1961, John F. Kennedy's popularity rating shot up dramatically. A stirring television performance where he admitted making mistakes had turned a foreign policy failure into a domestic political triumph. Mark Hertsgaard describes how Ronald Reagan undertook a PR blitz to stress his commitment to excellence in education. Viewers were treated to scenes of a seemingly activist president visiting classrooms, mingling with students, and talking to educators across the country. "The end result," according to Hertsgaard, "was to reverse the polling figures to a two-to-one support for Reagan, without the actual Reagan policy changing at all."[16] When White House aide Michael Deaver was asked by reporters about cuts that Reagan had made to the education budget, his reply was "You can say whatever you want, but the viewer sees Ronald Reagan out there in a classroom talking to teachers and kids, and what he takes from that is the impression that Ronald Reagan is concerned about education."[17] In fact, at one point, under questioning from reporters, Reagan could not even remember what his education policy was.

Hedrick Smith of *The New York Times* has commented on the difference between Reagan's commanding presence on TV and the hollowness he found on meeting Reagan in person:

> Reagan is unfailingly cheerful, gracious, polite; he makes people feel good. But to a reporter . . . he can sound wooden and staged at close quarters. I have interviewed him several times, all but once with frustration. His answers sounded like replays of a human cassette, his lines rehearsed, even the little jokes. He seemed to be reading a part. When I tried to probe Reagan's thinking . . . I heard a script.[18]

Similarly, public support for John Turner swung dramatically following his strong showing against Brian Mulroney in the 1988 election debates. Turner's performance, accomplished with the help of TV coaches, managed to supersede, at least for a brief period, the realities of a bitterly divided party, botched policy announcements, and a negative image built up over the previous five years. In one evening, Turner came close to turning his political fortunes around completely.

The other view is that television has little overall impact. The public, it is said, will judge leaders on their policies; their intelligence, ability, and trustworthiness; and the degree to which they can express and symbolize the national mood. Viewers can see through TV window-dressing and they arrive at decisions based on economic interests, beliefs, and ideology. Moreover, the modern political landscape has been and is filled with leaders who attained high office despite the fact that they were not highly telegenic. David Halberstam has written about Lyndon Johnson that whatever "was natural and human and alive in him froze" on television.[19] A rugged politician and master dealmaker, a man who bent many an adversary into submission by the sheer force of his personality, looked pleading and innocuous on the TV screen. Richard Nixon was elected president twice even though he was uncomfortable with and unappealing on TV. He almost always appeared nervous, often looked washed out and haggard, and perspiration would form on his upper lip. The congenial and shrewd Lester Pearson came across as cold and stilted and relentlessly uninspiring. Peter C. Newman has described Pearson's difficulties with the new medium:

> Expert after expert was given complete freedom to make him look as warm on TV as he was with small groups of friends. A voice coach was brought in from Toronto, and writers were hired to remove as many sibilants as possible from his scripts so that he could hide his speech problem. Toronto's MacLaren Advertising Company exhausted its considerable resources trying to improve his television manner. The TV manipulators tried a dozen different settings — intimate soirees, crowded scenes, living room shots, interviews with academics — but nothing really worked. Lester Pearson emptied many a living room in his time. "They're trying to make me look like 'Danger Man' but I feel more like 'The Fugitive'," Pearson complained to a friend about his TV advisors.[20]

Premiers William Davis of Ontario and Robert Bourassa of Quebec built powerful political machines and long terms in office despite their bland appearance on television. Both survived because they were able to carefully calibrate and then represent and appeal to the shifting moods of their electorates. The argument that television appearance is critical to success was once belittled by President Harry Truman when a TV director suggested that his necktie was inappropriate for television. Truman responded by asking whether it really mattered "Because if while I'm talking about Korea, people are asking each other about my necktie, it seems to me we're in a great deal of trouble."[21] Truman's view was that he would be judged on how he dealt with important issues and events and not by how his tie looked on television.

While the ability to project well on television may not be a prerequisite for attaining high office, most observers agree that the skilful use of television can yield enormous benefits to a politician. During Ronald Reagan's term of office, a conscious decision was taken "to make television the organizational framework" for his presidency.[22] Highly choreographed television performances became the principal means of communicating messages and selling policies. Much of his strategy was based on "the visual press release," giving TV reporters the visuals they required for the nightly news but under conditions dictated by the White House. TV reporters would be given access to staged events that made for "pretty" pictures but would not be given an opportunity to ask substantive questions. Presidential aide Michael Deaver became, in effect, the *de facto* producer of the evening news, dictating the story line by providing irresistible photo opportunities. As Deaver described his philosophy,

"You're always looking for a picture you don't ever have to explain. The picture tells the story regardless of what Ronald Reagan says."[23] William Boot has described the Deaver formula as "No access. Daily visuals. Simple message."[24] Under the tutelage of media advisor Roger Ailes, George Bush's presidency has also revolved around carefully staged and scripted visuals.

While the visual press release has become part of the media repertoire of Canadian prime ministers, in Canada the circumstances are different. Largely because of the institution of Question Period, where prime ministers are pressed into emotional exchanges, swept up in the frenzy of attack and counter-attack, and exposed fully to harsh questioning from the opposition, an immaculate television image is nearly impossible to maintain. Attacks by the opposition often make the best footage, and the prime minister is often shown in a less than flattering light. As the prime minister cannot control Question Period, he or she cannot control the television images that Question Period produces.

THE PRIME MINISTER'S MEDIA ARSENAL

As agenda-building is critical to the prime minister's survival, the office has developed formidable resources in dealing with the media. The prime minister has a director of communications, a press secretary, speech writers, and a battery of other staff to help formulate an overall media strategy and deal with reporters' daily news requirements. Cabinet documents now contain communications strategies that describe, often in considerable detail, how policies are to be sold. The Prime Minister's Office constantly monitors media coverage, wages image-building campaigns, and attempts to orchestrate issues, events, and situations so that the most favourable public relations juice is squeezed out. The art of media management rests on the ability to direct reporters to stories and points of view that the government wants reported, while hindering the coverage of events or perspectives that would detract from the government's message or prove to be embarrassing.

One weapon that is sometimes used is access to the prime minister. Under Trudeau, access was limited and held out as a reward to favoured reporters; Mulroney has also used this approach. The basic understanding is that access will be given in exchange for favourable coverage. Journalists who receive an exclusive tip or lead or are allowed to interview the prime minister have an advantage over other reporters and gain enhanced stature and credibility within their own news organizations. The news organization itself can benefit by co-operating with the prime minister. One network reporter remembers being upbraided by a member of Brian Mulroney's staff and told that "If you don't shape up (names a TV program) won't get an interview with the prime minister."[25]

Leaking a story to a favoured reporter has a number of advantages. A leak about an impending policy announcement, for instance, gives the government two opportunities instead of one to promote its policy. The first opportunity comes with the reporting of the leak. The second is the coverage that occurs when the policy is announced. As the first reports about a policy are often the ones that have the most impact on public opinion, the government has a great deal at stake in ensuring that these reports are favourable. Leaking information to reporters is also a means of testing public opinion. If news reports about a proposed initiative or appointment produce a hostile reaction from the public, then the government can deny the report's validity and retreat without losing face. The launching of "trial balloons" is undoubtedly the favoured aerial sport of Canadian politicians.

Leaking information to favoured journalists can also backfire, as it can arouse the resentment of other reporters. One CBC reporter interviewed for this study still retains a measure of resentment against Joe Clark because "he played friends."[26] Politicians also have to play the game with subtlety. Reporters are suspicious about being co-opted and resent attempts to manipulate them. Michael Grossman and Martha Kumar have described how White House officials would allay these fears among reporters by "letting them through the line."[27] Reporters would be permitted to "discover" a new development through questioning instead of just being handed the information.

Journalists who are seen as hostile risk being frozen out by the prime minister, as well as by ministers and key government and party officials. Being put in "deep freeze" can impair a reporter's ability to do daily reporting because reporters often need basic background information and facts confirmed before they file their stories. George Radwanski has observed that "nothing hurts a journalist more than being denied access, because we lose favour with our bosses."[28] He believed that journalists were constantly afraid of this kind of retaliation. "They watch for it to a degree you wouldn't believe," he said.[29] The danger is not only that other reporters will get the story at the expense of those frozen out but that even their own organizations may view them as abrasive and, hence, as a liability. In some cases, reporters will be frozen out for short periods, as a warning. TV journalist Mike Duffy recalls being on Mulroney's freeze list for over three months. Questions put to Mulroney were simply ignored. Then suddenly, for no apparent reason, Mulroney started talking to him again.[30] Sometimes the snub is so direct and brutal that there is no mistaking the degree of hostility involved. Claire Hoy recounts how in a scrum following a cabinet session that had been held in St. John's, Newfoundland, Canadian Press reporter Tim Naumetz asked Mulroney a question about a particular policy. According to Hoy, "Mulroney just glared at him, turned around, and walked away, ending the scrum on the spot."[31]

According to one knowledgeable Ottawa journalist, the severest form of retaliation is the "burn." In his memory it had only been used once. A reporter is deliberately fed false information and then burned when the story proves to have no basis in fact. The reporter is made to look foolish and his or her bosses are left wondering about the person's ability to carry out their job.

For some reporters the message is clear: conflict must be tempered by co-operation. Criticisms leveled at the government cannot be so harsh that they lead to a severing of communications. Their self-interest is to ensure that the bridges over which they must travel to do their work remain intact.

One well-worn tactic is to release information late on Friday afternoons. Correspondents facing deadlines have little choice but to go with the information that the government has supplied, for opposition MPs and interest group spokespeople who might have critical comments are likely to have left for the weekend. The end result is that the government has "at least a twenty-four hour free ride before the critics get their turn."[32] The item is also likely to receive greater media play because news organizations are often starved for news to report on weekends. The problem is particularly acute for newspapers that have large Saturday or Sunday editions to fill. One CBC producer who worked in Ottawa admitted that he always got edgy as Friday afternoons approached. By then everyone in the Press Gallery "was tired and didn't want to scramble."[33]

A related tactic is to make policy announcements close to the times when correspondents have to file their stories. Without the time required to analyse the substance or significance of the new policy or search out the opposition point of view, reporters often have little choice but to give verbatim accounts of the government's position and reasoning. Having been boxed in, they go with what they have—the government line.

Another well-known method of manipulating the media is for politicians to provide reporters with "pre-packaged" news. News is manufactured for the media; a story line is presented in briefings, photo opportunities are available so that reporters have good visuals, and press releases explain the background and significance of the event or policy that is being promoted. As reporters have to produce news stories almost every day, whether or not there is real news, some reporters depend on the government to serve up a steady diet of stories. Indeed politicians have come to expect, if not depend on, a certain degree of laziness and inertia among journalists: journalists who will take the path of least resistance and report the "news" they have been given. According to Michel Gratton, a former press secretary to Brian Mulroney, journalists "are considerably more docile when well-nourished with material."[34] A former Reagan press aide has described how the policy of "manipulation" was orchestrated in the Reagan White House: "You give them the line of the day, you give them press briefings, you give them facts, access to people who will speak on the record. . . . And you do that long enough, they're going to stop bringing their stories, and stop being investigative reporters of any kind, even modestly so."[35] Some reporters, of course, dismiss government press releases and pre-packaged news as "gainsburgers" and will vigorously pursue all aspects of a story.

Many reporters have come to view Question Period as an attempt to create pre-packaged news. Reporters are often forewarned about the questions that the opposition parties intend to ask so that they know when the sharp confrontations—the sparks that make for good visuals—are likely to occur and over which issues. The prime minister and cabinet ministers come well armed with answers that have been scripted and rehearsed in advance. The "House book" prepared for the prime minister and cabinet ministers contains dozens of answers to anticipated questions. Playing to the media's need for drama and sensationalism, snappy rejoinders, humorous one-liners, and bitter accusations have replaced any obligation to address the questions being asked. Question Period has become a kind of theatre where each side plays out the ritual of political combat for an audience of cameras and reporters. As Brian Mulroney once put it, "It's all theatre; once I understood that, I was all set."[36] Although journalists often see Question Period in terms of winners and losers, the reality is that Question Period doesn't necessarily produce a long-term winner or a positive image for any of the participants. The public is routinely exposed to shouting matches, insults, and the emotions of blind partisanship, and this can undermine attempts to build positive images.

Scrums, with reporters milling tightly around the person being questioned and jostling against each other for position, are also an opportunity for the prime minister or a party leader to convey a tightly scripted message. The line of the day has been well thought through, and key phrases are repeated so that reporters will include them in TV and radio clips or as quotes in articles. If the questioning becomes too intense or uncomfortable, the politician can cite pressing engagements and beat a hasty retreat. Colin Seymour-Ure warns, however, that scrums can prove dangerous: "An unstructured exchange increases the risks for the person giving out information: he is more likely to be caught off guard, or to make a mistake, or to be misunderstood—even at the simple level of the answer to one question being taken to refer to another. There may be difficulty in ending the exchanges, too, if the prime minister is almost literally boxed in."[37]

Diversions are another commonly used tactic. Governments often attempt to blunt the harmful effects of a negative story by scheduling a "good news" event for the same day. The hope is that more attention will be given to the news that shows the government in a flattering light than on the news that is damaging. For instance, the Mulroney government announced its new day care initiative on the same day as the release of the Parker Inquiry report into the activities of former cabinet minister Sinclair Stevens. That Mulroney announced a cabinet shuffle on the same day as Pierre Trudeau was scheduled to testify before a parliamentary committee on the Meech Lake Constitutional Accord, testimony that was scathing in its criticism, was unlikely to have been only a coincidence.

Above all, prime ministers attempt to set the ground rules for reporting. Interviews are only granted under conditions that are likely to produce favourable coverage. Prime ministers may insist that television interviews be done live, for example, so that the interviews will be aired fully and not extensively edited. One former press secretary to Joe Clark described how he arranged for a TV interview to run for the length of air time so that the producers were forced "to go with what had been said" rather than cutting and stitching the interview together to make it more sensational.[38] One of the cardinal rules of American media advisor Roger Ailes is to avoid having politicians appear on programs that are heavily edited. Ailes' experience is that "The network will use their most controversial 18 seconds. Those seconds could be remarks out of context or could be the one moment they lose their cool."[39] David Gergen, who worked in both the Nixon and Reagan White Houses, recalls the approach that Nixon used to avoid editing. Nixon would "go out and deliver one hundred words, and he'd walk out. Because he knew that they had to use about one hundred words. They had to use what he wanted to say. And if you gave them five hundred words, they would select part of it and determine what the point of his statement was."[40] Patrick Gossage, a press secretary to Prime Minister Trudeau, described the "old PMO trick" of stipulating that the text of an interview be published in its entirety as the condition for granting the interview. This ensured that "the PM's views get out clean."[41]

Another device is to do an "end-run" around the Ottawa Press Gallery by making key announcements outside Ottawa. The logic, according to Graham Parley of *The Ottawa Citizen*, is that "Moving out of Ottawa you get more uncritical coverage. Local reporters are not as informed on some of the issues and as familiar with the nuances."[42] While prime ministers cannot avoid being followed around the country by a caravan of Press Gallery reporters, some benefits can be garnered through favourable local coverage. The pace and pageantry of prime ministerial travel, rather than his pronouncements on issues, will sometimes dominate local reporting.

A new wrinkle in attempts to bypass the Ottawa media was developed during Brian Mulroney's first term in office. The Conservative party set up its own broadcast facilities and began to market interviews with ministers and MPs to TV stations across the country. A number of smaller stations, starved for access to leading newsmakers, regarded this as a bonanza; and being able to do a big Ottawa story seemed to outweigh any concerns they might have had about Liberal or NDP MPs not being given the same opportunity to appear. Among Ottawa reporters the Conservative operation became known as "the tiny Tory network" and was treated derisively as a marriage of party propaganda and bogus journalism.

A more subtle method of influencing media coverage is by creating a climate of expectations among reporters, expectations that become the standard against which the prime minister's or the government's performance will be judged. An attempt is made to condition reporters over weeks or months into accepting certain assumptions. Geoffrey Stevens has described how prime ministers can create a sense of crisis, for instance, that will make them appear to be the saviours of a particular situation.[43] Stevens remembers that during the battle over the Constitution in 1981, government representatives repeatedly stressed that a deadlock had been reached and that a resolution was virtually impossible. When an agreement was finally concluded, the media, having been conditioned to expect that the talks would prove fruitless, proclaimed it as a historic breakthrough even though Quebec had not given the deal its approval and the provinces had the power to sidestep the Charter of Rights and Freedoms. Nonetheless, the prime minister appeared to have triumphed over seemingly insurmountable odds. Similarly, the Mulroney government launched a major public relations campaign prior to bringing down its 1989 budget. The clear message was that the government was going to take action on the deficit and that the budget would contain "radical" cuts to government spending.[44] When the budget was finally brought down, reporters, who expected drastic spending cuts, tended to describe the reductions that were announced as moderate and relatively insignificant. Media coverage probably helped dampen public outcries.

Public relations experts suggest that there are a number of basic rules to successful political salesmanship. The message must be simple (message composition), it must be newsworthy (message salience), and it must be credible; it must ring true (message credibility).[45] Simplicity, newsworthiness, and credibility are the cornerstones of image-making. Without this basic formula, it is argued, threats, stunts, leaks, pre-packaging the news, and creating expectations will all, in the long run, fall short. George Reedy, a former press secretary to Lyndon Johnson, contends that at the end of the day the only thing that really matters about media relations is whether it is believable. As he put it, "When the press is satisfied that it is getting straight answers, even if it does not like the answers, everything has been accomplished that can be accomplished by the press office."[46] Attempts to manipulate situations artificially, or to pump up images that are not congruent with reality, are ultimately doomed to failure. Others would argue, however, that on the mean streets of Canadian politics, image, especially television image, has become reality.

EXPLAINING THE RELATIONSHIP BETWEEN PRIME MINISTERS AND THE MEDIA

Some analysts believe that relationships between politicians and the media are determined by factors and processes largely beyond the control of either party. In their study of media coverage of U.S. presidents, David Paletz and Robert Entman argue that reporting is conditioned by specific settings and circumstances, that is, coverage reflects the nature of the events and situations being reported. Three theories and conditions about media reporting emerge from their work that may be relevant to the Canadian political arena:

1. Coverage will vary depending on whether the president is at the beginning, middle, or end of term. If a president has just assumed office, the president's message is likely to be reported extensively and criticism muted. Criticism heightens only when the president has a record to defend.

2. During crises or on solemn occasions, the president's actions and appeals are likely to be widely reported and presented without critical comments.

3. The higher the level of popular support enjoyed by the president, the more attention his or her statements will receive and the more uncritical will be the coverage. The reverse is also true; "the greater the opposition is believed to be, the more emboldened network correspondents are in their analysis."[47]

Michael Grossman and Martha Kumar contend that the relationship between U.S. presidents and White House reporters changes according to the normal gravitational pulls experienced during a four-year term, and that the relationship is characterized by predictable phases. The first phase they describe is the "alliance." For a brief period, anywhere from six weeks to six months (although it can be longer in some cases), the interests of newly elected presidents and the journalists who are covering them coincide. The media's main interest is to convey the information that the public wants about the new president's character: family, friends, life-style, hobbies, personal style and a sense of his past. The media is also obligated to explain the values and objectives of the new administration and the policies that it intends to implement. In these circumstances, it is in the interests of the White House to ensure that reporters are supplied with as much information as they need and to co-operate with the media as much as possible. Almost invariably, personality profiles of the president are friendly and policies are treated with respect. A strong feeling exists among reporters that the new person should be given a chance to perform and that, until then, criticism would be unfair. Moreover, critics have little grist for their mills. As Grossman and Kumar explain:

> First, when reporters present criticism, they do so in the form of a comparison between the President's rhetoric and his record. Since the President has no record at this time, his rhetoric is presented as news. Second, critical stories seldom are written by reporters on their own authority—they prefer to pluck critical words from the mouths of public figures. At this early stage of the administration, however, most public figures are unwilling to criticize the President in strong and newsworthy terms because it is not yet clear which direction he is moving.[48]

Grossman and Kumar are careful to emphasize that what they are describing is not a "honeymoon" period because honeymoon suggests that the media have suspended normal routines and self-interest for a brief period. They argue instead that during the alliance phase both the president and White House reporters retain their own agendas.

The question for Canadian observers is whether a similar alliance phase exists for newly elected prime ministers. The answer gleaned from interviews with journalists is that a newly elected prime minister can expect a short period of uncritical coverage in which the spotlight is placed on the prime minister's personality, life-style, and ideas, and on the new policies that he intends to put into place. John Diefenbaker had a honeymoon period that lasted for well over a year. Pierre Trudeau's ascension to the prime ministership in 1968 ushered in a period of Trudeaumania in which journalists wrote extensively about Trudeau's supposed mystery and charisma. Trudeau's personality held a fascination for journalists. Brian Mulroney also enjoyed an alliance phase in his relationship with the media, albeit without the passion and exuberance that accompanied Diefenbaker's crusading style and Trudeau's "Camelot." For some prime ministers, an alliance with the media was either brutally short or non-existent. Although Joe Clark and John Turner benefited from a brief alliance period when they were first elected leaders of their parties, the media's good will and need for information about personalities and policies were exhausted long before they became prime minister. Both faced intense criticism and found themselves in the midst of media crises soon after taking power. To the media they were old horses, known quantities, and so the first phase of coverage lacked the sense of revelation and discovery that had existed with Diefenbaker and Trudeau.

A second stage in the cycle of coverage described by Grossman and Kumar is called the "competitive" phase. In this phase presidents are, in

John F. Kennedy's words, "reading more and enjoying it less."[49] They are under a constant barrage of criticism as opponents emerge to lead attacks on their policies; they have a record that has to be defended; and the journalists who take delight in exposing the clay feet of politicians now feel free to wield their scalpels. During the competitive phase journalists are no longer as interested in the president's personality or life-style as in his capacity to administer the government, manage the economy, and protect vital foreign policy interests. Poor performances, mistakes, and scandals become front page news and lead items on television and cause the president to lose his grip on the agenda. The president views the media as a principal competitor in getting his message through to the public and attempts to reassert control using some of the weapons described earlier. For some presidents, Lyndon Johnson and Richard Nixon, for example, media coverage became an obsession; and they saw themselves engaged against the media in a battle for survival. Virtually every modern prime minister has endured a competitive phase in his or her relationship with the media. The intensity of conflict may vary depending on the prime minister and the circumstances prevailing at a given time. But as will be shown later in this chapter, the battle for control of the agenda is endemic to prime ministerial politics.

Grossman and Kumar describe the third and last phase as "detachment." Relations are characterized by routine and formality; each side knows what it can expect to receive from the other. Contacts between the president and journalists are less frequent and occur in highly controlled settings. Some presidents attempt to retreat almost entirely from contact with reporters. Both sides know, however, that the relationship is too vital to be completely severed so that "strong elements of cooperation remain" even during the most intense periods of competitive struggle.[50] The passions ignited during the second phase have been allowed to cool.

Veteran observers believe that phases in the media's coverage of prime ministers are quite discernible, although not all would agree that Grossman and Kumar's description is applicable in Canada or that it explains the reporting of U.S. presidents accurately. Doug Fisher believes that "the fall from grace happened to everyone. It happened to Diefenbaker. It happened to Pearson. It happened to Trudeau. Pearson was very popular with the press but by the end they were snarling at him. Once Diefenbaker and Pearson got critical press, they got bitter but in different ways. Dief began to play favourites. Pearson would get hurt and withdraw and put up a screen. Trudeau got a tremendous lionization. He could walk on water. I was also there when it broke down."[51] According to Jim Coutts, a former chief of staff to Pierre Trudeau, "From the elation of election night there's a steep curve that takes you to paranoia six months later. Trudeau warned the party about Trudeaumania, that the euphoria would turn into something nasty. He was prophetic."[52] Anthony Westell argues that "There are waves within each cycle. There will be a period when the prime minister is generally being horse-whipped. Then there will be a drawing back from that. It has a lot to do with the herd instinct."[53]

Whether there are phases that are truly predictable remains an open question, as no serious study has yet been done to chart the peaks and troughs in the prime minister's relationship with the media. No prime minister, however, has been able to avoid either a period of bitter and hostile relations with the media or a relationship with the Press Gallery that has been tumultuous at the best of times.

PRIME MINISTERS IN THE MEDIA SPOTLIGHT: MACKENZIE KING TO BRIAN MULRONEY

The nature of prime ministerial-media relations has changed dramatically since Mackenzie King's day. There is little doubt that King would have had difficulty adapting to the media world of the 1990s. His "cant and humbug, his subtlety, his womanish manners, and his flaccid look,"[54] as well as his long, tedious speeches, his gift for well-timed inaction, and his bizarre personal life, would have made him almost impossible to "package" for today's media audiences. As Brian Nolan has argued, "In the age of television and Kennedy charisma, King would have probably failed miserably. A terrible orator, his flat, monotonous voice put to sleep friend and foe alike. . . . His speeches were unmemorable. He droned on interminably; his sentences were convoluted and their meaning nearly always ambiguous."[55] Yet the journalists with whom he dealt treated him with respect and caution, for the rules of engagement differed considerably from current practices. News conferences were held on only rare occasions and questioning was mostly confined to the subject that King had come to address. There was none of the aggressive pummelling and "quiz show" atmosphere that characterizes today's media "opportunities." Nonetheless, as W.A. Wilson remembers, "It was pretty hard to trap him. You would have to have gotten up pretty early in the morning."[56] "His thoughts slid out of your grasp like jelly," as Bruce Hutchison once put it.[57]

King could go about his daily routine unhindered by journalists lying in wait. Scrums were non-existent. When the prime minister spoke in the House of Commons, he rarely looked up at the Press Gallery; and he lived his personal life free from the excruciating scrutiny that today's politicians must endure. Still King was "sensitive to things that were written about him personally" and knew how to cultivate the sympathies of the small number of journalists who covered the Hill.[58] As Bruce Hutchison has described King's adroitness and charm:

> Even now the busy Prime Minister could take an hour to beguile an unknown young reporter, only because the remote Victoria Daily Times might come in

useful some day. . . . Today he was laying on the birdlime with a trowel and his trick of apparent candor easily ensnarled a new-hatched fledgling. To serve his immediate purpose, King talked at length, with frequent sighs, about the increasing difficulties of government, the nation's grave problems, so little understood, the Conservative Party's irresponsible criticism.[59]

W.A. Wilson, as a young man working for the family newspaper in New Brunswick, remembers interviewing King in 1935. For most of the interview King asked him about local politics and then "dropped four or so newsworthy statements—without me having asked him a question."[60] King's penchant for excessive flattery, however, was kept for press barons like Dafoe of the *Free Press* (Winnipeg) and Atkinson of *The Toronto Star*, with whom he kept close contact. He would ask their advice about government policy, would reveal his own thoughts and plans, and cemented these professional relationships into warm friendships.

Louis St. Laurent was another prime minister who would have had difficulties thriving under the glare of today's media spotlight. Dignified and gentlemanly, the great aristocrat of Canadian politics, he was also aloof, stodgy, colourless, and had a hot temper. St. Laurent did not have to contend until the end of his career with the intrusiveness and power of television; he governed at a time when relations between politicians and the Gallery were more congenial and respectful than they are in the 1990s. He could benefit from the image of "Uncle Louis," the patriarchal leader who stood above mundane partisan politics, without fear that the image would collapse under ruthless exposure by journalists. Although often possessing great "public charm," St. Laurent neither mingled with nor flattered reporters. He would walk right past waiting journalists and barely took notice of the Gallery when speaking in the House of Commons. According to J.W. Pickersgill, a leading cabinet minister in the St. Laurent government, he "didn't feel the need to cultivate anybody. He expected that if he did his job, he would be reported fairly."[61] Bruce Hutchison recalls what it was like to provoke St. Laurent's legendary temper:

> He answered all my questions with candor, sometimes with twinkling humor, until I came to a famous incident. Did he now regret his decision, as Minister of Justice, to arrest and hold incommunicado a company of alleged Russian spies? The smiling face hardened in a scowl. The kindly eyes seemed to congeal in black opacity. . . . St. Laurent paused for a moment, his scowl deepening, his eyes drilling mine. 'Sir, he said at last, I don't care to answer that question. . .'
>
> In print the incident seems trivial. In life it told me much about St. Laurent. His iron curtain not only excluded the offensive question, it nearly decapitated the questioner as it fell.[62]

W.A. Wilson also recalled that "if a reporter was going beyond the immediate need for information he could lose his temper sharply and deliver an angry rebuke."[63] St. Laurent and the journalists he dealt with both understood that the prime minister controlled the interview, a situation that might not be taken for granted today.

While St. Laurent was almost oblivious to relations with the media, John Diefenbaker was obsessed by them. The "Chief" constantly entertained, courted, charmed, cajoled, and manipulated members of the Gallery. He scanned between eight and ten newspapers daily, and his staff would collect clippings from other newspapers. He made a particular point of listening to "Preview Commentary," a CBC Radio program that featured journalists' views on the latest developments in Parliament. There was little news reporting or commentary that escaped Diefenbaker's ever vigilant eyes and ears.

Diefenbaker was a Gallery favourite long before he became prime minister. Indeed, Peter Dempson has recalled the warm hospitality extended to reporters who were invited to Diefenbaker's home and the sorrow felt throughout the Gallery when Diefenbaker's first wife, Edna, passed away.[64] The attraction to Diefenbaker was that he always made good copy. His oratorical flourishes, sense of drama, showmanship, and instinct for confrontation made him newsworthy almost every time he spoke. When Diefenbaker was elected prime minister, he sought and savoured the media's spotlight. Unlike St. Laurent, Diefenbaker encouraged the Gallery to follow him everywhere. He enjoyed being surrounded by reporters eager for his words, the give and take of scrums and, most of all, the constant attention. According to Charles Lynch, Diefenbaker's cravings for publicity changed the dynamics of Press Gallery reporting in a fundamental way. As Lynch argues, "his unprecedented accessibility not only gave reporters a field day but increased their work load and led to the expansion of Ottawa news bureaus. For the first time there was a major news source in the capital outside the Commons itself."[65]

Some journalists became part of Diefenbaker's inner circle and may have influenced some of the prime minister's decisions. A number of reporters, for instance, were invited to go fishing with Diefenbaker soon after the 1957 election, and prospective cabinet appointments were discussed on the trip.[66] Information about government business would be given to journalists that he trusted in exchange, of course, for favourable coverage. But, as described in Chapter Two, Diefenbaker could often be coy, using these reporters to float trial balloons and teasing them along with hints or small tidbits of information.

When criticism from the press increased sharply in 1959, Diefenbaker's mood turned ugly. As Anthony Westell has described Diefenbaker's about-face, "He was at first very popular with the press. He had a 'hail fellow well met' relationship of warmth and good humour. However, he viewed criticism as a betrayal. He soon believed in a conspiracy theory. He was completely convinced that the press was in a conspiracy against him."[67] His answer was to lash out at offending reporters, often in a torrent of rage. Peter Dempson remembers being summoned into Diefenbaker's office after an article critizing Diefenbaker and written by one of his colleagues at the *Telegram*, George Brimmell, appeared in the paper. The article was spread out on Diefenbaker's desk with the offending comments underlined in red. His hands shaking, Diefenbaker berated Dempson for half an hour.[68] When during the 1962 election campaign Charles King of Southam News wrote that the Diefenbaker "bubble" had burst, Diefenbaker again flew into a rage. In the presence of other reporters, he shouted at King, "I have nothing to say to you at all. Anybody can ask me questions but not you. . . . I mean that, too. That's final with you."[69]

The CBC became a particular target of Diefenbaker's anger. Once, when the teleprompter kept breaking during a TV appearance at the CBC's Ottawa affiliate, CBOT-TV, Diefenbaker threatened to fire the technicians. In 1959, "political pressure" persuaded CBC management to end "Preview Commentary." The program was soon reinstated, however, when thirty-five CBC producers resigned in protest and it became apparent that the network faced open rebellion.

Diefenbaker was the first prime minister to employ a press secretary. Jim Nelson, then the Ottawa bureau chief for the British United Press, was recruited in 1957. Nelson found the position frustrating and demeaning. Diefenbaker was not open to advice and couldn't resist making impromptu statements and announcements. He remained a one-man show. On one occasion, Diefenbaker handed Nelson a briefcase and told him to guard it carefully. Nelson was "absolutely shattered" when he found that the briefcase contained only a clean shirt.[70]

By the end of Diefenbaker's prime ministership, relations with the Gallery were strained to the breaking-point. Indeed, most reporters were probably in agreement with Val Sears' famous remarks made at the outset of the 1962 election campaign, "We've got to get cracking fellows. We've a government to overthrow."[71] Diefenbaker was convinced to the end that "the press gallery contributed to his losing office."[72]

Like his predecessor, Lester Pearson also enjoyed a friendly relationship with reporters for many years before he became prime minister. His wit, charm, and political acumen were on full display during the weekly press conferences that he gave first as assistant under-secretary of state for external affairs and then as under-secretary. As ambassador to the United States, he carefully cultivated relationships with leading American journalists such as James Reston and Walter Lippmann and with those Canadian reporters who had an interest in the new role that Canada was assuming in world affairs. Reston recalled that "Mike talked with reporters as people to be trusted. You could go and play pitch with him in the backyard of the embassy and he'd talk about anything, he didn't have to say some of it should be off the record—he knew it would be."[73] Nonetheless, he used his press contacts shrewdly. As historian Patrick Brennan has written, "One of his favourite tactics was to reveal 'off the record' any sensitive information he believed one or more reporters were on the verge of finding out on their own, safe in the knowledge that violating that confidentiality of sources was simply not done by a reputable Gallery man."[74] He was also aware that "a calculated indiscretion" in the form of a leak to the right journalist could work wonders in promoting a particular viewpoint or interpretation of events.[75] In Ottawa, Pearson would hold small dinner parties and soirées for friendly reporters. Romeo Leblanc found that Pearson was "seductive in small groups. He was self-deprecating, very civilized, and fun to be with."[76] He was available for interviews, and he knew the twists and turns of politics in the relatively insulated world of the Press Gallery.

When Pearson became leader of the opposition in 1958, he hired Dick O'Hagan, who had been working with MacLaren Advertising in Toronto, as his press secretary. O'Hagan held the position until 1966. O'Hagan quickly became part of Pearson's inner circle and, together with Keith Davey, the party's election impresario, was the guardian of Pearson's image. He tried to make Pearson into a more exciting television performer, a constant battle against Pearson's instinctive discomfort with television. Peter C. Newman has described O'Hagan's frantic efforts to produce and direct Pearson's televised announcement of the 1965 election: "O'Hagan stood in the control room, gesturing with his hands like some entranced faith-healer, a more convincing performance than Pearson was able to deliver. That night the Prime Minister looked like an unhappy puppet being manipulated by unseen influences . . . ."[77]

Another problem for Pearson was that during the 1960s the Gallery was undergoing substantial change. The old, comfortable milieu of shared experiences and confidences fell victim to the intrusiveness of a much larger number of reporters and a new aggressive style of reporting. Pearson had trouble adapting to the new rules. He disliked the scrums of waiting reporters that swarmed around him after cabinet meetings, fearing that he would be prodded into making off-the-cuff remarks he would later regret. He also felt that the pushing and frenzy of scrums was not in accordance with the dignity of his office. The solution recommended by O'Hagan was to hold regular press conferences and to turn his charm on with reporters whom he would meet in small groups.

Pearson, however, faced intense media criticism as his government was rocked by scandals, crises in Parliament, and heated jurisdictional battles with Quebec. Popular columnist Peter C. Newman and the television program *This Hour Has Seven Days* were particular thorns in Pearson's side. Charles Lynch argues that "It was the long years of having the press as a cheering section that made Pearson's plunge into politics so painful. He became prime minister, and suddenly all but a few special cronies turned critical and stayed critical."[78] As the attacks mounted, he retreated to the security of a small group of trusted friends in the media: Blair Fraser, Bruce Hutchison, and George Ferguson, among others. He avoided and attempted to bypass the Ottawa media whenever possible. Press conferences grew more infrequent, and he was reticent to grant interviews to journalists who had criticized his performance in office. When an important bill was defeated in the House of Commons in 1968, Pearson went on television to explain why he did not consider the matter a vote of non-confidence in his government. This was the first time that a prime minister had used television to appeal to the public directly. Pearson preferred addressing the public on TV to facing a raucous Parliament and a hostile Press Gallery. Similarly, he initiated the televising of constitutional conferences in the hope that the public would make their own judgements about his leadership rather than relying on press reports. Although Pearson benefited from the media's enthusiastic coverage of Canada's centennial celebrations in 1967 and from the huge international success of Expo 67 in Montreal, Pearson felt that his hard-won successes in building economic and social programs were never adequately recognized by the press. Indeed, as Diefenbaker before him, he "left office thinking that the press had done him in."[79]

Pierre Trudeau's relations with journalists were cool and distant. As a former professor steeped in the nuances of political philosophy and constitutional law, he disdained the media's tendency to simplify and sensationalize. He also resented their intrusions into his private life, particularly the circus-like coverage given to his wife, Margaret Trudeau; and at times his contempt was palpable. Although he had a few favourites such as Jack Webster, George Radwanski, Anthony Westell, and Jim Munson, Trudeau developed an intense antipathy towards journalists as a group during his tenure as prime minister. Ironically, during his formative years in Quebec before becoming prime minister, some of his closest associates—Jacques Hébert, Blair Fraser, and Gérard Pelletier—had been journalists. As prime minister, Trudeau made it known that he didn't care what was said or written about him, and he sometimes gave reporters "a detailed account of his low opinion of this or that story or comment that had reached his attention."[80] According to Brian Smith, Trudeau's attitude was that "If you are going to judge me, then I should be able to judge you."[81]

Trudeau's animosity and resentment were reciprocated by journalists. Clive Cocking found in an informal survey of the Gallery taken in 1978 that there was "not one reporter who likes Trudeau" and that "the gallery vultures seem distinctly bloody-minded."[82] Charles Lynch described the situation that prevailed in the late 1970s this way:

> It's been total war 'tween Trudeau and the press for a long, long time. . . . And the press gallery is just full of people who would love to get that sonofabitch, and who savour the fact that now he's on the skids they want to be there for it.[83]

There is little doubt, however, that Trudeau was also respected and feared. His intelligence, independence, and charismatic appeal won grudging admiration from the journalists covering him. *The Toronto Star's* Val Sears recalls that it was "always a delight to see him in a foreign country. He was always ahead of the pack."[84]

What sets Trudeau apart from virtually every other contemporary prime minister was that he made few efforts to cultivate good media relations. Only out of necessity, as part of struggles for political survival, did he swallow his natural feelings of enmity. Access to Trudeau was always difficult. When Geoffrey Stevens was the Ottawa columnist for *The Globe and Mail*, a position of considerable influence, his requests for an interview with Trudeau were repeatedly denied.[85] Former Trudeau press secretary Patrick Gossage recalls that the " 'Interview Request File' was definitely the office's most swollen and lethargic paper-collector. It was virtually a one-way dossier—in only!"[86] One journalist who did get interviews was Val Sears. Sears's impression was that "Trudeau was entirely indifferent to the press and to me. The interviews were no fun for him and no fun for me. He never let his guard down. The interview was filled with languid comments with Trudeau looking bored as if thinking 'When will this be over?' "[87] George Radwanski noted as well that "access to Trudeau's ministers was often difficult, largely because of the boss's view that we were dangerous idiots."[88]

Trudeau believed that he could be most effective if he bypassed the Ottawa Press Gallery and reached out to the public directly. He made as much use as he could of airtime to speak to Canadians and had federal-provincial first ministers' conferences televised. Most significantly, he had the proceedings of the House of Commons televised beginning in 1977.

During his long period in office, Trudeau was served by a succession of press secretaries. Romeo Leblanc, Peter Roberts, Pierre O'Neill, Courtney Tower, Jean Charpentier, Dick O'Hagan, Arnie Patterson, Patrick Gossage, Nicole Senecal, and Ralph Coleman each seemed to encounter numerous frustrations. Some enjoyed a place in Trudeau's inner circle, while others had little power at all. Joyce Fairbairn, a former reporter who served as Trudeau's legislative assistant, was in charge of briefing the prime minister before Question Period. Fairbairn prepared media summaries and helped think through various strategies for dealing with the media. The Trudeau government also set up a communications committee that met weekly and began the practice of devising a communications strategy to accompany new policies. When Dick O'Hagan was appointed press secretary in 1975 he again, as he had with Pearson, instituted regular press conferences. He reportedly told a resistant Trudeau, "Okay, so these aren't journalists of the caliber of those who work for *Le Monde* or the *London Times*. This is the press you have to deal with and it's necessary to respond to their needs at their level."[89] O'Hagan attempted to get Trudeau to acknowledge important reporters when they rose to ask questions, but the prime minister often forgot their names.

Trudeau's news conferences seemed to have a "chess-match" quality. Trudeau's answers were nimble but his tone often aggressive. He regularly challenged the intelligence and appropriateness of questions. According to Brian Smith, "He would dismiss questions as irrelevant, attack the premise and engage in the verbal jousting that he was well known for and it was quite biting. Reporters had to be intellectually up to it."[90] As George Radwanski described Trudeau's performance:

> He would answer parts of questions, walk right through them, or turn it around on you. You had to ask questions just right, shutting off avenues of escape, anticipating his getaway and shutting it down. It became a game.[91]

Radwanski noted, however, that Trudeau was more likely to respond if questions were challenging intellectually even if it was not politically advantageous for him to do so. On other occasions his instinct for political survival was put to the test. Mary Comber and Robert Mayne quote a former Trudeau aide as saying that Trudeau would

> have in reserve a number of dramatic and controversial declarations which he freely used ... to deflect questions away from ... sensitive areas. When particularly critical questions were expected, the Prime Minister would embellish his answer to a relatively innocuous question. This lively quote would then be picked up and become the theme for subsequent questions.[92]

Former Liberal cabinet minister Donald Johnson remembers the skill and ruthlessness with which Trudeau would debate his opponents: "He is a skilled debator, vicious with those whom he seeks to destroy in the parry and thrust of verbal exchanges. Time and again I have seen him seize one trivial exaggeration or inconsistency . . . skillfully dissect it, and watch as the whole merit of his opponent's argument collapses."[93]

Sometimes his zealousness, his need to win the argument and to lecture and correct others, however, undermined his attempts to build personal relationships. Christina McCall-Newman has described a lunch meeting held in Toronto in 1977 that brought together Trudeau and several prominent English-Canadian publishers. When one of the publishers joked that Quebec Premier René Lévesque had probably never been to a football game prior to the Grey Cup game of that year, Trudeau responded coldly, "Why should he have? I had never been to a football game myself until I was Minister of Justice. It may be difficult for you people to understand but football is not a French-Canadian sport."[94] Instead of letting the line pass, Trudeau had briefly turned pleasantries into confrontation.

There was little repair work that could be done during Trudeau's last term in office from 1980 to 1984. Both sides retained their earlier suspicions and animosities. Trudeau's public performances did become more effective as a result of advice, from Patrick Gossage in particular. After 1980, Trudeau used a podium more often, dispensing with the "gunslinger stance" that had not been terribly dignified. He also developed a more relaxed delivery for television. A sophisticated transcription service was introduced and a "Visiting Editors" program started. On the whole, though, Trudeau's distaste for the media fostered his reliance on a repertoire of formal media-management tactics, with little attempt to build interpersonal skills or relationships. He remained a distant and little understood figure, disliked but also admired by the Gallery.

Perhaps no modern Canadian prime minister was as accessible to journalists as Joe Clark. Clark scrummed outside the House almost daily when Parliament was in session, held a weekly press conference, and granted frequent interviews. Yet despite — or perhaps even because of — his availability, Clark received harsh treatment. Clark's difficulties began when he invited journalists to accompany him on his world tour in 1978. The tour was designed to familiarize Clark with international problems and trouble spots. As there were no policy statements or substantive issues or events to report, journalists were left with little to focus on except Clark's personality and whatever "human interest" stories the tour could provide. The tour soon became a public relations disaster. Luggage was lost, Clark nearly walked into a soldier's bayonet while reviewing Canadian troops in the Golan Heights, and his comments and behaviour seemed awkward and unsophisticated. To the seasoned reporters who covered him he quickly became a caricature, an object of derision and ridicule.

To compound his troubles, Clark did not come across well on television, which magnified his weak chin, stilted laugh, and gawky movements. Clark began his prime ministership with an image of ineptitude that seemed to take on a life of its own. As Val Sears has described the situation, "The perception early on was that he was a bumbling twit. It snowballed. There was no way to get out of it. There never was a great deal of sympathy. The guy was never in the real world in his life. He was like the fat kid in the school yard waiting to be beaten up."[95] Desmond Morton argued that:

> Whoever it was who decided that Joe Clark was a wimp established a framework of interpretation in which every action, in victory or defeat, could be located. The image, at least in my view, preceded the evidence and distorted it.[96]

There is a suspicion that some media managers began soliciting stories about Clark's alleged ineptness from their reporters because they thought that these stories were popular with audiences. Hubert Gendron, who covered Clark during the 1979 federal election campaign, admitted that the psychology among reporters was such that "during the tours of Maritime steel mills and shipyards everyone was looking for him to fall into a steel vat or something."[97] Journalists who reported on Clark began to refer to their task as the "wimp watch."

That the Tories were able to win power (albeit a minority government) in 1979 despite Clark's negative image and bad press suggests that the media may not be as powerful a force in determining the outcome of Canadian elections as some believe. It might be argued, however, that voters thought even less of Trudeau, who had also been pummelled by negative media coverage, than of Clark. The electorate may have been determined to defeat Trudeau, whatever the consequences.

Clark did not enjoy any appreciable period of alliance with the media upon becoming prime minister. Clark's personality held little fascination for reporters or the public, and the new government was given little reprieve from criticism. According to Stephen Handelman:

> The seeds of ridicule and disbelief planted in the public mind long before he became Prime Minister grew until they choked off the life of his government when it barely got started. . . . Long before the press had come to accept and respect Clark's ability as Prime Minister the public was still looking at him with a jaundiced eye. Clark's jerky awkwardness became a metaphor for his government.[98]

One former press secretary, Jock Osler, complained that "The more he was open, the more they attacked. The bastards trashed us."[99]

It might be argued that had Clark won a majority, the media might have been more prudent about making early judgements about his government's performance. There might have been more respect and circumspection had his victory been more substantial and journalists known that the government would serve a full term. But as the Conservatives were not in a secure position and appeared weak and inexperienced, some journalists began to believe that the government was not going to last for long. The government's prospects for survival became a focus of attention. The Conservatives made the mistake of making few firm policy decisions during their first months in office and then taking over four months to call Parliament into session. Journalists were left with little to report except the government's apparent in-fighting and indecision.

John Turner, while prime minister for only a brief period in 1984, received an extraordinary amount of harsh coverage. As was the case with Joe Clark, Turner never enjoyed a full alliance period with journalists. While as a dashing young cabinet minister in the late 1960s and early

1970s he had been a Gallery favourite, his long absence from politics had left him strangely inexperienced and rusty. The mood of the Gallery had also changed considerably in the intervening years. As Doug Fisher described the attitude that greeted Turner on his return:

> Turner had been the golden boy early on but lost it when he went off to Bay Street. By the time he came back, we had a much more left-wing gallery with a lot of younger people who didn't remember Turner the golden boy. All they knew was that he came from Bay Street. Gee! Look at the suits on him and look at his wife. So he got the . . . kicked out of him very early. I thought he was lucky to survive the leadership race the way we were going after him.[100]

According to Stephen Clarkson, "John Turner had failed utterly to respond to the changing nature of the press corps. Having been described for years in flattering terms by reporters who built up his myth as dauphin in exile, he was unnerved by their switch to a more critical stance once he re-entered the political ring. . . . The reality of Turner the politician so clashed with the previous image the same media had sustained that reporters could barely disguise their contempt."[101] Fred Fletcher noted that Turner's nervousness and awkwardness were ridiculed openly by reporters, and that the leader's tour during the 1984 election became "a kind of trial by ordeal."[102] Much of the blame lay with Turner himself. There were numerous gaffes and inappropriate gestures, not the least of which was the damaging "bum-patting" incident during the 1984 election. Turner was also hindered by his intense and "fire-breathing" appearance on television. His burning stare, staccato speaking style, and stiff movements made viewers feel uncomfortable. According to one leading Liberal, "John was bewildered by his TV problem. His life-time act had been to be Mr. Glad."[103] Years of television coaching finally produced a more polished, "cooler," and more comfortable television performer during the 1988 federal election. In a survey of how party leaders were covered by the CBC and *The Globe and Mail* during the 1984 election, Comber and Mayne found that in stories that gave assessments Turner received negative treatment 90 percent and 84 percent of the time, respectively.[104] Coverage remained harsh during his years as opposition leader as he faced internal party upheavals, bitter differences over party policy, and a constant questioning of his leadership. A study done of the 1988 election by the National Media Archive of the Fraser Institute found that CBC and CTV were "slightly more critical than favourable to Turner," while CBC Radio's *The World at Six* provided "twice as many negative as positive statements."[105] The once powerful Bay Street baron had been put through the media grinder.

Brian Mulroney's relationship with the media seems to have gone through all of the phases described by Grossman and Kumar. Mulroney benefited from a healthy period of alliance in which he received favourable coverage, endured a harsh competitive phase during which he felt that his government was under siege and, at the end of his first term and during his second mandate, entered a detachment phase where relations remained controlled, formal, and distant.

Mulroney has been more conscious of the importance of media relations than any other prime minister. During the years spent in the political wilderness after losing the 1976 Conservative leadership race, Mulroney sought to rebuild his political fortunes by ardently courting leading journalists. He was always available for interviews, tried to befriend influential journalists, and was a source for inside information on developments in the Conservative party. In a book on the 1983 Conservative leadership race, Patrick Martin, Allan Gregg, and George Perlin wrote:

> Quick to contact journalists with whose work he agrees and equally quick to call those who disappoint, Mulroney cajoled and bullied, leaked and stonewalled his way into the professional lives of many journalists, until he became able to do a little "trafficking" of his own.[106]

When he became prime minister, a number of journalists took positions in his government: L. Ian MacDonald, Bill Fox, Dalton Camp, Bruce Phillips, and Luc Lavoie, among others. Moreover, in his first years in office Mulroney was virtually obsessed with media coverage; anything that was written or said about him was devoured voraciously. Even when he travelled, videotaped newscasts and accounts of newspaper articles were sent to him daily.[107] Michel Gratton, a former press secretary, described him as a "media junkie."[108]

Yet relations with the media were to sour within Mulroney's first year in office. His government was wracked by scandals and resignations among his cabinet ministers, and he seemed to use the levers of partisan patronage with extraordinary abandon. He soon faced a barrage of negative reporting and commentary that stung him deeply. As Gratton has written:

> ... when they started sticking the knives into him, they did so in a merciless frenzy. Since he attached so much importance to the media, the wounds went all the deeper, and left him with a deep resentment at having been betrayed by people in whom he had invested a portion of his soul. He started to hold them responsible for all his problems, rather than seeking out the truly guilty parties within his own administration. I can't remember how often he railed against the media, calling the reporters ignorant fools who didn't understand anything.[109]

Angry and exasperated, Mulroney would phone publishers, editors, and reporters to complain. Bill Fox, his first press secretary, sometimes got into heated battles with reporters over the tone of their stories. Journalists who were considered unfriendly were frozen out.

Part of the problem was that having made patronage a main issue during the 1984 election, Mulroney had set the standard by which he would be judged. Journalists felt that they had every right to attack him on this ground. The Gallery also became suspicious of Mulroney's penchant for exaggeration and bluster, his syrupy pretentions, and his slickness. Mulroney's "blarney" aroused considerable cynicism and invited attempts to hold him accountable for his words.

By his third year in office, relations between Mulroney and the press had hardened into cold formality. Although Mulroney had once promised that press conferences would be held twice every month, Mulroney did not hold a formal press conference in the press building amphitheatre from early 1987 to early in 1990. He had chosen, instead, to engage the media in a somewhat different way. After leaving the House, he speaks briefly to reporters from the stairs that lead to his office. *The Globe and Mail's* Craig McInnes has described how this technique maximized Mulroney's control over the exchanges with reporters:

> As he ascends, reporters bark out questions, like hounds baying at a fleeting fox. If Mr. Mulroney hears one he wants to answer, he will pause on the stairs and throw a few words back down to the crush of reporters and photographers. Only the quick and the well-placed get close enough to hear them.
>
> Some days the Prime Minister seems to hear nothing and goes up the stairs with the questions of reporters falling impotently in his wake.[110]

Another example of detachment was his choice of Marc Lortie, an external affairs officer, as his press secretary following Gratton's departure. Fox and Gratton had both been journalists and were intensely partisan. Lortie, however, saw his "role more as providing a service."[111] Lortie stayed through the 1988 election. When he returned to the public service following the election, Gilbert Lavoie, a former national editor of *La Presse*, became press secretary.

What distinguishes Mulroney's media relations system is the degree to which it is planned and centralized. While there was a good deal of coordination under Trudeau, Mulroney seems to give higher priority to the communications committee of the cabinet, whose job is to plan media strategy on a regular basis. The rationale, according to Marc Lortie, was that "the prime minister wanted to make sure that every time a cabinet minister was dealing with a policy, the communications aspects would be a factor in the policy. Too often things were announced in an uncoordinated way. If you made two different announcements on the same day about two different policies, very likely one will suffer because the media will cover one announcement and not the other."[112] The media outlets that are to be targeted, when and where announcements are to be made, and the manner in which information is released are planned well in advance.

Despite the centralized flow of government information through the press office and attempts to stage events so that the prime minister speaks in carefully controlled settings where a dignified image can be preserved, Mulroney's instinct for partisan attack, embellished rhetoric, and jabs at the opposition often upset the best planning. He seems torn between the formal, restricted, and ritualized structures of media relations and his desire to play to the crowd and seek affirmation from the journalists who cover him; it appears that he is often tempted to break free of the structures that he himself has created in order to survive in the battleground of media relations.

CONCLUSION

The media environment has changed dramatically since Mackenzie King's days as prime minister. Today government leaders are aware that they can only reach their publics and build consensus through the media. Agenda-building, public relations, and effective television performances are the prerequisites for gaining and maintaining power. Getting the message through the media filter means understanding the media's requirements and using those requirements to one's own advantage.

Little can be taken for granted, however, against a critical press. Party leaders, and especially the prime minister, engage in numerous media management exercises; indeed, much of their day is devoted to staged media events, including Question Period. Yet they inevitably face bruising criticism, much of what they say and do never reaches the public in the way they intended it to, and they can expect to endure a media crisis at some stage during their period in office. No prime minister since St. Laurent has been able to win the media battle, and St. Laurent governed amid very different circumstances. Prime ministers must govern in a harsh journalistic climate that, in Joshua Meyrowitz's words, "lowers the political hero to our level."[113]

NOTES

1. Frederick Fletcher, "The Prime Minister as Public Persuader," in *Apex of Power*, Thomas Hockin ed., 2nd ed. (Scarborough, Ontario: Prentice-Hall, 1977), pp. 86-111.
2. Quoted in Shanto Iyengar and Donald Kinder, *News That Matters: Television and American Opinion* (Chicago: University of Chicago Press, 1987), p. 126.
3. Thomas Griffith, "More Professional, Less Human," *Time*, 16 November 1987.
4. Fletcher, pp. 99-100.

5. Mary Anne Comber and Robert Mayne, *The Newsmongers* (Toronto: McClelland and Stewart, 1986), p. 13.
6. The concept of a "press crisis" is introduced by F. Christopher Arterton, "The Media Politics of Presidential Campaigns," in *Race For The Presidency*, James David Barber, ed. (Englewood Cliffs, New Jersey: Prentice-Hall, 1978), p. 28.
7. Mark Hertsgaard, *On Bended Knee: The Press and the Reagan Presidency* (New York: Farrar, Straus, Giroux, 1988), p. 18.
8. Quoted in Alan Frizzell and Anthony Westell, "The Media and the Campaign," in *The Canadian General Election of 1988*, Alan Frizzell, Jon Pammett, and Anthony Westell, eds. (Ottawa: Carleton University Press, 1989), p. 78.
9. S. Robert Lichter, Stanley Rothman, and Linda Lichter, *The Media Elite* (Bethesda, Maryland: Adler and Adler, 1986), p. 10.
10. Joshua Meyrowitz, *No Sense of Place* (New York: Oxford University Press, 1985), pp. 275-80.
11. Ibid., pp. 284-5.
12. Interview with Romeo Leblanc, Ottawa, 26 May 1987.
13. Max Atkinson, *Our Masters' Voices* (London: Methuen, 1984), p. 174.
14. Ibid., pp. 175-76.
15. "The Remaking of the Candidate: Part II: C & E Interviews Michael Sheehan," *Campaigns and Elections* (May/June 1988), p. 28.
16. Hertsgaard, pp. 48-9.
17. Hedrick Smith, *The Power Game* (New York: Random House, 1988), pp. 418-19.
18. Ibid., p. 428.
19. David Halberstam, *The Powers That Be* (New York: Alfred A. Knopf, 1979), p. 430.
20. Peter C. Newman, *The Distemper of Our Times: Canadian Politics in Transition: 1963-1968* (Toronto: McClelland and Stewart, 1968), p. 69.
21. Quoted in Joyce Nelson, "Packaging the Populace: Polling in the Age of Image Politics," *Fuse* (August 1989), p. 21.
22. Smith, p. 402.
23. Ibid., p. 420.
24. William Boot, "Campaign '88: TV Overdoses on the Inside Dope," *Columbia Journalism Review* (January/February 1989), p. 24.
25. Confidential interview.
26. Confidential interview.
27. Michael Grossman and Martha Kumar, *Portraying the President* (Baltimore: Johns Hopkins University Press, 1981), p. 174.
28. Interview with George Radwanski, Toronto, 23 May 1986.
29. Ibid.
30. *TV Guide*, 18 June 1988, p. 9.

31. Claire Hoy, *Friends in High Places* (Toronto: Key Porter Books, 1987), p. 310.
32. Interview with Jeff Dvorkin, Toronto, 21 May 1986.
33. Ibid.
34. Michel Gratton, *"So What Are The Boys Saying?"* (Toronto: McGraw-Hill Ryerson, 1987), p. 110.
35. Hertsgaard, p. 52.
36. Graham Fraser and Ross Howard, "Commons Floor a TV Studio Where MPs Play to Camera," *The Globe and Mail*, 4 April 1988, p. A1.
37. Colin Seymour-Ure, "Prime Ministers, Political News and Political Places," *Canadian Public Administration* (Summer 1989), p. 313.
38. Interview with Jock Osler, Calgary, 10 July 1986.
39. Fred Barnes, "Pulling the Strings," *The New Republic*, 22 February 1988, p. 12.
40. Smith, p. 406.
41. Patrick Gossage, *Close to the Charisma* (Toronto: McClelland and Stewart, 1986), p. 112.
42. Interview with Graham Parley, Ottawa, 9 July 1987.
43. Interview with Geoffrey Stevens, Toronto, 22 May 1986.
44. Claire Hoy, *Margin of Error* (Toronto: Key Porter Books, 1989), p. 90.
45. W. Lance Bennett, *News: The Politics of Illusion* (White Plains, New York: Longman, 1988), pp. 73-74.
46. Grossman and Kumar, p. 88.
47. David Paletz and Robert Entman, *Media Power Politics* (New York: Free Press, 1981), pp. 69-70.
48. Grossman and Kumar, p. 277.
49. Quoted in Grossman and Kumar, p. 279.
50. Ibid., p. 295.
51. Interview with Doug Fisher, Ottawa, 27 January 1988.
52. Interview with Jim Coutts, Toronto, 3 June 1987.
53. Interview with Anthony Westell, Ottawa, 28 January 1988.
54. Bruce Hutchison, *The Far Side of the Street* (Toronto: Macmillan of Canada, 1976), p. 70.
55. Brian Nolan, *King's War* (Toronto: Fawcett Crest, 1988), p. 5.
56. Interview with W.A. Wilson, Ottawa, 18 April 1989.
57. Hutchison, p. 220.
58. Interview with J.W. Pickersgill.
59. Hutchison, p. 69.
60. Interview with W.A. Wilson.
61. Interview with J.W. Pickersgill.
62. Hutchison, p. 220.
63. Interview with W.A. Wilson.
64. Peter Dempson, *Assignment Ottawa: Seventeen Years in the Press Gallery* (Toronto: General Publishing Co., 1968), p. 88.

65. Charles Lynch, *The Lynch Mob* (Toronto: Key Porter Books, 1988), p. 53.
66. Dempson, p. 95.
67. Interview with Anthony Westell.
68. Dempson, p. 114.
69. Ibid., p. 120.
70. Laurie West, "The Man in the Middle: The Role of the Prime Minister's Press Secretary," Honours Research Project, School of Journalism, Carleton University, April, 1986, p. 6.
71. Dempson, pp. 119-20.
72. Quoted in Clive Cocking, *Following the Leaders* (Toronto: Doubleday Canada, 1980), p. 33.
73. Norman Smith, "Pearson, People and Press," *International Journal* (Winter 1973-4), pp. 16-17.
74. Pat Brennan, " 'A Responsible, Civilized Relationship': Reporting the Nation's Business, 1937-1957," Ph.D. diss, York University 1989, p. 294.
75. Ibid., p. 299.
76. Interview with Romeo Leblanc.
77. Newman, p. 344.
78. Lynch, p. 70.
79. Quoted in Cocking, p. 33.
80. Lynch, p. 89.
81. Interview with Brian Smith, Toronto, 16 July 1987.
82. Cocking, p. 31.
83. Quoted in Cocking, p. 33.
84. Interview with Val Sears, Ottawa, 26 May 1987.
85. Interview with Geoffrey Stevens, Toronto, 22 May 1986.
86. Gossage, p. 24.
87. Interview with Val Sears.
88. Interview with George Radwanski, Toronto, 23 May 1986.
89. Quoted in West, p. 28.
90. Interview with Brian Smith.
91. Interview with George Radwanski.
92. Comber and Mayne, p. 134.
93. Donald Johnson, *Up the Hill* (Montreal: Optimum Publishing International, 1986), p. 96.
94. Christina McCall-Newman, *Grits* (Toronto: Macmillan of Canada, 1982), pp. 57-58.
95. Interview with Val Sears.
96. Desmond Morton, "Television: Does the Image Reflect Reality?" in *Politics and the Media* (Toronto: Reader's Digest Foundation of Canada and Erindale College, 1981), pp. 43-44.
97. Quoted in Cocking, p. 139.

98. Quoted in Frederick Fletcher, "The Contest for Media Attention: The 1979 and 1980 Federal Election Campaigns," in *Politics and the Media* (Toronto: Reader's Digest Foundation of Canada and Erindale College, 1981), p. 134.

99. Interview with Jock Osler.

100. Interview with Doug Fisher.

101. Stephen Clarkson, "The Dauphin and the Doomed: John Turner and the Liberal Party's Debacle," in *Canada at the Polls, 1984*, Howard R. Penniman, ed. (Durham, North Carolina: Duke University Press, 1988), p. 113.

102. Frederick Fletcher, "The Media and the 1984 Landslide," in *Canada at the Polls, 1984*, p. 169.

103. Interview with James Coutts.

104. Comber and Mayne, pp. 131-32.

105. "Campaign '88," *On Balance* (January 1989), pp. 2-3.

106. Patrick Martin, Allan Gregg, and George Perlin, *Contenders: The Tory Quest for Power* (Scarborough, Ontario: Prentice-Hall, 1983), p. 96.

107. Claire Hoy, *Friends in High Places* (Toronto: Key Porter Books, 1987), p. 312.

108. Gratton, p. x.

109. Ibid., p. xi.

110. Craig McInnes, "Scrums a Tradition But Point is Obscure," *The Globe and Mail*, 2 December 1989, p. A3.

111. Interview with Marc Lortie, Ottawa, 26 January 1988.

112. Ibid.

113. Meyrowitz, see Ch. 14.

6

The Television Election

For politicians, elections are the ultimate tests of power and survival. Party leaders are personally on trial, living by their wits and instincts, nerves and endurance, and ultimately by their capacity to touch voters in some way. The conventional wisdom among political consultants has always been that the campaign reflects the candidate. Indeed, Larry Sabato believes that at least in the United States, where parties are weaker and candidates have a greater capacity to be entrepreneurial, "In the end, in most cases, the candidate himself or herself wins or loses the race; his or her abilities, qualifications, communications skills, and weaknesses have far more impact on the shape of the vote than all of the consultants and technologies combined."[1] The organizational weight and effectiveness of the political parties can also be decisive. Parties run polling, advertising and direct mail campaigns, orchestrate national leaders' tours, mobilize funds and volunteers, and direct images and messages with military precision. Planning begins more than a year before an election is expected. Party election structures, largely dormant in the periods between elections, are fueled and cranked up and parties begin to call in their "markers" to get the candidates, personnel and, most importantly, the money that makes fighting an election campaign possible.

Virtually every aspect of the election campaign will involve the media; in fact, to a large degree the media are the stage on which the election is fought. Whether through the filter of television and newspaper reporting or by buying time and space on television and in newspapers, parties must use the media to reach voters. The media, however, are not just the stage for the election drama. Media organizations are themselves participants, actors in the drama. Elections are an opportunity for news organizations to display their journalistic fire-power: star reporters are showcased, poll results are commissioned, and "in-depth" coverage provided. News organizations sell themselves to audiences and advertisers at least as much as they cover the election. Their own image and prestige are on the line. Inevitably, individual journalists want to grab the spotlight by breaking a big story, pinning politicians down with aggressive questions, and promoting their own views and reactions. The media has its own agenda; reporting is invariably sensational, dramatic, and confrontational, and contains as many jolts as possible. For the media, the focus is on the horse-race among the leaders. Leadership is the lens through which the election is reported.

The election is largely decided by whose agenda becomes the dominant one. Each party wants to move the election battle to its territory by fighting the election on its themes. The party that sets the context and frames the issues is the most likely to win. To do this a party not only has to wage an information campaign against the other parties, it also has to get the media to adopt its logic, its vocabulary, its version of issues and events. Party election planners have devised a series of strategies for both maneuvering the media into reporting the story that they want and bypassing the media to get their messages "out clean" to the public. The success of these strategies can largely determine the results of the election.

THE CONDITIONING CAMPAIGN

It is a mistake of the highest order to analyse elections only during the official writ period. The real election campaign begins weeks or even months before the formal election period when elaborate and sophisticated conditioning campaigns are launched. For instance, during the summer of 1988 in the run-up to the federal election campaign held in the fall, Brian Mulroney's Conservative government undertook an extensive "image-building" campaign. In order to "kickstart the numbers," i.e., the level of Conservative support as measured in public opinion polls, the prime minister travelled extensively across the country presenting himself as energetic and hard-working, someone with a strong vision of the future. A trip to Washington, the pageantry of the Toronto Summit, and visits by Ronald Reagan and Margaret Thatcher helped create a sense of "visible action."[2] During this period, over seventy new projects and initiatives were announced by the government, including funding for several large energy projects and the strengthening of farm programs, and new money for the film industry, AIDS research, and regional development. An Angus Reid poll conducted in July 1988 for the federal government, but apparently used for partisan purposes, revealed widespread public concern over the environment and issues such as housing.[3] In late summer Mulroney became a champion of the environment, announcing clean-ups of Halifax harbour and the St. Lawrence River, and suddenly created a new position, the minister of housing. Each promise was unveiled amid great fanfare and widely reported in the media. The Conservatives went from third place in the polls in March to first place by September[4]; they had laid the groundwork for their re-election.

The other parties also engaged in conditioning campaigns, although being out of government and without the ability to "buy off" interest groups and regions of the country, their campaigns were much more limited. Nonetheless, party leaders met with journalists and editorial boards and spoke to business and community groups, trying to sell themselves and plant seeds—relationships, commitments, and ideas— that they would soon try to harvest. John Carey calls this process the "metacampaign": "The metacampaign is waged not so much to win public support as to convince the big contributors, party workers, reporters, and the other attentive political elites of the actual campaign's credibility. If the metacampaign succeeds, money and volunteers will flow in; the press and the opinion makers will promote the desired positive image."[5] According to R. Jeremy Wilson, it is "a campaign about the campaign."[6] Some parties have, in the past, been so amateurish in their devising of strategy that they haven't realized that an extensive "seasoning" period is now a part of most successful election campaigns. The formal election campaign that takes place during the writ period is really only the final phase in a longer and more protracted effort. The party that wins the conditioning campaign is also likely to win the election.

The informal rules that normally govern the media's coverage of elections, particularly those that provide for equal coverage, do not apply in the conditioning period. For months preceding an election, the media spends much time and space speculating about when the election will be called and gearing up for the campaign. Many media organizations do not seem to realize that the election that they are waiting for has, in a sense, already begun. In 1988, the Conservatives received extensive coverage as they bombarded the public with promise after promise; policies announced by a government inevitably make headlines. Ironically, many of the promises announced in the pre-conditioning phase were abandoned by the Conservatives after they were re-elected in November. The Conservatives had reaped a windfall of favourable publicity from a media that was waiting for the election to begin.

THE LEADERS' TOUR: HOW THE PARTIES MANIPULATE THE MEDIA

The national leaders' tour is the basic building block of Canadian elections. The tour is thought to accomplish at least two things essential for a democracy: it gives voters the opportunity to see the party leaders first hand and therefore be in a better position to make up their minds about whom to vote for; and second, it is believed that the leaders themselves benefit from the hurley burley of the hustings. The tour is supposed to be a broadening experience that allows leaders to learn about the country, to see things from a fresh perspective, to grow and be tested through contact with the people. Both of these original purposes have been undermined by the highly orchestrated television packaging of the modern leaders' tour.

In John A. Macdonald's day, the intention was to personally speak to and greet as many voters as possible. During the Confederation era, leaders were often forced to hold "joint" or "contradictory" meetings; there were few public buildings so that leaders frequently held debates on or spoke from the same stage.[7] One of the great innovations was the campaign picnic; there were speeches, brass bands, ham and cold chicken, and people milling about waiting to talk to the leaders. Travel was by coach and train and, at least during one election, the winter election of 1887, by sleigh. Macdonald was often so "worn out that he could do nothing but tumble into bed" after so much travel.[8] On some days "he would injure himself beyond recovery by these tremendous exertions."[9] One of Macdonald's favourite tactics on the campaign trail was to make fun of the reports that appeared in the opposition press. During the 1887 campaign, for instance, he reminded voters that *The Globe* had reported his suicide in 1873 and that ". . . on various occasions since, had announced his approaching demise through cancer of the stomach or paralysis of the brain."[10] He told his audience that "he was enjoying a few lucid moments" before the next "attack of frenzy."[11]

Wilfrid Laurier's contribution was the "whistle stop" campaign. In 1895 and 1896 Laurier, travelling by train, raced to between 200 and 300 rallies and met, by one estimate, nearly 200,000 voters.[12] The whistle stop featured an informal reception at the platform of the train station where Laurier would make some pleasant remarks before making his way through the waiting crowd, grasping and shaking hands. "To those he could not reach, he gave a kindly nod of the head or smiled his best political smile," according to Michael Nolan.[13] A small group of journalists would accompany the whistle stop tour, recording what took place in the breathless, emotional style of the partisan press.

The train remained the principal means for campaigning well into the 1950s. But with the growth of large circulation general service newspapers, the advent of radio, and the fading of the partisan press, the events of the tour became less important than how those events were reported. The press had to be courted, and the daily struggle to position the campaign so that it received the best possible coverage was begun. During the 1957 campaign, for example, Tory leader John Diefenbaker crossed the country twice by train, following Prime Minister St. Laurent across the country, refuting his claims, and getting in the last word. During the 1965 election Diefenbaker whistle-stopped through 196 cities, towns, and villages.[14] The press travelled in its own railway car, and party officials took care of hotel accommodations when the tour stopped over in a major city and made sure that reporters were amply supplied with food and "liquid refreshment."[15] On at least one leaders' tour prostitutes were sent to reporters' rooms.[16] Party leaders and journalists travelled together in a largely self-contained world. The party's message was not difficult to discern as politicians and journalists often shared each other's company at the end of the day, if not each other's purposes.

The arrival of television changed the nature of the leaders' tour dramatically. By the late 1960s, the tour had become a television production with everything geared to reaching the audience at home with a potent visual message. The tour itself is a prop used by leaders to package themselves for television. According to Craig Oliver, who covered the Mulroney campaign in 1988 for CTV, "The idea is to control the agenda by controlling the pictures. Everyday they'd give us a pretty picture of some kind. Some of the rallies were theatricals; thousands of balloons, laser lights, pounding theme music. It's a created event in which the audience is a prop, they're just sets and actors. Cecil B. DeMille should have been there."[17] Oliver also observed that "If newspaper people didn't get on the campaign plane they [the party] couldn't care less."[18] Terrence O'Malley of the advertising firm Vickers and Bensen, who has worked on several ad campaigns for the Liberal party, argues that "Advertising and the campaign tour have moved closer together. In a sense they both produce a controlled and crafted message. The campaign tour is a daily 30 second commercial. The campaign itself has become advertising."[19]

The basic formula consists of presenting what Anthony Westell and Alan Frizzell have called "pre-packaged news."[20] The objective is to ensure that at least one newsworthy item of the party's choosing is made available to the media each day under conditions that make it difficult for the media to resist reporting what has been presented to them. The basic technique is a form of political jujitsu first devised by the Republicans in the United States during Richard Nixon's campaigns for the presidency and later perfected in the Reagan and Bush campaigns. As in jujitsu, where you use the size and strength of your opponent to your advantage, parties use television's own requirements and characteristics as their main weapons in getting their message on the news. Television journalists are trapped into reporting the party's pre-packaged news because their own medium demands dramatic visuals, leaders in conflict, and highly charged sound bites or clips.

In packaging themselves as news or, as O'Malley has pointed out, as a kind of TV commercial, the parties prepare a tightly scripted message each day that can be reduced to a single phrase or comment. If their remarks are going to be reduced to a nine- or eleven-second clip for radio and television, then there is little purpose in leaders discussing the rationales, assumptions, or philosophy that underlie their policies or promises. The short barb, the snappy line, the smart remark are what counts. Perhaps most important is that the message be presented against a compelling visual background. During the 1988 election, John Turner spoke about environmental policy against the backdrop of a forest of maple trees ravaged by acid rain. When talking about the advantages of free trade, Brian Mulroney would appear at plants where workers were producing goods destined for American markets. George Bush talking tough about crime while surrounded by uniformed police officers and Michael Dukakis riding a tank before discussing defence issues are two of the most vivid images of the 1988 American presidential election. The idea is that TV reporters needing good visuals will find the pictures irresistible and report the message that the party wants presented. As CTV reporter Alan Fryer has put it, "If you control the pictures you control the message getting out."[21]

Another part of the strategy is to avoid being caught in situations that detract from the message being delivered or, as Craig Oliver has put it, "knocks you off the high ground"[22] by allowing the media to set the agenda. Access by reporters to the leaders is restricted to brief encounters, and leaders appear in controlled settings in front of friendly audiences. The key element is the choreographing of relations with the press. As Elly Alboim, the Ottawa bureau chief for CBC Television News, has expressed it, "The struggle over the access that reporters have with the leaders is really a struggle for the agenda. The media want access so that they can have the opportunity to force their own agenda."[23]

During the first weeks of the 1988 federal election, Mulroney's "peekaboo" relationship with the press became a source of considerable irritation to journalists. To protect Mulroney's staged performance—what Graham Fraser described as "the Papal Tour"—reporters had been kept behind ropes at party rallies and the prime minister was largely unavailable for questions from journalists.[24] The Liberals' strategy was to contrast the closed cocoon that enveloped the prime minister with the openness of their campaign. But Turner's openness was contrived as well, an optical illusion. The Liberals had campaign staff whose job it was to find out what questions were on reporters' minds. Based on this information and their own campaign goals, Turner's advisors would suggest a "line of the day." At the daily scrums, which were the symbol of Turner's openness, the Liberal leader answered only five or six questions from reporters who were not allowed to ask follow-up questions. One reporter, Alan Fryer of CTV, complained that Turner simply "didn't answer questions he didn't like."[25] Turner did, to his credit, appear on radio hot line shows and in front of high school and university audiences.

The NDP's campaign was as controlled and rehearsed as the others. AnnaMaria Tremonti, who covered Broadbent's campaign for CBC television, was critical of the New Democrats for having "talked about Broadbent as being the man who could relate to ordinary Canadians. But they didn't let him do it. I felt for people who had waited to meet Broadbent and left disappointed because he didn't bother to mingle or shake hands."[26] The name of the game is to avoid confrontations or gaffes, embarrassing situations, or unwanted questions. Even innocent situations can blow up in a politician's face. Jeffrey Simpson recalls that the "cruellest piece of television footage in the 1979 campaign" was of Tory leader Joe Clark approaching a bikini-clad woman on a beach. "The camera soaked up Clark's running style and the woman's embarrassed reaction as the stranger in the carefully pressed suit . . . stuck out his hand while the woman's hand recoiled to cover the upper half of her body."[27] The picture of Conservative leader Robert Stanfield dropping a football, which appeared in *The Globe and Mail* during the 1974 election, made Stanfield an object of ridicule and derision. The Liberals were to complain bitterly about the coverage that Turner received during the first weeks of the 1988 election campaign. Turner's chief of staff, Peter Connolly, contends that "For two weeks Turner performed very, very well— and got awful, awful, awful, awful coverage." On one occasion he had overheard TV journalists telling their camera people "He's limping! He's limping! Shoot that!"[28]

The tours make sure that reporters are elaborately courted and taken care of. The parties try to create a sense of shared experience, fun, and good feeling on the planes and buses. The reporters are well looked after in terms of food and drink and the campaigns even try to "orchestrate" parties. The Liberals, for instance, put on a "beach night" with everyone wearing beach shirts and sun glasses. During the 1988 election "spin doctors" were always there to feed information and try to put the right spin, i.e., the party's perspective, on the stories that reporters were working on. Reporters would be told what was important, why charges and claims by the other parties were untrue, and how well the leader was doing. Reporters were charmed, worked on, frozen out, praised, and manipulated continually. The CBC's AnnaMaria Tremonti remembers how the spin doctors would give her inflated figures about how many people were in an audience or attending a rally.[29] According to Tremonti, the sense of being watched and under constant surveillance was pervasive: "There were people watching you. They wanted to know your reaction to how their leader was doing. You were under constant scrutiny."[30] Craig Oliver observed that on the Conservative plane, party press people "were constantly offering suggestions, assessing the mood all the time, gauging your views, letting you know that they were watching you. If the Prime Minister liked what you did they'd tell you. What was new was the scope of it."[31]

Media managers in Toronto were also the targets of spin tactics. The Conservatives, in particular, phoned frequently with comments and criticisms about news coverage. The Liberals and the NDP were not as aggressive. In the case of the Liberals, this was largely because top

Liberals broke off contact with the media after the CBC and other news organizations ran stories about an insurrection against John Turner's leadership, which was allegedly discussed among top Liberal strategists in the first weeks of the election. The purpose of the phone calls was to put media organizations on the defensive, to make them "double think and justify" their reporting.[32] Rumours about the opposition would be floated, there would be tips about future developments, and claims always that the other parties were getting off too easily and that the leader concerned was not being treated fairly. Sometimes rough pressure tactics were used. The Conservatives, for example, tried to get the CBC to take reporter Wendy Mesley off the prime minister's plane because they felt that she had been too critical in her reporting. According to Arnold Amber, executive producer of News Specials for CBC Television, "there were entire days that they wouldn't talk to her"[33] after a story she did about Mulroney's inaccessibility to reporters at the beginning of the campaign. At the same time as the Conservatives complained about Mesley's reporting, they also played up how well AnnaMaria Tremonti had done when she had reported on Mulroney.[34]

The Conservatives also had an extensive media monitoring operation in place. The contents of the major television newscasts and twenty-four newspapers were analysed and two reports prepared each day of the campaign. The purpose was not only to see what trends were emerging but also to try either to smother or redirect unfavourable reporting. As one of the party's media analysts described the process, "Stories move from east to west because of the time zones. If you have good information early in the morning on a story that's developing, you can catch an issue and deal with it before it rolls across the country. It comes down to how do you launch a strategic response."[35] New technologies such as fax machines and cellular phones helped the Conservatives to react virtually instantly to media stories that were developing. By issuing a press release, putting information on the wire, or intervening with reporters or media managers directly, the party could launch a pre-emptive strike to knock out potentially damaging coverage.

THE LEADERS' TOUR: HOW JOURNALISTS SEE THEIR ROLE

Media organizations cover elections through their own "frames" and bring independent agendas to their reporting. As mentioned earlier, their reputations and prestige are at stake to some degree, and there is much to gain in terms of self-promotion by trumpeting their influence and the talent of their journalists. Much of the conventional wisdom about how elections should be covered by the media stems from two different sets of problems that occurred in the 1974 and 1980 federal elections.

During Pierre Trudeau's re-election campaign in 1974, the Liberals slickly outmanoeuvred journalists by issuing a series of complex policy proposals just as reporters' deadlines approached. Some of the policy statements were fifty pages long.[36] Without the time or resources necessary to check facts, determine the implications of the proposed policies, or have access to critical comments from opposition politicians or experts, journalists were "sandbagged" into giving verbatim accounts of the Liberals' policy announcements. By the time news organizations put together a well-rounded analysis of a particular policy, which often took three to four days, the Liberals would move on to announce another major policy. There was a barrage of ten announcements in a three-week period. As part of this strategy, the prime minister only appeared in controlled settings where he could avoid reporters' questions. As Frederick Fletcher described the situation, ". . . reporters would cover Trudeau's activities without being able to either interrogate him or to spend much time analyzing what he was doing."[37] The result was that Trudeau dominated the headlines and airwaves but received little critical coverage. Stanfield's campaign seemed lost amid the publicity given to the Liberal policy announcements, and his plan for wage and price controls was subject to an avalanche of criticism. Jim Coutts, who helped devise the strategy, has blamed the media for having brought the situation on themselves. According to Coutts, "At one time parties revealed their platforms at the beginning of campaigns. The media found this boring and the platforms went unreported and were quickly buried. We decided then to reveal the platform over time. Had it been one page in a twenty-page platform, it wouldn't have been covered."[38]

After the 1974 experience, a consensus seems to have emerged among the major news organizations that they had to be better prepared and more rigorous in their coverage. They were determined not to be outmanoeuvred again. By the 1979 election the major news organizations had repositioned themselves. Seasoned reporters were assigned to the leaders' tours, reporters were encouraged to comment on the tactics that were being used by the parties, issues teams were established, and research back-up was provided. They could now react quickly to any new developments. Moreover, journalists felt that they had an obligation to introduce issues that were not being dealt with by the parties, and to press what they felt were the public's real interests. Part of their role was to force a discussion about issues, an agenda of national concerns, on the politicians. Vince Carlin, the CBC's head of television news from 1980 to 1985 and now CBC Radio's chief correspondent, describes this new imperative: "We had our own agenda of issues that we felt were important. Our job was to provide context and analysis. . . . You have to point out that a statement may have contradicted a statement made two weeks before. It would be misleading if we didn't do that."[39] This new style of election coverage also coincided with the rise in the use of public opinion polls by the media. Polls allowed the media to gauge and publicize voters' concerns and helped them legitimize their role as delegates of the public, with the right to press politicians to respond to issues that the voters saw as important.

A second issue emerged with regard to television coverage during the 1974 election. The question was whether the leaders' tour would be treated as regular news and have to compete for a place in the newscast against other items, including terrorist bombings, plane crashes, or sensational murders, or whether party leaders would be guaranteed special coverage. Controversy erupted when Conservative leader Robert Stanfield did not appear on television for several days at the height of the election. The NDP's final campaign rally, an event that NDP leader David Lewis considered to be one of the emotional highlights of his career, was also not covered.[40] During the 1980 election, the NDP's campaign director Robin Sears complained vigorously to the CBC when that network repeatedly showed film of NDP leader Ed Broadbent but did not carry his actual words. Sears threatened to publicly denounce the CBC if it did not report the election campaign fully.[41] Since 1979, the CBC's policy has been that elections receive "special prominence," although in-fighting over how the policy was to be implemented occurred during the 1980 election. The network's long-standing policy has been "to ensure that party leaders would be given, on a general basis, an equal amount of airtime."[42] Allen Garr, who reported for the CBC on the media's reporting of the 1988 election, has described the "rules" that are now in place: "The media interprets its mandate differently during a campaign. The politicians know that baby whales are not going to push them off the air and that the media find it incumbent to cover items that wouldn't ordinarily be covered. So the parties know that during the campaign there are going to be three hits per newscast and that they and the other parties will receive daily coverage."[43] The "bean counting" that now goes into ensuring an equal quantity of coverage for each of the parties does not, however, guarantee that the tone, the footage chosen, the selection of sound bites, or the willingness of reporters to take on the leader by making critical comments in their pieces are distributed equally or fairly.

An interesting development during the 1988 federal election was that the cost of having journalists cover the leaders had risen to such an extent over previous elections that only wealthier news organizations could have journalists on all three leaders' tours for the entire campaign. The cost of a seat on a campaign plane was $12,000-13,000, not including meals, accommodation, and other travel expenses. As television crews normally consist of a reporter, producer, sound editor, and camera person, the cost to follow only one of the leaders was well over $100,000. Under these conditions some news organizations decided not to cover the campaign fully. Radio-Canada did not send reporters on the tours for the first two weeks of the election; *Le Devoir* and *La Presse* only covered the leaders for three and four weeks, respectively; and the fifteen newspapers in the Southam chain pooled their resources to place nine reporters with the leaders at the beginning of the election.[44] The French language television network, TVA, assigned reporting teams to the Conservative and Liberal campaigns only for the last four weeks and to the New Democrats only for the last three weeks of the campaign. Global Television covered the leaders' tour for five of the election's seven weeks.[45] By contrast, *The Globe and Mail* had seven reporters with the leaders and the CBC a full complement of journalists from both radio and television through the entire election.

One effect of these cut-backs by news organizations was that the power of larger and wealthier organizations, the big media—the CBC, CTV, *The Globe and Mail, The Toronto Star*, etc.—to set the agenda was considerably magnified. The big media players loom even larger and are even more influential than they are in other news situations. Small and medium size news organizations are reduced to getting their information secondhand, either through the Canadian Press wire service or through the filter of the larger and wealthier news organizations.

Journalists who cover the tour are subject to a number of often contradictory pressures in producing their stories. They are caught in the cross-currents between the priorities of their own news organizations, the sway of pack reporting, and the manipulated environment created by the political parties. Each of these tugs them in a different direction.

The first of these pressures are the expectations and norms imposed on them by their own news organizations. During the 1988 election, most news organizations sent young and relatively inexperienced reporters on the leaders' tour. Part of the reason for going with younger reporters, in contrast to the more seasoned group of journalists who had covered previous elections, was the shattering pace and exhaustion of the tour. Numbing weariness and the disruption to family life have discouraged older reporters from wanting the assignment. Another important factor was that changes in technology—satellites, fax machines, microcomputers, cellular phones—allowed media managers to maintain control from a distance. Reporters were continually messaged, and stories and scripts could be checked in advance and videotape seen long before any narrative was written. As Allen Garr observed, "the strategy this time was to put young people on the planes knowing that their work could be controlled by all of the grey heads back at the office controlling the phones."[46] While journalists often had considerable discretion over their own stories, they were also part of an organizational web that required them to continually negotiate with superiors. Each organizational culture had different expectations. At CBC Television, an election team headquartered in Toronto co-ordinated the news traffic between planes and attempted to develop a story-line each evening. As Elly Alboim has described the process, "You could hijack a leader's campaign on any given day by forcing them to respond to a contradiction that had emerged or to statements by other leaders."[47] Cocooned on the planes, reporters often had little sense of the wider chess game that was being played. For example, Keith Boag, the CBC reporter on the Liberal plane, was not told about a major story being prepared in Toronto about rumblings within the Liberal campaign against John Turner's leadership. As one member of the election team explained the decision not to tell Boag, "We didn't want it leaking out anywhere. He was surprised when the story hit."[48]

A second influence is pack journalism. The theory is that reporters sealed off together for an extended period of time, covering the same events, talking to the same sources, will share views, information, and impressions, develop the same hypotheses, and ultimately produce the same stories. The pack is held together by fear, fear that a competitor will break a story or develop a new angle, somehow get the edge. Finding out what your rivals are thinking, trading information and perspectives, and matching their work becomes the safest course, the better part of valour. Within the pack, opinion is often set by veteran reporters. As Craig Oliver has described it, "You're all in the sphere together—a world of its own. You're covering the same event, seeing the same thing, so a pack mentality is almost inevitable to some degree. The homogenized view is the product of covering the same events in the same insulated environment. I could see other reporters agonizing over what their lead should be. As the veteran, I would have younger reporters asking me for my views."[49] Jeff Simpson has recalled the effect that star columnist Allan Fotheringham's presence had on other reporters during the 1979 election: "Fotheringham would enter the room and every reporter would go over and form a scrum around him. . . . Foth was leading the pack."[50]

One example of the pack forming during the 1988 election was when reporters, as a group, decided to zero in on the cost of Liberal campaign promises. According to Alan Fryer, "At a few points we said, let's organize this. We sort of agreed. I'd pop a question. Someone else would follow up. It was an agreement to keep going at him. This was the pack at work and in this circumstance it was positive."[51]

Some reporters make a conscious effort to break from the pack and not go with the consensus view about how to interpret a particular event. As more reporters are the products of journalism school training, there is greater awareness of the dangers of falling into a "group think" situation. The pull of central organizations, strengthened by the instant nature of new communications technologies, has also helped to weaken the grip of the pack mentality.

The third influence is that of the political parties who control the environment within which journalists must operate. As discussed earlier, journalists are constantly being monitored, manipulated, and "set up" by the parties. Many reporters are aware of and refuse to fall into the traps that are laid out for them. The pretty visual backdrops, the quote of the day, the pre-packaged news event presented on a silver platter, however, cannot always be ignored. Journalists are often put in a "take it or leave it situation": either they go with the scripted event or they face having nothing else to report. Still, attempts at overt manipulation often work against the parties. On one occasion during the 1988 election, the Liberals took reporters to a water-treatment plant in Quebec City. Instead of being pictured against the backdrop that the Liberals had planned, John Turner was shown trudging through mud, a metaphor, perhaps, for the political quagmire that he found himself in.[52] Similarly, Turner's announcement of the Liberals' child care policy, announced with some bravado, quickly turned into a fiasco as reporters pounced on faulty arithmetic. The child care disaster reverberated for days. Brian Mulroney's attempts to run a formula campaign in 1988 became an issue in itself, as reporters refused to be cordoned off behind ropes and prevented from having access. The Conservatives were also upset that so much attention was given on television to hecklers (some of whom were obvious plants) and to demonstrators, often at the expense of the prime minister's message. They complained that Mulroney was receiving less "clip time" than the other leaders and that he was often cut off in mid-sentence. Time and time again choreographed scripts and staged events simply fell flat.

Politicians tend to feel that the media's reporting of elections is almost always negative and sensational. Roger Ailes, George Bush's media advisor, accused the American television networks of covering only "visuals, attacks and mistakes," while Robin Sears of the NDP has described Canadian television reporting as little more than "punches, polls and pictures."[53] As discussed in Chapter Two, many journalists believe that their reporting has to be critical. CTV's Alan Fryer is concerned about the tone of some of the reporting: "There are different types of reporters. You see the reporters who report it straight. Then there are those who are analytical and critical. And there are other reporters who just want to dump on the candidate. They see themselves as adversaries."[54] Comber and Mayne interviewed a number of journalists who covered the 1984 federal election and found that many of them "were comfortable with the adversarial role." One told them that his task was to find "the chinks in the armor" of the leaders.[55]

A study of samples of radio, television, and newspaper coverage during the 1984 election by Wagenberg, Soderlund, Romanow, and Briggs revealed a remarkable amount of criticism levelled by the media at John Turner. In evaluating Turner, negative coverage outpaced positive coverage 85 percent to 15 percent. Brian Mulroney also received more negative than positive reporting, although Ed Broadbent received mostly favourable treatment. Commenting on the media's relentless criticism of Turner, they observed that "Members of the media judged Turner's performance to be poor, and like the 'wimp' tag attached to Joe Clark and the football 'fumbler' image of Robert Stanfield, such pictures tend to persist in the absence of overwhelming evidence to the contrary. . . . Thus, the most positive comment about Turner as the campaign wore on was 'he's doing better,' a phrase which conveyed all the implications of damning with faint praise."[56]

Alan Frizzell and Anthony Westell of Carleton University found in studies of reporting in selected newspapers during the 1984 and 1988 elections that while party leaders were most often described in neutral tones, unfavourable depictions were far more numerous than favourable ones. Data taken from seven newspapers showed that during the 1988 election only 3.2 percent of reporting about Brian Mulroney was favourable, as against 32.9 percent that was unfavourable. John Turner received the highest percentage of favourable comments at 9.5 percent, but this was overshadowed by the 23.5 percent of coverage that was unfavourable.[57] A study done of media coverage of the 1988 election by the National Media Archive of the Fraser Institute discovered that CBC's *The National* and *The Journal*, the *CTV National News*, *The Globe and Mail*, and CBC Radio's *The World at Six* gave both Mulroney and Turner more negative than positive coverage. Ed Broadbent received more favourable than unfavourable comment on CBC and CTV television, but this was reversed in *The Globe and Mail* and on *The World at Six*.[58] Of course, it can be argued that the critical coverage received by the party leaders reflected their poor performances. Campaigns that were contrived, lack-lustre, and unimaginative deserved to be treated as such.

One consequence of this critical tone in reporting is that the parties and the media seem to be locked in a vicious circle of accusations and distrust. One commentator has likened it to a "Lebanese retribution situation."[59] The parties contend that when they discuss issues seriously and in-depth, their arguments often go unreported or are ripped out of context. Gaffes, personal attacks, hecklers and demonstrations, internal party battles and dropped footballs make news. Hence they have no choice but to wage the kind of campaign that fits the media's insatiable hunger for jolts and entertainment. Journalists argue that if all the parties are going to present are contrived events with pretty pictures and canned one liners, if content is foresaken, then they will find other things to cover. As tensions on both sides have increased, the democratic process has suffered. As Robin Sears has put it, "The public is left with watching baby kissing and cheap shots from reporters."[60]

Perhaps the greatest problem with the leaders' tour as an institution is that it has made leadership into an all-consuming issue and, to some degree, "presidentializes" the Canadian political system. In the eye of the television lens, the party literally becomes the leader. Television's need to focus on individuals and to personify complex issues, and the need of the parties in the face of this to provide a single spokesperson and a neat, tightly-wrapped message, have elevated party leaders to be the supreme contestants of elections. The leaders' tour is the source for almost all news, and the leaders' debates a gladiatorial contest on which the hopes of the parties sometimes rest. In his study of the 1984 election, Frederick Fletcher found that the issue of leadership was discussed in 26 percent of television and front-page newspaper stories, and in 31 percent of newspaper columns and editorials. Statements by leaders accounted for half of front-page newspaper stories during the 1980 and 1984 elections.[61] According to Frizzell and Westell, during the 1988 election approximately 62 percent of CBC television coverage, 58 percent of CTV's coverage, and 72 percent of Global Television's coverage focused on the leaders in some way.[62] Even when there are highly-charged issues that capture the public's imagination, as free trade did during the 1988 election, the issues are largely presented as articulated by the leaders. The leaders become the symbols of the policies being proposed.

Some have argued that this fixation on leaders has led to dangerous distortions in the Canadian political system. As media attention is riveted on party leaders, local candidates and even prominent members of the party who are likely to become powerful cabinet ministers are ignored. They are, except in unusual circumstances, invisible in the national media. Studies done by Frederick Fletcher of the 1980 and 1984 elections found that local candidates accounted for only 5.4 and 4.3 percent of front-page newspaper coverage in those elections.[63] Where local candidates were once assured of local television coverage, this is no longer the case. Local television stations now devote a great deal of attention to the national campaign, for satellite feeds have made the local supper hour newscasts prime time for reporting the leaders' tour. Geoffrey Stevens has described the frustration felt by local candidates:

> The role of the local candidate in an election now is if he's lucky he gets to introduce his leader, if his leader happens to come to his town. But if he does get to introduce his leader, he can be darn sure that he's not going to get on television; television isn't going to cover the introduction of the leader. Most of the time his job is simply to keep out of the way of the television cameras so he doesn't block the view of the leader and the band and the balloons.[64]

To compound the situation, current election spending restrictions mean that most local candidates are unable, on their own, to buy television advertising. The link between MPs and their ridings, which is the linchpin of the election system, is to some degree no longer intact. Moreover, local organizations have become weak and hollow as television has supplanted their primary role of reaching voters with the party's message.

One is tempted to say that the old wisdom that all politics is local has been turned on its head and that now, because of television, all politics is national. Even powerful cabinet ministers, once able to assure their election because of the control over local party machines, must depend for their survival on their leader's coat-tails. During elections political power is where the cameras are, and the cameras are almost exclusively on the party leaders; and television's focus on the leaders is never sharper than during the leaders' debates.

TELEVISED DEBATES: POLITICAL RITUAL AND MEDIA SPECTACLE

Televised debates among the party leaders have become one of the basic rituals of democracy. It is a supreme test of nerves, of skill and instincts, a trial by fire through which the leaders must pass if they are to be credible to the media and to the public. The ordeal is fraught with dangers. For most of the campaign the leaders appear in controlled settings where their performances are heavily managed and choreographed. Debates, however, force the leaders to step out of their protected cocoons and expose them to the glaring spotlight of prolonged public scrutiny, probing questions from journalists, and venomous attacks from opponents. Their composure, facial expressions, and the way they glance at the camera; their mastery of issues and party positions; and their ability to touch the audience emotionally and make themselves liked are all part of the performance. The public is given the opportunity to compare leaders directly, and to see them explain their policies and proposals in their own words rather than through reporters' words or in ten- or twelve-second radio and television clips. For the media, with their craving for drama, personalities, confrontation, and winners and losers, the debates are the pre-eminent campaign story. With virtually half of eligible voters watching at least part of the debates they have become the central fixture of the campaign, and how media commentators explain and interpret them can be critical in deciding the outcome of the election.

There is considerable disagreement among scholars about what effects the debates have. In a study of the 1979 leaders' debate, Lawrence Leduc and Richard Price found that the debate had little impact because "a high proportion of debate watchers had already decided on their vote at the time of the debates."[65] They argue that views about and images of the candidates had been largely determined before the debate; the debate served to reinforce rather than alter these preferences. Yet scholars also contend that there are circumstances when performances in a debate can be decisive: when one or more of the party leaders is not well-known and is in a sense being introduced to large numbers of voters for the first time; or when one of the party leaders acts out of character, breaks the mould of their existing image either by an unexpectedly brilliant performance or by committing unexpected errors or appearing weak. As Marjorie Hershey has written, "debates matter when they teach some voters something new about a candidate."[66] Practitioners have tended to see debates as potentially decisive turning-points. For instance, Hugh Segal, a member of the Conservative debate preparation team in the 1988 election, has argued that debates were so important in both the 1984 and 1988 elections that the parties were compelled to virtually redraw their strategies after the debates took place. Segal's view was that "Debates either gell the existing situation or shake it up."[67] In a survey conducted for *Maclean's* following the 1988 election, 45 percent of respondents said that the TV debates had helped them decide how to vote.[68]

John F. Kennedy's performances in debates against Richard Nixon in the first series of televised presidential debates in 1960 are seen as having been a critical factor in Kennedy's victory. The telegenic Kennedy, appearing tanned and relaxed and conveying warmth and confidence (one recent account claims that Kennedy spent time with prostitutes prior to the debates),[69] was preferred by an overwhelming number of viewers to Nixon, who looked shifty and awkward. Remarkably, radio listeners believed that Nixon had won the debates; his answers to questions were thought to be clearer and more decisive.[70] A blunder made by President Gerald Ford during his 1976 debate with challenger Jimmy Carter—he seemed to suggest that Poland was an independent country free of Soviet influence—may have been a factor in Ford's defeat. Ironically, in surveys taken immediately following the debate most respondents thought that Ford had won. It was only after the media began reporting that Ford had made a mistake that opinion about who had won shifted to Carter.[71] During the Carter-Reagan debate in 1980, Carter committed the famous "Amy" gaffe when he said that he consulted with his adolescent daughter about nuclear policy. In addition, his attempts to paint Reagan as a "mad bomber" backfired when Reagan appeared reassuring and congenial, the neighbour across the fence rather than an impassioned cold war ideologue. Contrary to expectations, it was Reagan who came across as "presidential" and Carter who seemed mean-spirited and pedestrian. Reagan's confidence was undoubtedly bolstered by the fact that his advisors had obtained copies of Carter's briefing book before the debate and so he knew what Carter was going to say.[72] Carter's fortunes declined rapidly following the debate.

The style and structure of televised debates in Canada has differed considerably from that of U.S. presidential debates. Where American debates have become little more than "joint appearances" or "parallel

Confrontation is a major feature of Canadian TV debates.

press conferences,"[73] with little opportunity given for direct exchanges or confrontation, in Canadian debates party leaders have been able to tangle aggressively with each other as they stand almost toe to toe. Neither country, however, has established official rules governing debates. During each election, the political parties and the television networks negotiate over whether there will be debates at all, the number that will be held, when they will be held, and the formats that will be followed. Each side brings its own immediate interests to these negotiations. The first televised debate in Canada at the federal level was in 1968 between Pierre Trudeau, Robert Stanfield, David Lewis, and Réal Caouette, the Social Credit leader. More a joint appearance than a real debate, leaders had the option of speaking in either English or French. There were no debates held during the 1972, 1974, and 1980 elections. A single, two-hour English language debate took place in 1979, while in 1984 there were two network debates (one in French and the other in English) and a third debate on women's issues that was carried but not sponsored by the networks. In 1988 there were two debates, one in each language. The format featured two three-hour debates, each divided into nine seventeen-minute segments with two party leaders squaring off against each other in each segment while the third leader remained on the sidelines.

Considerable criticism has been directed at the networks for the way that they handled the debates in 1988. One accusation is that the "nets" were so concerned about losing advertising revenue that they refused to consider holding more than one debate in each language and insisted that no debates take place on the largest revenue-producing nights. Robin Sears, who has negotiated with the networks on behalf of the NDP in a number of elections, claims that the parties "were a product to be packaged as a television program. This had never been the approach in the past. We were cast in the role of talent for their production. . . . The most offensive remarks were that we wouldn't be an entertaining product."[74] Michael Kirby, who was a member of the Liberal debate preparation team, believes that the networks formed "a cartel" to ensure that little advertising revenue would be lost. When, at one stage, the political parties reached agreement to hold two debates in each language, the networks blocked the proposal.[75]

To prepare for the debates, leaders study briefing books that review the issues likely to be raised, hold extensive strategy sessions with their advisors and, in some cases, receive lessons from television consultants or language teachers. Mock debates pitting the leaders against stand-ins have been held, and handlers and speech-writers script opening and closing remarks and hard-hitting one-liners. Leaders may also need to be "cooled out" so that they are not overly tense or exhaust themselves before their performance. Prior to the 1988 debates, John Turner was coached by television consultants Henry Comer and André Morrow. Comer worked for months to change Turner's intense and overheated television style, modifying his voice pitch and the pace of his delivery, and trying to contain his large gestures and big body turns and fit them "into the frame of the TV box."[76] For instance, Comer had noticed "that when one is asked a question that requires thought or reflection, one's eyes move; instinctively, someone who replies to a question without any pause or eye movement appears less thoughtful or reflective."[77] Mulroney did not need the same television coaching as Turner did; his main problem was finding the time to do the necessary brainstorming with his debate advisors and homework on issues amid a crowded and jumbled schedule. The debates became an obsession. According to his former press secretary, Michel Gratton, Mulroney "relived" the 1984 debates "hundreds of times," replaying questions and answers endlessly in his mind.[78] The circumstances in 1988 were much different than they had been in 1984, when Turner was prime minister and Mulroney leader of the opposition. Now the roles were reversed. As Hugh Segal has described the situation facing Mulroney in the second confrontation, "Mulroney went into the debate with numbers showing that he could win up to 210 seats. He had to be prime ministerial, he couldn't risk appearing emotional or shrill."[79] His preparations centred around this cautious strategy.

Leaders who have strong leads in the polls have little to gain and much to lose by debating. Opponents gain increased publicity and enhanced prestige because of the equal status that the debate gives them, but for leaders in the polls there is the possibility of committing gaffes that will cost votes. Knowing how to avoid debates can be one of the keys to electoral survival. Writing partly in jest, Jeff Greenfield has the following advice for politicians wanting to duck debates:

> If, for example, you are genuinely afraid of a debate, if you believe you are running ahead and have nothing to gain from such a clash, if you believe yourself incapable of coherent speech in a tense situation, then the proper move was to take the position of an ardent advocate of debates, but to do it in a way that made the holding of them impossible. If, for example, your rival suggested a series of six debates, you would thunder that this was inadequate, a sham, a circus; only fifteen debates would really give the people of Furburg a real chance to hear the issues. If a debate was proposed on one issue, you would demand to know why the people were not entitled to hear your views on all the critical issues. If a wide-ranging debate was proposed, you would insist that this scattershot approach would deprive the people of an intelligent discussion.[80]

With a large lead in the polls during the 1980 federal election, the Liberals obfuscated in a not dissimilar way. None of the formats proposed could fulfill their requirements for a "real" debate. Throughout the 1970s and 1980s Alberta Conservative Premiers Peter Lougheed and Don Getty, buoyed by large leads in the polls, maintained a no debates policy. The argument was that Conservative leaders were too busy meeting voters to debate their opponents. Ironically, the policy stemmed from Peter Lougheed's easy victory over Social Credit Premier Ernest Manning in a televised debate during the 1967 election; although Manning won the election, Lougheed's performance in the debate added immensely to his prestige and popularity. The lesson learned was that you never debate when you are ahead.

Once a debate has been agreed to, there are a number of tactics commonly used to win. The first is to be able to deliver one-line zingers that defuse your opponent's attack and make it onto the television newscasts. Television reporters and producers play a particularly critical role when only twenty or thirty seconds out of a two- or three-hour debate are replayed as the highlights. The leaders and their handlers know that it's sharp confrontations and biting one-liners that will make the TV news clips, and that those clips will be shown many times during the remainder of the election. As Michael Kirby wrote in a memo to John Turner before the 1988 election debates, "No-one who is an uncommitted voter will watch the whole debate, so the key will be the 30-second clip. . . . This means that we must give the leader a set of one-liners which he can fit into his answers."[81] The accepted wisdom is that being the first to attack is dangerous because one risks appearing mean or aggressive, thus offending viewers. The best zingers are usually counter-attacks, the poised or deft response to an opponent's attack.

Election battlefields are littered with those felled by a single quip or exchange. John F. Kennedy used this devastating reply to rebut claims that Richard Nixon made about his policies: "Mr. Nixon has distorted my position. I always have difficulty recognizing my positions when they're described by Mr. Nixon."[82] Ronald Reagan's carefully prepared zinger "There you go again," used in response to an attack on his record by Jimmy Carter in 1980, became magnified in importance by repetition on television. Reagan's humorous remark to Walter Mondale during their 1984 confrontation, "I am not going to exploit for political purposes my opponent's youth and inexperience," which was designed to deflect Mondale from making Reagan's age an issue; Walter Mondale's "Where's the beef?," used against Gary Hart in a critical debate during the race for the Democratic presidential nomination in 1984; and Lloyd Bentsen's "You're no Jack Kennedy" retort to Dan Quayle, made during the vice-presidential debates in 1988, were the equivalent of knock-out punches because of television's need for the "demon" clip.[83]

During the 1984 leaders' debate in English, the clips chosen were of Mulroney delivering a stinging lecture to Turner about patronage. When Turner said that he had no option but to accept a series of highly questionable patronage appointments made by his predecessor, Pierre Trudeau, Mulroney tore into him: "Well, you had an option, sir. You could have said 'I'm not going to do it. I'm not going to ask Canadians to pay the price.' You had an option to say no and you chose to say yes to the old activities and the old stories of the Liberal party. That, sir, if I may say respectfully, is not good enough for Canadians. . . . That is an avowal of failure. That is a confession of non-leadership and this country needs leadership. You had an option, sir. You could have done better. . . ."[84] In 1988 a heated clash between Turner and Mulroney over free trade, in which Turner charged that Mulroney had "sold us out to the Americans," provided the highlights. According to Elly Alboim, journalists in the CBC news-room recognized immediately "that that was the enduring clip."[85] While the parties try to influence judgements about the debate by sending "spin doctors" to hustle reporters covering the event at the studio, they can rarely reach the editors and producers who often make the key decisions.

A particular problem in Canadian debates is that television's focus on a single, hot button clip can have a devastating impact on party leaders not involved in the exchange. The networks send a message to voters, however inadvertently, that the leader who is not in the clip is not an important factor in the election. While the networks have taken pains after debates to replay clips that involve clashes between each of the leaders, a single clip tends to endure and resonate through the campaign. Terry O'Grady, the NDP's Communications Director, describes the frustration of being a helpless onlooker to clip decisions made by television journalists: "We watched the debate in a room above the studio. As soon as we saw the Turner-Mulroney exchange on free trade we knew instantly that that was the clip and that we were not in it."[86]

A second tactic is called the "shotgun" blast.[87] The objective is to raise doubts in the voter's mind about the policies and character of your opponent by launching a full broadside attack. Although the tactic can be dangerous because it might be seen as overly aggressive, even brutal, the aggressor has the advantage of being able to set the agenda. George Bush's relentless denunciation of Michael Dukakis's liberal views during the 1988 presidential debate—at one point using the word Liberal three times in a single sentence—proved effective in tarnishing Dukakis's image and record with voters. Polls show that after the debates the number of respondents who considered Dukakis to be a Liberal, and hence would vote against him, rose substantially.[88] Dukakis seemed shocked by the nature of the attack. His only defence was to argue that labels were not useful. Similarly, John Turner's prolonged, bludgeoning assault on the NDP's policy towards Canada's membership in NATO, made during a confrontation with Broadbent in the 1988 English debate, was intended to remind voters about the NDP's socialist ideology and plant kernels of doubt in voters' minds about whether the NDP would savage Canada's traditional alliances.

A favourite technique used by Pierre Trudeau was to take his opponent's position on an issue and exaggerate its consequences out of all proportion. He would then ruthlessly demolish his opponent by attacking the exaggeration as absurd. Trudeau's "mopping up" could go on at some length.

A third tactic is commonly known as "bridging." The ploy is to deliver the message you intend regardless of the question that is asked. Leaders "start responding to the question, then branch off to a topic they want to address."[89] The question is used as a bridge to get back to the issues and arguments that the leader wishes to emphasize. Greenfield gives the following example:

Reporter: Mr. Smithers, how would you preserve the housing stock in our central cities?

You: I think we have to face the reason why forty years of federal housing programs haven't worked. And the reason is that the key to decent housing in our cities is an effective fight against crime—because the fear of crime is why middle-class and stable working-class citizens flee our neighborhoods and our cities. So the real question you have to answer about our housing dilemma is what to do about crime. I believe there are five practical, tough, immediate steps we can take. . . ."[90]

Leaders who actually respond to the specifics of the questions being asked risk losing control over the agenda.

Turner's television advisors devised a number of other tactics to unnerve Mulroney during the 1988 debates. Unnoticed by viewers was that Turner stared "malevolently" at Mulroney whenever the prime minister looked at him, and that Turner remained standing "to give himself an air of authority."[91] During the French debate, Turner tried to upset Mulroney's composure by setting a fast tempo; against Broadbent, however, Turner slowed the pace of the debate down and tried to get the NDP leader to do most of the talking in the hope that Broadbent's lack of facility in French would be fully exposed.[92]

The debates in 1984 and 1988 seem to have been decisive turning-points in both elections. Mulroney's stinging rebuke to Turner in 1984 produced sudden and dramatic shifts in voter intentions and perceptions. Poll results showed that the belief that Turner could produce change plummeted from 60 percent to 40 percent in two days.[93] Within three days of the first two debates, the Conservatives overcame the Liberal's lead in the polls. Hard-hitting television ads prepared by the Conservatives to undermine Turner's credibility were shelved before they could be shown because, as Tory advertising director Tom Scott put it, "the debate did the work for us."[94]

In 1988, the debates hit all the campaigns like an earthquake. Turner's impassioned attack against the free trade deal struck a chord of fear in a large number of voters. The percentage of poll respondents who thought that Canada's social programs would be placed in jeopardy by the Free Trade Agreement rose from one-third to one-half.[95] More importantly, Turner had set the agenda; his issue, free trade, was to be the battleline over which the rest of the election would be fought. In the view of Tom Scott, "The gold standard for appearing prime ministerial changed during the debates. Turner was passionate, heroic, emotional, hysterically defending the country."[96] Scott describes the reaction that took place among Conservative strategists: "After the debate we had to regroup, we were berserk, we didn't know what to do next. Everybody felt helpless."[97] The biggest loser in the debates was the NDP. Not only was Broadbent not in "the clip" after the English debate but his faltering French was put painfully on display during the French debate. Looking gray, stilted, and exhausted, Broadbent was off form in both encounters. His performance damaged the party's prospects as the Liberals ate into a part of the anti-free trade vote that might otherwise have gone to the NDP; and in Quebec, where so much of their efforts and resources had been concentrated in the hopes of making an historic breakthrough, party support evaporated quickly. According to AnnaMaria Tremonti, who covered the NDP for CBC television, after the debates the party seemed to reach a "glass ceiling."[98] As Tremonti described the situation, "They didn't know what to do. You could see it on their faces. You could see it in Broadbent. They didn't know how to deal with free trade. They had expected to do better and they knew that the other parties had eclipsed them. They didn't have the intellectual and strategic capacity to deal with it."[99]

One school of thought holds that the public decides on a winner based on the consensus that has formed in the media. Opinion solidifies among editorial writers, columnists, commentators, and reporters and spreads rapidly to the man and woman on the street. In this sense, the media "declares" the winner. A variant of this view is that "the clip" decides the winner. Through sheer repetition the demon clip becomes inscribed indelibly in the public's consciousness. A third perspective is that media opinion follows public opinion. Journalists hold off making "big pronouncements" not only out of a sense of responsibility but also because they know that poll results are likely to prove them wrong. Viewers who see the debates for themselves are unlikely to be swayed by media commentators whose views they don't always respect.

CONCLUSION

The leaders' tours, polling, and targeting and the televised debates are vehicles that allow political parties to set the agenda. In most circumstances, however, party messages must pass through the media's filter to reach the public. The leaders' tour is the aspect of the campaign that seems the most vulnerable, the most dependent on the media's editorial decisions. Finding ways to outmanoeuvre television journalists, in particular, the use of jujitsu tactics, has become a key element in planning the tour.

Televised debates give voters a unique opportunity to see and evaluate the leaders in an unhindered way. Recent debates suggest that voters' perceptions of the campaign can be altered at least for a short while. The media's role in interpreting the leaders' performances and, most importantly, the television clips chosen for highlight packages allow the media to influence dramatically how voters see the debate.

The power of the media to edit or recontextualize a party's election message has forced parties to play the game by the media's rules. One is tempted to argue that the media no longer report the campaign—they have become the campaign. The media mirror their own reflection.

The question is whether the electorate is adequately served by a process that is so blatantly manipulative and quirky. Instead of learning more about the country and its problems, politicians are focusing almost exclusively on the media. News organizations, for their part, see elections as an opportunity to celebrate their own interests and credentials, to make headlines, declare winners and losers, and ridicule, however correctly, the falseness of politicians. What's lost in the jumble and frenzy of the encounters between some politicians and the media is any sense that elections are meaningful, even sacred events, that must not be taken for granted.

NOTES

1. Larry Sabato, "Magic . . . or Blue Smoke and Mirrors? Reflections on the New Campaign Technology and the Political Consultant Trade," in *Campaigns and Elections*, Larry Sabato, ed. (Glenview, Illinois: Scott, Foresman and Co., 1989), p. 3.
2. Graham Fraser, *Playing for Keeps* (Toronto: McClelland and Stewart, 1989), p. 150.
3. Christopher Waddell, "PCs Tipped on Pollution by Survey; Public Paid," *The Globe and Mail*, 30 December 1988, p. A3.
4. Alan Frizzell, "The Perils of Polling," in *The Canadian General Election of 1988*, Alan Frizzell, Jon Pammett, and Anthony Westell, eds. (Ottawa: Carleton University Press, 1989), p. 92.
5. Edwin Diamond and Stephen Bates, *The Spot* (Cambridge, Massachusetts: Massachusetts Institute of Technology, 1988), p. 6.
6. R. Jeremy Wilson, "Horserace Journalism: The Media in Elections," *Journal of Canadian Studies* (Winter 1980-81), p. 66.
7. Michael Nolan, "Political Communication Methods in Canadian Federal Election Campaign 1867-1925," *Canadian Journal of Communication* (May 1989), p. 31.
8. Donald Creighton, *John A. Macdonald: The Old Chieftain* (Toronto: Macmillan, 1955), p. 469.
9. Ibid.
10. Ibid.
11. Ibid.
12. Nolan, pp. 33-4.
13. Nolan, p. 35.
14. Ross Laver et al., "The New Tricks in an Old Trade," *Maclean's*, 31 October 1988, p. 16.
15. Peter Dempson, *Assignment Ottawa: Seventeen Years in the Press Gallery* (Toronto: General Publishing, 1968), p. 97.
16. Ibid.
17. Interview with Craig Oliver, Ottawa, 17 April 1989.
18. Ibid.
19. Interview with Terrence O'Malley, Toronto, 12 December 1988.
20. Alan Frizzell and Anthony Westell, "The Media and the Campaign," in *The Canadian General Election of 1988*, Alan Frizzell, Jon Pammett, and Anthony Westell, eds. (Ottawa: Carlton University Press, 1989), p. 75.

21. Interview with Alan Fryer, Ottawa, 8 December 1988.
22. Interview with Craig Oliver.
23. Interview with Elly Alboim, Ottawa, 21 April 1989.
24. Fraser, p. 187.
25. Interview with Alan Fryer.
26. Interview with AnnaMaria Tremonti, Ottawa, 17 April 1989.
27. Jeffrey Simpson, *Discipline of Power* (Toronto: Personal Library, 1980) pp. 76-77.
28. Fraser, p. 232.
29. Interview with AnnaMaria Tremonti.
30. Ibid.
31. Interview with Craig Oliver.
32. Interview with Elly Alboim.
33. Interview with Arnold Amber, Toronto, 13 December 1989.
34. Interview with Allen Garr, Toronto, 13 December 1988.
35. Confidential interview, 9 June 1989.
36. Frederick Fletcher, "The Mass Media in the 1974 Canadian Election," in *Canada At The Polls: The General Election of 1974*, Howard R. Penniman, ed. (Washington: American Enterprise Institute, 1975), p. 254.
37. Fletcher, "The Mass Media in the 1974 Canadian Election," p. 253.
38. Interview with James Coutts, Toronto, 3 June 1987.
39. Interview with Vince Carlin, Toronto, 5 June 1987.
40. Interview with David Lewis, Ottawa, 11 August 1980.
41. Interview with Robin Sears, Toronto, 4 June 1987.
42. Interview with Arnold Amber.
43. Interview with Allen Garr.
44. Patricia Poirier, "Quebeckers to Get Less of Leaders' Campaigns as Media Cut Coverage," *The Globe and Mail*, 5 October 1988, p. A9; and Stevie Cameron, "New Generation of Reporters Following the Leaders this Election," *The Globe and Mail*, 13 October 1988, p. A2.
45. Bruce Wallace, "And Now, the News," *Maclean's*, 31 October 1988, p. 25.
46. Interview with Allen Garr.
47. Interview with Elly Alboim.
48. Interview with Don Newman, Ottawa, 9 December 1988.
49. Interview with Craig Oliver.
50. Clive Cocking, *Following the Leaders* (Toronto: Doubleday, 1980), p. 95.
51. Interview with Alan Fryer.
52. Norman Snider, "Turner's Last Hurrah?," *Saturday Night*, February 1989, p. 34.
53. Dan Goodgame and Naushad Mehta, "The Made-for-TV Campaign," *Time*, 14 November 1988, p. 63; and interview with Robin Sears.

54. Interview with Alan Fryer.
55. Quoted in Frederick Fletcher, "The Media and the 1984 Landslide," in *Canada at the Polls, 1984: A Study of the Federal General Elections*, Howard R. Penniman, ed. (Durham, North Carolina: Duke University Press, 1988), p. 169.
56. R.H. Wagenberg, W.C. Soderlund, W.I. Romanow, and E.D. Briggs, "Campaigns, Images and Polls: Mass Media Coverage of the 1984 Canadian Election," *Canadian Journal of Political Science* (March 1988), p. 129.
57. Frizzell and Westell, p. 89.
58. "Campaign '88," *On Balance* (January 1989), pp. 1-3.
59. Interview with Robin Sears, Toronto, 14 June 1989.
60. Ibid.
61. Quoted in Frederick Fletcher, "Mass Media and Parliamentary Elections in Canada," *Legislative Studies Quarterly*, vol. 12, no. 3 (August 1987), 359-360.
62. Frizzell and Westell, p. 84.
63. Frederick Fletcher, "The Media and the 1984 Landslide," p. 174.
64. Geoffrey Stevens, "Prospects and Proposals," *Politics and the Media* (Toronto: Reader's Digest Foundation of Canada and Erindale College, University of Toronto, 1981), p. 102.
65. Lawrence Leduc and Richard Price, "Great Debates: The Televised Leadership Debates of 1979," *Canadian Journal of Political Science* (March 1985), p. 153.
66. Marjorie Hershey, "The Campaign and the Media," in *The Election of 1988*, Gerald Pomper, ed. (Chatham, New Jersey: Chatham House Publishers, 1989), p. 89.
67. Interview with Hugh Segal, Toronto, 26 April 1989.
68. "The Voters Reflect," *Maclean's*, 5 December 1989, p. 19.
69. C. David Heymann, *A Woman Named Jackie* (New York: Carol Communications, 1989), p. 242.
70. Austin Ranney, *Channels of Power: The Impact of Television on American Politics* (New York: Basic Books, 1983), p. 15.
71. Ranney, pp. 25-26.
72. Diamond and Bates, pp. 287-88.
73. Leduc and Price, p. 138; and Doris Graber, *Processing the News* (New York: Longman, 1988), p. 123.
74. Interview with Robin Sears.
75. Gerald Caplan, Michael Kirby, and Hugh Segal, *Election* (Scarborough, Ontario: Prentice-Hall Canada, 1989), p. 231.
76. Interview with André Ouellet, Ottawa, 18 April 1989. See Jaimie Hubbard, "Votes Can Hang on the Image-Maker's Skill," *The Financial Post*, 10 October 1988, p. 13.
77. Fraser, p. 271.

78. Hugh Windsor, "The Battle of the Potential Network Stars," *The Globe and Mail*, 22 October 1988, p. D2.
79. Interview with Hugh Segal.
80. Jeff Greenfield, *Playing to Win* (New York: Simon and Schuster, 1980) p. 201.
81. Caplan, Kirby, and Segal, p. 136.
82. Greenfield, p. 233.
83. William Boot, "Campaign '88: TV Overdoses on the Inside Dope," *Columbia Journalism Review* (January/February 1989), p. 26.
84. Quoted in Greg Weston, *Reign of Error* (Toronto: McGraw-Hill Ryerson, 1988), p. 86.
85. Interview with Elly Alboim.
86. Interview with Terry O'Grady.
87. Myles Martel, *Political Campaign Debates* (New York: Longman, 1983), p. 85.
88. Barbara Farah and Ethel Klein, "Public Opinion Trends," in *The Election of 1988*, Gerald Pomper, ed. (Chatham, New Jersey: Chatham House Publishers, 1989), p. 111.
89. Jaimie Hubbard, "Leaders Learn to Play it Cool, Calm for TV Debate," *The Financial Post*, 24 October 1988, p. 16.
90. Greenfield, p. 209.
91. Fraser, p. 276.
92. Ibid., p. 277.
93. George Perlin, "Opportunity Regained: The Tory Victory in 1984," in *Canada at the Polls, 1984: A Study of the Federal General Elections*, Howard Penniman, ed. (Durham, North Carolina: Duke University Press, 1988), p. 87.
94. Interview with Tom Scott, Toronto, 24 April 1989.
95. James Bagnall and Hyman Solomon, "How the Tories Turned the Tide," *The Financial Post*, 28 November 1988, section II, p. 13.
96. Interview with Tom Scott.
97. Ibid.
98. Interview with AnnaMaria Tremonti.
99. Ibid.

7

"If You Fly by Your Guts, You're Nuts"

A party's election strategy is largely dictated by its assessment of voters' perceptions and opinions. Messages are geared to the public mood and specific groups of swing voters are targeted. As polling is the best instrument for gauging public opinion, it has become the navigational equipment that guides election strategy. Through polling, parties are given a map of the electorate and its concerns: the suitability of campaign themes and issues, views about the strengths and weaknesses of the leaders and parties and the effectiveness of advertising campaigns, where the key ridings and the swing voters are, and the anatomy of opponents' campaigns and their vulnerabilities. How well party strategists interpret their data, the intelligence that is applied to solving strategic problems that are revealed through polling, and the accuracy of the survey instruments available to the parties can be critical determinants of the election outcome. Joe Napolitan, one of the founders of the political consulting industry in the United States, contends that "Polls don't win elections. What wins elections is the use you make of the information you get in a poll and probably the least important information in a poll, especially early on in a campaign, is who's ahead at a given moment."[1] According to Ian McKinnon, until recently Chairman of Decima Research, the Conservative Party's pollster, "The tools themselves do not win or lose elections. They can give you an advantage. You can know better what people are thinking, talking about, what they want to hear, what issues concern them. You can portray your candidate in a more effective fashion. . . . Modern campaigning is not about the supremacy of the tools. It's about adept politicians using the tools well."[2] The election aircraft isn't flown by the instruments, it's flown by the pilot. But it's also the case that, as political consultant Lionel Sosa has put it, "If you fly by your guts, you're nuts."[3]

Polls are also a major focus in the media's coverage of elections. By commissioning their own polls during elections, media organizations have the power to create news, gain publicity and prestige, and affect the flow of the campaign itself. Polls are irresistible to the media. They create dramatic headline stories where winners and losers are declared, and they allow news organizations to demonstrate that they are on top of the latest information. In a crude sense, they become a form of advertising. Polls have clearly become a media obsession. During the 1979 and 1980 federal elections news organizations commissioned eight and ten polls, respectively; by the 1984 election the number had mushroomed to four-teen and during the 1988 election the results of at least twenty-four national polls were released.[4] There were at least two or three major polls reported every week, each of which created "an echo," reports about and reactions to results, that often reverberated for days afterwards. Frizzell found that polls were mentioned in one in five television news stories during the 1988 election.[5]

PARTY POLLING AND DIRECT MAIL

Polling in Canada began during the Second World War when Ottawa commissioned surveys of opinion on the home front, the Gallup organization did polls during the Ontario election of 1943, and the advertising agency of Cockfield, Brown polled forty-three ridings for the Liberal Party in 1945.[6] The original impetus for polling had come from powerful Liberal cabinet minister Brooke Claxton, and was largely abandoned after Claxton's departure from the national stage. It was to be two decades before polling was again a regular feature of political campaigning. There was virtually no polling done in any of Louis St. Laurent's or John Diefenbaker's election campaigns, although a primitive poll was conducted for the Conservatives by McKim's, an advertising agency, in 1953.[7] Diefenbaker's contempt for polling was such that he often remarked that "polls were for dogs."[8] The change came when Keith Davey, the Liberals' national director, became impressed with the way that John F. Kennedy had used polling during his run for the presidency in 1960. Davey commissioned Kennedy's pollster, Louis Harris, to do surveys during the 1962 and 1963 elections. At one point, Davey even asked Harris to test reactions to Lester Pearson's characteristic bow-tie. (People disliked it, considering it effeminate.)

   The Liberals became infatuated (some would even say obsessed) with polling during the 1970s. The party surveyed extensively, with pollster Martin Goldfarb receiving a lion's share of the party's business. Goldfarb soon became part of the party's inner circle, and his influence on strategy was reputed to be enormous. In fact, Joe Clark once accused the Liberals of operating a "government by Goldfarb" because they polled so extensively before making decisions.[9] Yet while some policies may have been shaped or at least packaged according to what the polls prescribed, Pierre Trudeau's obstinate disregard for anything that didn't accord with his convictions is legendary. According to Keith Davey, "He liked to know what he could do to improve his image, how he could improve his style. But what he wouldn't do was take policy decisions based on the data from the surveys."[10] Jim Coutts observed that, "Trudeau wasn't going to change on the constitution if it was 90 percent to 10 percent against him."[11] After Trudeau's departure, and with the party out of power, the Liberals became increasingly divided and disorganized and the party plummeted into debt. During the 1988 election the party was reduced to a "low rent" polling operation, were outspent by the Conservatives by at least five to one, and seemed to have fallen far behind the Tories in integrating polling with campaign strategy.[12]

The Conservatives, by contrast, have developed an enormous polling capability, one that infuses almost every aspect of how their campaigns are run. The Conservatives presently have two significant advantages. As the government in power, they have access to polls commissioned by government departments and paid for by taxpayers. According to one account, almost 800 polls were conducted for the Mulroney government during its first term in office.[13] Second, the Conservatives have been able to nurture Decima Research from a fledgling makeshift operation into a polling powerhouse with an international reputation. Largely the creation of company President Allan Gregg, a former party researcher, Decima has been able to attract a large number of prestige corporate accounts even as it has remained the party's "in-house" pollster. Now owned by a British firm, WPP Group PLC, and run through an American subsidiary, Hill and Knowlton, Decima is considered by many to be the "state of the art" political pollster in Canada, with a sophisticated data base and a wealth of campaign experience. As research, i.e., polling, does not constitute a campaign expense under the current Election Act, and the Conservatives have had the largest war chest, they have been able to use polling far more extensively than the other parties. Unlike the other parties, they have had a full menu to choose from. For instance, in 1988 Decima began polling months before the formal campaign began and during the election did tracking polls nightly, conducted four national surveys, analysed twenty-five "representative" ridings, and ran dozens of focus groups. Decima was an on-going resource to the campaign, the campaign's "brain trust." In addition, Allan Gregg has been credited with devising the "bombing the bridge" advertising strategy, which used TV spots to assault John Turner's credibility and tilted the election to the Conservatives in the final two weeks. As Ian McKinnon has described the role played by Gregg following Turner's debate victory, "You do strategic research right away and be prepared to set course. Allan designed the research, analysed it and designed the strategy. He was the intellectual creator of the ad strategy."[14] The CBC's Arnold Amber believes that "In this last election Decima might have been worth a 15 to 25 seat advantage. A different polling organization might have blown it for the Tories."[15]

By comparison, the NDP has had an ambivalent attitude to polling and less money to spend on it. As a party with an ideological commitment to socialist principles and to maintaining a grassroots party organization, party activists have viewed polling with some suspicion. As Robin Sears has described this sense of unease, "Our problem in the NDP is that polling is still seen as a black art by a significant part of our core that adheres to the fundamentalist thesis that polling is somehow wicked. Many of our activists see polling as anti-democratic because they believe it tends to enhance central control, shape policies and lead to principles being fudged."[16] According to one estimate, the NDP spent $300,000, a relatively meager sum, during the 1988 federal election, enough to do nightly tracking polls and focus groups but little else.[17] The NDP has not cultivated a strong link to any one polling firm. During the 1988 election they used Fingerhut/Madison Opinion Research of Washington, D.C., and Access Survey Research of Winnipeg, a subsidiary of the Angus Reid Group.

There are basically seven types of polls used in election campaigns. While not every campaign will use the full complement of techniques, most will use at least some of them.

1. *The Bench-mark Study*

Usually conducted months before an election, the bench-mark study attempts, through in-depth interviews with a large random sample of prospective voters, to assess the general mood of the public towards issues and candidates. The idea is to gain an appreciation of the landscape on which the election battle is to be fought by obtaining a "map" of the electorate.

2. *The Follow-up Survey*

As parties and politicians sometimes act upon the findings in the bench-mark study, repositioning themselves on issues or trying to recast their images, the follow-up survey is used to verify if these changes have been accepted by the electorate or whether opinion has shifted since the bench-mark study. The sample is usually much smaller and entirely different from the one used for the bench-mark poll.

3. *Omnibus Polls*

An omnibus poll is a multi-purpose poll in which a variety of questions are asked about a number of issues or products. The omnibus poll allows survey organizations to service a number of clients at the same time with the same sample. Questions about voting intentions may be asked together with questions about deodorant or toothpaste. Political questions are sometimes tagged on at the end of surveys on other topics because the political client may only have commissioned a small number of questions and it is easier for a pollster to add the political questions to a larger survey.

4. *Panel Surveys*

A portion (sometimes up to half) of those interviewed in the bench-mark or follow-up survey are contacted weeks or months later in order to detect changes in opinion that have taken place in the interim. Panels are an effective way to measure shifts in mood and gauge the reasons why changes are occurring. The problem with panels is that, having been interviewed once, respondents are more likely to pay attention to politics and thus can no longer be considered representative of the Canadian population.

5. *Tracking*

During the election campaign, different samples of 100 to 500 individuals are phoned each day and asked about developments in the campaign. The purpose is to create a "trend line" monitoring the "pulse-rate" of voters. Tracking allows the parties to measure even slight movements of opinion and to know in what direction opinion is heading.

6. *The Riding Study*

Since percentages of the vote do not translate directly into the number of seats that will be won or lost, polls of demographically "representative" ridings, either "bellwether" ridings that traditionally vote for the winning party or "key" ridings where close contests are expected, are undertaken. Riding surveys tell parties where to concentrate their efforts.

7. *Focus Groups*

A small group of people—usually no more than a dozen or so—are selected non-scientifically at shopping centres, through brokers who have lists of people on file, or as a result of telephone interviews and paid a small amount of money to participate in discussions led by a trained leader. Researchers and party officials can observe the focus group from behind a one-way mirror. The purpose is to gain "insights that go beyond your numbers"[18] by understanding how people make connections between issues or events and the emotions and instinctive reactions that are often the mainsprings of opinion. Dozens of focus groups are conducted in different cities across the country during a major product marketing or political campaign.

Two of these methods, tracking and focus groups, are especially critical to the winning of elections. Tracking is important because it is a particularly sensitive barometer of sudden changes among an increasingly volatile electorate. Where voting was once securely attached to the anchors of family, religion, language, and class, these moorings have been loosened as increased mobility, the emergence of a consumer culture, the anonymity of urban life, and the power of mass communications have eroded traditional values and perceptions. Only about 40 percent of the electorate can now be described as having fixed allegiances to a particular party.[19] Most voters are to some degree "free agents," willing to shift their vote depending on the circumstances in each election; indeed, in recent years politicians have seen sizeable leads in the polls washed away literally overnight by volcanic shifts of opinion. Prime Minister John Turner had a healthy ten-point lead in the polls when he called an election in July 1984. Within two weeks his campaign had capsized, and on 4 September the Conservatives won the largest majority in Canadian history. Ontario Premier Frank Miller had a huge twenty-point lead entering the 1985 provincial election, only to lose power to Liberal David Peterson. Newfoundland Conservative Premier Tom Rideout also had a twenty-point lead going into the April 1989 provincial election. He was defeated convincingly by Liberal Clyde Wells. Voting intentions in the 1988 federal election fluctuated wildly, with polls indicating that at various points both Conservative and Liberal majorities were possible. More than a quarter of respondents in one survey admitted to having changed their minds at least once during the campaign.[20] The value of tracking is that it allows the parties to detect trends early, make a diagnosis, and administer treatments quickly.

Focus groups are a means of gauging not only the currents of opinion but the undertows that may be sweeping powerfully below the waterline. They are used extensively in planning overall strategy, particularly the themes to be used in the advertising campaigns. According to NDP Communications Director Terry O'Grady, focus group testing helped the NDP devise its 1988 election theme of "fairness for average Canadians." Groups were asked to picture three people walking into a room: a Conservative, a Liberal, and a New Democrat. They saw the Conservative as "straight-laced, an accountant type,"; the Liberal as somewhat of a yuppie, but not someone totally trustworthy; while the New Democrat was seen as "an ordinary guy" with whom you could "hoist a few at the local pub."[21] Focus groups told the Conservatives when to switch off free trade as a main theme in their campaign. The Conservatives found that "After the debate there was such a need for information that people in focus groups would exchange information about what they knew about free trade. After three weeks we had the opposite reaction. People had heard enough. They were putting their hands over their ears."[22] The idea of calling John Turner a "liar" as a way of shaking his credibility after his triumph in the debates had also been tested in focus groups.[23] In the American presidential election in 1988, George Bush's strategists "felt they had struck gold" when focus group testing revealed that Michael Dukakis's positions on the Pledge of Allegiance and on prisoner furloughs raised doubts about his patriotism and his ability to maintain law and order. The Republicans devised a brutal campaign to blacken Dukakis's record that centred on these themes. In William Safire's words, they "threw red meat to the Yahoos."[24] Focus groups were also used as "checks" on the television advertising campaigns. Groups were shown storyboards that described potential ads and asked about the best wording for the dialogue, and pre-tested ads that the parties had prepared. Ads done by other parties would also be shown. According to Terry O'Malley, the creative director of the Liberal ad campaign in 1988, the reaction of focus groups convinced the Liberals to go with ads that said "Say one thing, mean another. Don't let Mulroney deceive you again." The original dialogue, "Don't let Mulroney fool you again," was rejected by the groups.[25]

The ultimate aim of election polling is to develop the most effective targeting strategy: which messages and techniques will sway which group of voters. Polling tells the parties where the swing votes are—in which regions and among which income, ethnic, and age groups—and the messages that are most likely to move those votes. The skill is to direct scarce resources—advertising, direct mail, phone banks, appearances by leaders, and the most persuasive messages—to where they will have the most impact. With advances in technology, targeting has become much more refined. One of the more recent developments is direct mail. Using specialized lists of voters cobbled together by the parties or obtained through brokers, the parties mail letters that contain customized messages. The advantage of direct mail is that it goes directly from party to voter with no intermediary. The media filter is bypassed. And where traditional campaign techniques are labour intensive, requiring large numbers of canvassers to go door-to-door, direct mail is technology driven; millions of voters can be reached using relatively few people. The Conservatives were the first to use direct mail, adopting it in the mid-1970s when, being out of power, the party had difficulty raising money from large contributors. Direct mail techniques learned from the Republicans in the United States allowed the Conservatives to widen their fund-raising base and to build a formidable party infrastructure. The other parties were much slower to realize the potential of direct mail, although they have caught up to some degree. During the 1988 federal election millions of pieces of mail were sent out.

The Conservatives organized a computerized direct-mail system that reached 200,000 undecided voters in forty ridings.[26] Using riding profiles prepared by Decima Research, voters with certain life-styles—for instance, single mothers with jobs—were targeted. A letter with Brian Mulroney's signature was sent to each person on the list, asking them to write back with their views and concerns. The letter was followed by a phone call that asked about the voter's concerns and then by a second letter with a response, one of thirty-three prepared beforehand, tailored to the person's specific problems or opinions. A second phone call followed the second letter, and finally a third phone call was made on election day. A consultant on the project described the process as "Chinese water torture. Except that you're not bugging people when you get hold of them during a campaign; they expect it. The more you see them, bug them, phone them, show you want their support, the more likely they are to vote for you."[27]

THE USES AND ABUSES OF MEDIA POLLING

While party polls are kept private, the results of polls done for the media are blasted across headlines and trumpeted at the top of newscasts. As mentioned earlier, the media's stake in polling reached unprecedented proportions in 1988, with virtually all of the major news organizations becoming players in the game. Goldfarb Consultants polled for the Liberals as well as for Baton Broadcasting, owner of several CTV stations. Southam commissioned four polls by Angus Reid Associates; soon after the election, the polling firm was taken over by Southam. Gallup Canada did surveys for *The Toronto Star* and their polls were carried in other newspapers as well. *The Globe and Mail* featured four polls conducted by Environics. Canadian Facts and Insight Canada Research did surveys for the CBC and CTV, respectively. The mating dance between polling firms and news organizations is facilitated by the fact that polling firms often agree to do polls for media outlets at bargain basement prices in the hope of gaining a windfall of publicity. Using polls as a vehicle for self-promotion, news organizations often celebrate with great fanfare the results of polls that they've commissioned but downplay or ignore entirely polls done by other news organizations.

Academic observers have tended to be critical of the way the media report polls. While some news organizations have gained a great deal of polling expertise and have become sophisticated and professional in the way they present results, others seem oblivious to what Alan Frizzell calls "the perils of polling."[28] Robin Sears describes what many see as the main problem: "I could count on one hand the number of journalists that are competent to analyse polls. They write high profile stories about poll results but wouldn't know an aspect of polling methodology if it came up and bit them."[29] Jeff Simpson's view is that:

> Just as love is often wasted on the young, so polls are often wasted on the media. . . . Many journalists, including those who write about political matters, are unschooled in Canadian history, in polling methodology, in an understanding of any part of the country but their own. Yet the beguiling simplicity and easy accessibility of polling data embolden all journalists to become instant pundits, or worse still, experts. They can pontificate on the meaning of this, the likely outcome of that, the significance of everything, on the basis of a few stark numbers.[30]

Indeed, many journalists seem unaware of the large number of "entry points for errors in the polling process" and the extent to which polls can be manipulated for partisan purposes, opinion created, and results over-sold.[31] The following are some of the main methodological problems that can occur in polling.

1. *Margin of Error*

A poll is based on a random sample that gives each person in a target population an equal statistical probability of being interviewed. The margin of error depends on the size of the sample. A sample of 1500 individuals is accurate within three or four percentage points, nine-teen out of twenty times. Larger samples will have a smaller margin of error, and smaller samples a larger margin of error. News organizations may not be aware that a poll's scientific validity is conditioned by the size of the sample. During the 1984 federal election, one television station reported a poll based on a sample of 200 indi-viduals, a poll with a margin of error so enormous that it made the entire exercise meaningless.[32] News organizations usually fail to point out that if there is a 4 percent margin of error and the Conser-vatives, for example, have 36 percent, then the Conservatives' score may be as high as 40 percent or as low as 32 percent. News organiza-tions also routinely report regional breakdowns—which party is lead-ing in different provinces or parts of the country—when the sample size and hence the margin of error in that particular "sub-set" does not warrant drawing conclusions. As Claire Hoy has written, "We have the absurd excesses of media polls breaking vote preferences down into provincial units, say Manitoba, where the national sample means that only about 54 Manitobans were asked and the margin of error for that result is 18, plus or minus."[33]

Samples may also be "contaminated" by the method used to select those who are interviewed. When pollsters are pressed for time they may not make "call-backs" to people who could not be reached the first time. Pollsters should make at least four attempts to reach a prospective respondent in order to maintain the integrity of the sample. During the 1988 federal election one poll was conducted during the day, with the result that seniors and non-working women were oversampled; a survey done in the evening, when a broader section of voters were at home, would have been more accurate.

Moreover, any shift at all from one poll to another, however statistically insignificant, is often reported as a change in opinion in the electorate. The media do not comprehend that differences be-tween two polls might be due more to sampling error than to voter response. It takes a good many polls to really establish a trend.

2. *Wording*

The way that questions are worded can dictate the kinds of answers that are given. Indeed, the substitution of a single word, the word "job" for the word "work," for example, can lead to a difference of over 20 percent in the responses obtained.[34] Sometimes questions contain a preamble to educate respondents about the topic, which may inadvertently create opinions or deliberately "load the dice." Not educating respondents also has its risks, as respondents need some basic information in order to assess issues. One poll commissioned to determine whether Canadians approved of the purchase of nuclear submarines mentioned the costs of the submarines in the question and found that Canadians were strongly opposed to the submarines being bought. Another poll that didn't mention cost showed that Canadians supported the purchase.[35]

3. *Question Order*

Some questionnaires direct respondents to intended answers by leading them through a series of sensitizing or softening-up questions. Again, pollsters can subtly prompt their respondents into giving the "correct" answer by building a case for a particular position in questions. One poll done before the 1988 election found the NDP receiving significant popular support. Angus Reid had asked respondents about voting intentions only after a series of prior questions about Ed Broadbent's attractiveness as a leader.[36] Survey researchers are also aware that if given three choices of amount or degree in questions, most people will select the middle alternative.[37] They can get the answer they want by merely lining up choices in a particular order.

4. *Lying*

Studies indicate that between ten and fifteen percent of respondents routinely lie to pollsters.[38] Some people prefer to keep unpopular extremist or racist views to themselves, are embarrassed to admit that they may not know about a particular topic, or will give what they think is the expected or socially acceptable answer. As Nelson Wiseman, a University of Toronto political scientist, points out, "A lot of people see surveys as a test. They don't want to flunk. They don't want to sound stupid. And they also want to sound like they're responsible citizens."[39] In one poll, respondents were asked about whether a fictitious group called "Danarians" would be acceptable as neighbours and whether people wanted their children to marry Danarians. Pollsters were astonished to find that significant anti-Danarian feelings existed. People obviously were afraid to admit that they did not know who the Danarians were. On another occasion a poll found sizeable support for a non-existent cabinet minister whose name had been invented by a researcher.[40]

5. Voter Turnout

A particularly difficult problem during elections is the number of people who tell interviewers that they intend to vote but are, in fact, non-voters. A number of other questions have to be asked to shake loose those who are unlikely to vote. Polls that accept respondents' words at face value, without gauging the depth and intensity of their commitments, can be misleading. Moreover, there is even difficulty determining how people voted in previous elections—often the gauge of how they will vote in a forthcoming election—because people change their votes in retrospect. A standing joke is that American pollsters have found that everybody voted for Kennedy and that nobody voted for Nixon.

6. Undecideds

Dealing with the "undecideds" is one of the most perplexing problems that pollsters face during elections. Some polling firms eliminate undecideds from their samples entirely, while others do the deciding for the respondent by weighting factors such as how they say they voted in previous elections, their position on key issues, and which way they appear to be leaning. How the undecideds are dealt with can sometimes affect the overall result.

7. Seats vs. Popular Vote

Being ahead in popular vote does not necessarily mean that a party will win the most seats in an election. A party can win the most seats and even form a government without winning the most votes. On many occasions, the size of a party's popular vote is inflated by a strong showing in a given region of the country. At the same time that it "wastes" votes winning overwhelming victories in that region, it can lose close contests elsewhere. By stressing popular vote rather than the number of seats likely to be won, media pundits may mislead their readers or audiences about the outcome of the election. Using only a few polls of 1,000 Canadians, for instance, it is impossible to determine the breakdown of seats.

Even with the most scrupulously unbiased and methodologically rigorous pollster, the problems of lying, estimating turnout, and failing to measure seats continue to plague the industry. Neophyte journalists are often unaware of (or completely oblivious to) the importance of the technical aspects of polling. Two days before voting day during the 1988 federal election, *The Toronto Sun* ran a full-page story based on an "unscientific poll" of 100 voters in a close Toronto riding. A reporter had simply been sent out to talk to voters. The story featured a large photo of "winner" Barbara McDougall.[41]

The major complaint about the media's treatment of polls, aside from the tendency of some journalists to fall into methodological traps, is that findings are sensationalised; results presented out of context and without the necessary nuances, cautions, and "shades of grey"; and that the "horse-race"—who is leading and by how much—is hyped to the point that political analysis comes to resemble sports reporting. There is also the fear that the shower of publicity given to polls blankets out coverage that could be given to issues and policy pronouncements, and that polls colour how journalists report the campaign. What politicians say about the deficit or health care is unlikely to make it on to the news on a day that a major poll is released. As Alan Fryer of CTV has commented about his experience during the 1988 election, "When there's dramatic new poll results, that becomes your story. Polls affected the type of story you did . . . more than in any previous campaign. As long as they're there you have to respond to them."[42] Frederick Fletcher found in his study of the 1984 federal election that some reporters "lost interest in reporting the issue positions after it became clear that the Conservatives would win."[43] The possibility also exists that having invested so much of their prestige in the polls that they've commissioned, news organizations will develop a stake in and become attached to the findings that emerge. A poll can then become a self-fulfilling prophecy: the news organization, unconsciously perhaps, frames its coverage to give an advantage to the party that it has "declared" the winner. It becomes locked into its own projections, and its reporters chase the losing party leaders to get their reactions on why they are behind and on what's gone wrong with their campaigns. The effect on the parties that are behind can be devastating.

Media executives argue that even if news organizations did not publicize the results of their polling, they could not cover elections properly without access to poll data. Polling is as essential to *their* election campaigns as to those of the political parties. As the CBC's Elly Alboim has expressed it, "The only way I can evaluate what you're doing [politicians] is by mirroring your polling. The only way I can evaluate what is really germane to vote choice, so that I can provide information that the people really want to know about, is by polling. I have to see what the issue sub-set is, I have to know what the rank order is, I have to understand the relationship between leadership and issues in order to intelligently plot out an election campaign."[44] In describing the CBC's coverage of the 1988 election, Alboim admitted that "once we discovered through polling the astonishing illiteracy rate on free trade, it really did reposition our coverage. We did much more substantive, detailed reporting on the issue."[45]

REPORTING POLL RESULTS: THE ELECTION WHEEL OF FORTUNE

The larger concern is whether the media's reporting of polls has a direct effect on the outcome of elections. Some have argued that the reporting of polls creates a "bandwagon" effect: the party that is ahead in the polls receives a shot in the arm, stronger candidates come forward, there are more campaign workers, major financial contributors climb on board, and there's a lift in terms of image and morale. The bandwagon also works in reverse. The "losing" party develops a losing psychology. Every downward shift in the polling trend line is a dagger in the heart of the party's campaign, each poll a new cut that adds to the party's bleeding. In the view of André Ouellet, co-chair of the Liberal campaign in 1988, "It has a tremendous effect on the results of an election because it discourages some candidates from running, discourages and destabilizes candidates that are running, and creates a bandwagon effect. It's human nature to want to be on the winning side. It creates a trend which could make the difference between majority and minority governments."[46] Elly Alboim argues that poll results helped produce an abortive rebellion against John Turner's leadership in the midst of the 1988 election. According to Alboim, "They horribly demoralized the Liberals and created the kinds of discussions that hurt Turner so terribly. The MPs seeing the polls began to wonder what they could do to prevent disaster. Moreover, the media's reporting criteria changed. We began to focus on the party's fortunes and soul-searching about the leader."[47] Polling done for the Ontario Liberal Party during the 1985 provincial election found that virtually every news report about poll results that showed the Conservatives floundering produced a new surge in support for the Liberals.[48]

During the provincial election in Nova Scotia in 1988, an Angus Reid poll published five days before the election showed the Conservatives with an eleven-point lead, a four-point gain from an earlier Reid poll. The Liberals, who felt that they were closing in on the Conservatives, saw the poll as a virtual disaster. As Ron Macdonald, the Liberals' campaign manager, explained their predicament, "The one thing which might kill us was the perception people had we couldn't win. We had to get them to start thinking of us as winners."[49] Macdonald believes that "In a close, volatile election, a pollster can have a tremendous impact. He can play God. I think in that election he [Reid] saw the opportunity to play God and he issued the numbers."[50] The Liberals finished just three percentage points behind the Conservatives.

Some argue that the reporting of so many polls has an anesthetizing effect on voters. People become fixated on the "score-card" and lose interest in other aspects of the election or in becoming directly involved. As Terry O'Malley has put it, "People don't have to go to the game, they can just tune in the score."[51]

Those who believe that polls affect the outcome of elections tend to feel that the reporting of polls should be banned either entirely or at least during the latter stages of election campaigns. This proposal is vigorously opposed by those who feel that any ban on information available to the public is harmful. As Tory pollster Allan Gregg has argued, "It's hard philosophically to say there's intrinsically something evil about telling people what they're thinking. Philosophically . . . I find it repugnant."[52] It's also believed that polls help voters make better, more rational decisions. Voters with access to poll results are likely to be "strategic voters." An example that has often been cited was the apparently last-minute decision by voters in Vancouver's Quadra riding to elect Liberal leader John Turner in 1984.[53] Seeing that the Conservatives were about to win a landslide victory across the country, Quadra voters could cast a sentimental vote for Turner in their own riding. It's also thought that during the 1988 election, some of those opposed to free trade attempted to maximize the impact of their vote by choosing the candidate from either of the parties that intended to block the deal, the Liberals or the NDP, whoever had the best chance of winning in their ridings. A point made by Robin Sears, however, is that the NDP, as the third party, is the one most likely to be hurt by reported polls. He asks whether "anyone's fortunes should be determined by what is intended to be a measuring device, not a vote determining device."[54]

Several surveys have been done on how voters perceive the effects of polls. The 1988 National Election Survey is likely to produce the most interesting results on the effects of polling, but the results will not be published for some time. A *Maclean's*/Decima poll conducted in the aftermath of the 1988 election found that a relatively small number of respondents, 23 percent, felt that polls had been "helpful" to them in making their voting decisions. Sixty-five percent said that polls had made no difference.[55] An Environics poll taken during the election, however, produced a different result. Although only 13 percent of those interviewed would admit to being influenced by poll results, 64 percent felt that others were affected.[56] This may be the so-called "third-person effect" that researchers often find in testing public responses to sensitive issues like pornography. Respondents resist saying that they personally have been affected because of their need to retain self-esteem; but they view third parties such as friends and neighbours as being easily swayed.

Some countries have acted to limit the extent to which the media's handling of polls might affect the outcome of elections. In France, the publication of poll results are banned in the seven days preceding an election; and in West Germany, a self-imposed limit agreed to by the polling industry bans the release of poll results during the last week of an election. The CBC will also not "commission or conduct polls for broadcast" during the last ten or fourteen days of an election campaign, depending on the length of the campaign.[57] Most Canadian news organizations, however, recognize no boundaries in their pursuit of sensational, audience-grabbing stories.

Lastly, there is concern about the impact that polls may be having on the political system as a whole. Some observers believe that polls have turned leaders into followers. Knowing which way the tide is running, politicians are afraid to make unpopular decisions or take a stand based on principles that may not be in fashion. Polls tend to fix a politician's gaze on the immediate and the short term, the election just around the corner, rather than on long-term problems that need attention. The argument, in short, is that polls have helped to elevate a disturbing kind of politics and politician. As Daniel Greenberg has written, "Polls are the life-support system for the finger-to-the-wind, quick-change politics of our time and, as such, are the indispensable tools for the ideologically hollow men who work politics like a soup-marketing campaign."[58] Jim Coutts believes that polling allows such politicians to "skew public policy to the ten percent of the voters that are up for grabs" and that, as a consequence, "the have-nots are forgotten."[59] Others argue against this pessimistic view. They contend that it is the public and not the technology that is supreme. According to Ian McKinnon, "One of the things that one often hears that I think is very incorrect is that the technology takes a nameless, faceless, directionless candidate, packages them and presents them to the electorate and that's how to win a campaign. People see through that . . . they can penetrate any artificial facade reasonably well."[60] A more cynical reply is that "In the free market, you can fool some of the people some of the time, but in a political campaign, you only need to fool half of the people once."[61]

NOTES

1. Joe Napolitan, "Television and the Democratic Process," *Banff Television Festival*, 6 June 1989.
2. Ian McKinnon, "Television and the Democratic Process," *Banff Television Festival*, 6 June 1989.
3. Quoted in John Witherspoon, "Campaign Commercials and the Media Blitz," in *Campaigns and Elections*, Larry Sabato, ed. (Glenview, Illinois: Scott, Foresman and Co., 1989), p. 62.

4. Frederick Fletcher, "Mass Media and Parliamentary Elections in Canada," *Legislative Studies Quarterly* (August 1987), p. 360; and Alan Frizzell, "The Perils of Polling," in *The Canadian General Election of 1988*, Alan Frizzell and Anthony Westell, eds. (Ottawa: Carleton University Press, 1989), p. 95.
5. Frizzell, p. 99.
6. Interview with J.W. Pickersgill, Ottawa, 8 December 1988; and Reginald Whitaker, *The Government Party* (Toronto: University of Toronto Press, 1977), p. 232.
7. Dalton Camp, *Gentlemen, Players and Politicians* (Markham, Ontario: Penguin, 1988), p. 99.
8. Claire Hoy, *Margin of Error* (Toronto: Key Porter Books, 1989), p. 79.
9. Jeffrey Simpson, "The Most Influential Private Citizen in Canada," *Saturday Night*, July 1984, p. 11.
10. Hoy, p. 30.
11. Interview with James Coutts, Toronto, 3 June 1987.
12. Interview with Robin Sears, Toronto, 4 June 1987.
13. "Ottawa's Polls are Expensive," *Calgary Herald*, 22 December 1987, p. A11.
14. Interview with Ian McKinnon, Toronto, 24 April 1989.
15. Interview with Arnold Amber, Toronto, 13 December 1988.
16. Interview with Robin Sears.
17. Charlotte Gray, "Purchasing Power," *Saturday Night*, March 1989, p. 17.
18. Quoted in Larry Sabato, *The Rise of Political Consultants* (New York: Basic Books, 1981), p. 77.
19. George Perlin, "Opportunity Regained: The Tory Victory in 1984," in *Canada at the Polls, 1984*, Howard R. Penniman, ed. (Durham, North Carolina: Duke University Press, 1988), p. 95.
20. "The Voters Reflect," *Maclean's*, 5 December 1988, p. 19.
21. Interview with Terry O'Grady, Ottawa, 18 April 1989.
22. Interview with Tom Scott, Toronto, 24 April 1989.
23. Ibid.
24. Marjorie Hershey, "The Campaign and the Media," in *The Election of 1988*, Gerald Pomper, ed. (Chatham, New Jersey: Chatham House Publishers, 1989), pp. 81, 86.
25. Interview with Terry O'Malley, Toronto, 12 December 1988.
26. Graham Fraser, "Tories Took Aim at Undecided Voters with Target '88 Mail Scheme," *The Globe and Mail*, 4 September 1989, p. A4.
27. Ibid.
28. Frizzell.
29. Interview with Robin Sears.
30. Jeffrey Simpson, "Pollstruck," *Policy Options* (March 1987), p. 6.
31. Sabato, p. 93.

32. Barry Kiefl, "Must Have Professional Polls in Media, CBC Official Says," *The Globe and Mail*, 11 September 1984, p. 7.
33. Hoy, p. 88.
34. Alex Michalos, "If Only the Public Understood Opinion Polls," *The Financial Post*, 15 February 1988, p. 31.
35. John Lamb, "A Price Tag Hard to Ignore," *Maclean's*, 20 June 1988, p. 4.
36. Hoy, p. 56.
37. Sabato, p. 94.
38. I. Lewis and William Schneider, "Is the Public Lying to the Pollsters?" *Public Opinion*, vol. 5, no. 2 (April/May 1982), 42-47.
39. Hoy, p. 93.
40. Lewis and Schneider.
41. Hoy, p. 215.
42. Interview with Alan Fryer, Ottawa, 8 December 1988.
43. Frederick Fletcher, "The Media and the 1984 Landslide," in *Canada at the Polls, 1984*, Howard R. Penniman, ed. (Durham, North Carolina: Duke University Press, 1988) p. 171.
44. Elly Alboim, "Television and the Democratic Process," *Banff Television Festival*, 6 June 1989.
45. Hoy, p. 212.
46. Interview with André Ouellet, Ottawa, 18 April 1989.
47. Interview with Elly Alboim, Ottawa, 21 April 1989.
48. Rosemary Speirs, *Out of the Blue* (Toronto: Macmillan, 1986), p. 122.
49. Hoy, pp. 144-145.
50. Ibid., p. 145.
51. Interview with Terry O'Malley.
52. Barbara Yaffe, "Pollster Surprised by Quebec Shift, Turner's Victory," *The Globe and Mail*, 12 October 1984, p. 5.
53. Mary Anne Comber and Robert Mayne, *The Newsmongers* (Toronto: McClelland and Stewart, 1986), p. 73-4.
54. Interview with Robin Sears.
55. "The Voters Reflect," p. 19.
56. Michael Adams and Donna Dasko, "If Polls Persuade the Voters, Few Will Admit It," *The Globe and Mail*, 25 November 1988, p. A7.
57. Canadian Broadcasting Corporation, *Journalistic Policy* (1982), p. 38.
58. Quoted in Herbert Asher, *Polling and the Public* (Washington, D.C.: Congressional Quarterly Press, 1988), p. 15.
59. Interview with James Coutts.
60. McKinnon.
61. Quoted in Witherspoon, pp. 61-62.

8

In the Eye of the Beholder: The Power of Election Advertising

Politicians consider television ads or spots to be uniquely powerful weapons. Parties spend roughly half of their total election budgets on advertising, with most of the expenditure going towards buying television ads.[1] During the last four weeks of a campaign, the period during which television advertising is allowed under the Election Act, viewers are battered by a relentless downpour of ads. The allure of the ads is that they allow the parties to reach voters directly without having to pass through a journalistic filter. Ads give the parties the opportunity to define themselves by setting their own priorities and projecting an attractive image. Spots also allow parties to define their opponents, presenting them in a less than favourable light by raising uncomfortable issues. According to Dorothy Nesbit, "videostyle" campaigning resembles a courtship where parties woo and romance voters with enticing promises and hot emotional appeals.[2]

Television advertising has been the subject of considerable controversy. Some observers consider it inherently manipulative, a vehicle for deception, distortion, and mud-slinging. Jeffrey Simpson has described fifteen- to thirty-second spots as "the antithesis of intelligent discussion of complex issues" because they are based on snippets of information that either sell the coronas of personality or cruelly ridicule opponents, not on a reasoned comparison of records and positions on issues.[3] The American television analyst Jeff Greenfield describes how images can overwhelm substance in the ads:

> The television advertisement is indeed an advertiser's dream, because it is the first time in history that every appeal—save those of smell or touch—can be packed into a single message. Light can glimmer off trees, music can suggest fun, romance, intrigue, danger, satisfaction; . . . In political terms, it is possible—literally—to wrap candidates around an American flag, while patriotic music swells around them; they can be photographed striding purposefully up the steps of the Capital, even though they have no more idea of what is inside the building than a child does; they can be surrounded by the *sense* of an issue rather than offering any ideas about it.[4]

Defenders of television spots argue that today's voters were raised on television and are, as a consequence, sophisticated TV viewers hardened against manipulative advertising. Video-literate voters know the difference between image and reality and can see through attempts to deceive them. As political consultant David Sawyer has argued, "There's no way you can go back now and show the candidate wandering down the beach, with his jacket over his shoulder and a dog running by his side. These are the clichés from the period when political television was naive. People now are looking with sophistication at your messages. Put out a message to con them, and they'll figure it out like that."[5] It's also pointed out that although spots are only fifteen to thirty seconds long, "people make judgments about other people in less time than that *routinely* in their daily lives."[6]

Advertising has always been a part of Canadian politics. During the era of the party press, newspapers were the propaganda arms of the parties with which they were aligned. During elections a newspaper's election coverage was itself a kind of advertising. But parties also used slogans, pamphlets, posters, and buttons to promote their causes. The early campaign posters were colourful and eye-catching and often very clever. Perhaps the most famous one was produced by the Industrial League for the 1891 election and features John A. Macdonald being carried on the shoulders of eager supporters under a slogan that reads "The Old Flag, The Old Policy, The Old Leader." During the 1911 election, when the Conservatives were urging voters to have "No Truck or Trade with the Yankees," a poster depicted Uncle Sam tapping a tree with the words "Canadian raw material — maple" scrawled on it. Uncle Sam declares, "Gol Darn His Old Tree. I Want The Sap."[7] Another poster shows Wilfrid Laurier and two Liberal colleagues sawing the "Canada" branch off the "British Empire" tree. The caption beneath the poster reads "Sir Wilfrid: 'Bear down, you fellows, and she'll fall like ripe fruit from the parent tree.' "[8] In a poster from the 1930 election, Mackenzie King is a muscular welder forging a united Canada.

A number of posters depict Canada as an innocent and helpless woman. In a 1891 poster entitled "The Way He Would Like It," a young female Canada is being delivered to a greedy and sinister-looking Uncle Sam. A more robust Miss Canada is featured in a Liberal campaign poster from the 1930 election. She is shown opening the doors to the opportunities presented by the British preferential tariff.

It's interesting to note that while posters have disappeared from use in Canadian elections, "les affiches" remain "the most omnipresent medium of communication" during French elections, plastered on virtually every available wall space, billboard, utility poll, and store-front.[9]

Newspapers, magazines, and free time slots on radio were the principal means of political advertising in the 1940s and 1950s. As ad campaigns grew in sophistication, two new players emerged at the forefront of politics: the ad executive and advertising agencies. Advertising agencies formed alliances with parties based on a spoils system. An agency

THE OLD FLAG,
THE OLD POLICY,
THE OLD LEADER.

VOTE LIBERAL

THE WELDER

would do party work at a discount in exchange for lucrative government advertising contracts if and when their party came to power. Reg Whitaker has described how the relationship was welded together: ". . . the relationship was to be a patronage one, party work in return for government contracts. This has indeed been the classic arrangement with ad agencies in Canadian politics. . . . The use of political advertising as a 'loss leader' by agencies is thus no longer a very startling piece of news. What is murky, however, is the exact nature of the bargain."[10] According to Keith Davey, the logic was that the agency that helped promote a party's policies during an election was in the best position to sell them once they became government policies.[11] Davey also observed that the agencies that worked first for the parties and subsequently for governments were always "blue-ribbon" agencies who were qualified to receive the contracts that they did.[12] Jim Coutts has described the situation that currently exists in blunt terms, "There are Liberal agencies and Tory agencies. That's the way advertising works in Canada."[13]

Perhaps the best example of successful image politics in the post-war period was the "Uncle Louis" campaign devised for Prime Minister Louis St. Laurent by the Cockfield, Brown agency during the 1953 election. St. Laurent, a man of austere tastes, aristocratic bearing, and a sometimes explosive temper was sold to the Canadian public as a warm and effusive family man. Conservative Dalton Camp has described St. Laurent's dramatic transformation:

> The Liberal Party seized the new instruments of communication and used them confidently, deliberately and effectively. Where the former leader, Mr. King, had been a man of mystique, mystery and, some said, intrigue, his successor, thrust into an age of growing media sophistication, became a man of a familially common mould, everyone's handsomely aging uncle, doting on the children, whimsical, a little patronizing and a whole lot more visible . . .
> . . . while this was happening in the campaign of 1953, none of us at Tory headquarters seemed aware of it. While the advisors and strategists poured over every published word uttered by the Prime Minister and his cabinet, no one looked up to see that the Liberal leader had changed his clothes.[14]

Cockfield, Brown's position in the Liberal campaign was such that it was given advance knowledge of the timing of the 1953 election, information that up to then had been the preserve of the cabinet alone. According to Whitaker, Cockfield, Brown and the other agencies within the Liberal orbit—MacLarens and Walsh and Ronalds, among others—were "very handsomely compensated" for "their rather modest political investment."[15] He estimates that Cockfield, Brown received between $1.5 and 2 million annually in government advertising contracts during the 1950s.

Dalton Camp, who with Allister Grosart spearheaded Conservative ad campaigns in the late 1950s and brought together agencies such as McKims, Fosters, Burns, O'Brien, and Locke Johnston, argues that the arrival of the ad executives aroused the suspicions of the old ward-healer, back-room politicians, who saw that these "young men with alien manners, full of self-assurance and incomprehensible jargon" were beginning to usurp their role.[16] Election organizations were soon dominated by a new generation of technocrats, advertising people and pollsters, who saw elections as more of a science than an art.

Television was first used during the 1957 federal election, when parties were allowed to make free-time broadcasts and could also purchase advertising time. Prevented by the CBC from using dramatizations of any kind, the leaders could appear only as "talking heads" addressing the camera directly. Not all politicians could make the transition to the new medium, and Prime Minister St. Laurent was among those who stumbled badly. St. Laurent's stilted and impersonal performance was nothing less than disastrous. *The Winnipeg Free Press* observed that St. Laurent "refused to make any concessions to the television camera" and advised him that "If you cannot loosen up and act like ordinary people, it would be decidedly to the advantage of the Liberal party to give up the television time that has been allotted to you."[17] St. Laurent may have felt as President Dwight Eisenhower did when he was making his first campaign commercials on television. Eisenhower is reputed to have said, "To think that an old soldier should come to this."[18] By contrast, Diefenbaker's eloquence and forcefulness made him an effective TV performer. In his free-time appearances during the 1957 election, the Tory leader railed against a government run by the "power lust of a few men" whose "control was more and more absolute."[19] He asserted with considerable passion that the Conservatives were the party of destiny and had become "the party of the people."[20] According to Dalton Camp, "The trial lawyer won hands down over the corporate lawyer on TV."[21] Whether television played a decisive role in Diefenbaker's triumph is difficult to determine, but almost everyone realized that the nature of political campaigning had changed.

AMERICAN POLITICAL COMMERCIALS FROM "DAISY" TO "WILLIE HORTON"

The most important developments in the evolution of election advertising occurred in the United States in the 1960s. Television ads done in the 1950s for Dwight Eisenhower and Adlai Stevenson were, at best, a novelty with parties and consultants still experimenting with ways of reaching audiences effectively. In the campaigns waged in 1960 and 1964 by John F. Kennedy and Lyndon Johnson, respectively, political advertising on television came of age. Kennedy used a TV spot to help diffuse the controversy that had arisen over whether a Catholic should be elected president. In that ad, Kennedy was filmed addressing a crowd, imploring them "You cannot tell me the day I was born it was said I could never run for president."[22] Kennedy also used negative advertising to ridicule his opponent, Vice-President Richard Nixon. Film was shown from a press conference where President Eisenhower was asked whether Nixon had contributed any major ideas while he was vice-president. Eisenhower replied, "If you give me a week, I might think of one. I don't remember." An announcer then told viewers that "President Eisenhower could not remember. But the voters will remember. For real leadership in the sixties, help elect Senator John F. Kennedy president."[23] Lyndon Johnson's ad campaign relied on scare tactics and placed what Diamond and Bates have called "dirty pictures in the public mind" to a degree that still remains unprecedented.[24] The goal was to portray Republican Barry Goldwater as a mad bomber who could bring nuclear war.

Johnson's "Daisy" commercial is one of the most famous ads in history, although by design it aired only once. The ad featured a young girl picking petals off a daisy flower and counting the number that she had removed. Then an announcer dramatically takes over the count, "Ten, nine, eight, seven . . ." and then the screen is filled with the shock of a nuclear explosion. The announcer goes on to explain, "These are the stakes—to make a world in which all God's children can live. Or to go into the dark. We must love each other, or we must die. Vote for President Johnson on November 3rd. The stakes are too high for you to stay at home."[25] The ad was so controversial that it continued to be shown on newscasts for days afterward despite the fact that the Democrats had pulled it and had intended to pull it after one broadcast. A week later, the Johnson campaign struck again with an ad that showed a young, blond-haired girl licking an ice-cream cone while a woman's voice warned of dairy products contaminated with Strontium 90 and Cesium 137. "They can make you die," she explained sadly. "There's a man running for president who wants to go on testing more bombs. His name is Barry Goldwater."[26] The creator of the ads, Tony Schwartz, believed that ads that brought new information to voters were not as successful as commercials that appealed to images and ideas already existing in voters' minds. The goal was "not to get something across to people as much as it is to get something out of people."[27] Schwartz had brought to the surface fears about Goldwater that many voters already had. He had also permanently altered the nature of election advertising.

During the late 1960s and early 1970s, the "clean, unemotional, 'factual' presentation" dominated the election airwaves.[28] Voters would be told about some aspect of a candidate's record or about her or his policy proposals as part of a tightly-wrapped direct appeal. Typical of the genre was a commercial run by Democrat George McGovern in his race against Richard Nixon in 1972. The rise in the cost of various food products since Nixon had become president in 1968 was announced as the foods were shown on the screen. The ad concluded by stating "So the next time you are in a supermarket, ask yourself: Can you afford four more years of Mr. Nixon?"[29]

By the late 1970s, American election commercials had become large-scale theatrical extravaganzas. The strategy, attributable in large part to political consultant Robert Goodman, was to fill the screen with powerful images and feelings, to show rather than tell voters what the message was. Goodman's spectacles invariably included large crowds, stirring music, dramatic effects, and expensive production techniques. The politician would be presented in heroic terms—larger than life, someone shrouded in historic greatness and charisma. In one ad created by Goodman his client was shown leading a cavalry charge, while in another the client was shown at first sunlight as an eighty-piece orchestra played triumphant music. The work done for Ronald Reagan in 1984 by Hal Riney, creator of the successful Gallo Wine ads, is considered by some to be the pinnacle of spectacle advertising. Reagan never appears nor is his name ever mentioned in Riney's famous "Morning Again" spot. We see splendid scenes of men and women beginning their day—hugs, homes, flags—all to the strains of upbeat patriotic music. The film was processed to reflect a golden glow. Riney intended to create the sense of a country rising again—powerful again, but yet tranquil and at peace. The audience was told at the end of the commercial that the United States had come a long way in "four short years."

Although negative or "black" ads have been a feature of American campaign advertising virtually from the outset, some have argued that with the "black flight" (a flight is a series of ads aired together) launched by George Bush's campaign during the 1988 election, the practice reached a new and sinister level. In Bush's spots, Michael Dukakis's record as Governor of Massachusetts was systematically and brutally misrepresented by what one observer called "scorched-earth negative ads" and "pit-bull politics."[30] In one of Bush's commercials, entitled the "tank ad," Dukakis is shown "grinning goofily" as he rides in a tank. The ad claimed that Dukakis opposed a number of weapons systems when, in fact, he supported them. Bush's most astonishing commercials featured a convicted killer, a black man named Willie Horton. The commercial claimed that while Bush supported the death penalty for first degree murderers, Dukakis not only opposed it but allowed first degree murderers to receive weekend passes from prison. The commercial showed a picture of Willie Horton while an announcer solemnly recounted that Horton, who was serving a life sentence for murdering a boy whom he had stabbed nineteen times, had kidnapped a young couple, stabbing the man and repeatedly raping the woman, while out on a weekend furlough. What the ad failed to mention was that most states had similar prison furlough schemes, and that an equally controversial federal program existed under the Reagan-Bush administration. Moreover, the crime rate in Massachusetts had actually fallen during Dukakis's term as Governor. The ad, which played on racist stereotypes and fears, is thought to have produced a visceral response in some voters.

The conventional wisdom among veterans of American ad wars is that negative spots can be so devastating to the candidate who is attacked that a response or counter-ad has to be launched within twenty-four to forty-eight hours. The smear has to be erased, the distortions refuted or ridiculed, and the record somehow set straight. Although studies indicate that voters have ambivalent views about negative ads and that they often backfire on the attacker, making the attacker seem "sleazy" and mean-spirited, ads, as Tony Schwartz points out, that address instincts and perceptions that already exist in voters' minds often hit their mark. Politicians must have the capacity, resources and ingenuity to launch a forceful reply, something that Dukakis was unable to do. In the high noon atmosphere of American electoral politics, politicians are either "quick or dead," with political consultants and ad people being the hired gunslingers.

THE TILTED GAME OF CANADIAN ELECTION ADVERTISING

When it comes to television advertising, the current election law gives the party in power enormous advantages. The networks must provide paid-time and free-time advertising based on the number of seats that each party has in the House of Commons at the time of dissolution, each party's percentage of the vote in the last election, and the number of party candidates running for election. Altogether, 6.5 hours of paid time and 3.5 hours of free time are made available to the parties. Since the governing party can buy more time and also receives a larger share of the free-time broadcasts than the other parties, the game is tilted in its favour. Having won a landslide victory in the 1984 federal election, the Conservatives were allowed to buy 195 minutes of television time during the 1988 election compared to eighty-nine minutes for the Liberals, sixty-seven minutes for the NDP, and nineteen minutes for other parties.[31] The amount of time allotted dictates to some extent the nature of the strategies that can be employed and the structure, pace, and depth of a party's ad campaign. Terry O'Malley, the creative director of the Liberal advertising campaign during the 1988 election, has commented on the inequalities that are built into the Canadian system: "It's a 100-yard dash except that we started forty yards behind."[32]

The three parties operate very different advertising "shops." The Conservatives have the largest and most experienced organization. Largely the brainchild of Senator Norm Atkins and Tom Scott, the Conservatives' current advertising structure goes back to the 1971 Ontario election. It is a consortium of people and agencies that, in Tom Scott's words, come together "to form a complete and temporary entity which is part ad agency, public relations firm, broadcaster, and political consulting company—all rolled into one."[33] The advantage enjoyed by the Conservatives is that the volunteers donated by ad agencies work full time for the party during the election. Although the party has had to buy the services of individuals, sometimes paying top dollar, the Conservatives are able to put into place a "twenty-four hours a day, seven days a week" organization.[34] In 1988 the ad campaign was buttressed by a large research effort: polling, focus groups, and an audio and video library. As the Conservatives are far wealthier than the other parties and the current election law does not limit the amount that can be spent on research, they had a substantial research advantage during the 1988 election. Until the 1988 election, ads in both English and French were done through the central organization; in 1988 a Quebec campaign, with its own independent budget, was established.

The Liberals set up Red Leaf Communications using the consortium model pioneered by the Conservatives. Volunteers from a number of agencies are brought together temporarily, except that "no person gives up the job they have."[35] So unlike the Conservative operation, which is built around full-time personnel, the Liberals depend on "after hours" efforts from people who give up nights and weekends and fit in time between hectic schedules and their other advertising projects. Red Leaf resembles a regular advertising agency, with separate creative, media, accounting, and research staffs. The Liberals have taken a different tack from the Conservatives with regard to Quebec advertising, however: the Quebec campaign was run independent of Red Leaf until 1988 when a Quebec agency, Groupe Morrow, was included as part of the national advertising effort.

The New Democrats, as a third party with little chance of forming a government, have not been in a position to create an advertising consortium similar to the other parties. Agencies expecting government contracts are unlikely to flock to the NDP campaign. For a time, the NDP was able to benefit from a provision in the Election Act that reimbursed the parties for one-half of their radio and television advertising expenditures. As that provision (which had much to do with getting parties "hooked" on TV ad campaigns) is no longer in effect, the NDP has had to buy the services of advertising agencies at competitive prices. During the 1988 election, the account went to Michael Morgan and Associates and Nouvelle Société.

How parties schedule their advertising "buy" is a key component of election strategy. As TV advertising is limited to the last four weeks of what is normally an eight-week election and is prohibited in the final forty-eight hours of the campaign, the "air wars" take place over a relatively brief period. Most analysts agree that party ad campaigns can be roughly divided into three distinct phases, each lasting for approximately seven to ten days. Depending on the strategy employed, parties can either be "first out of the gate" — spending a great deal at the beginning in the hope of setting the agenda and defining the terms on which the election will be fought—or can "hold their fire" for a blitz in the last week. Most campaigns begin with a sizable buy, have a lull in the middle, and build towards a climax at the end. To "backload" the buy in order to maintain a defensive capability for the final week is considered the safest strategy.

Traditionally the best buys are during sports events, on either side of the news, and before and after news breaks. Some parts of the country may be targeted for heavier than usual buys: areas where there are close contests, where votes are soft and need to be consolidated, or in large population centres. Certain ads might not run at all in some areas. Ideally, the buy is integrated with the achievement of wider campaign objectives: the themes hammered home in the TV campaign should be co-ordinated with speeches and announcements on the leaders' tour, appeals made by local candidates, and the content of direct mail and other kinds of advertising.

During the 1988 federal election, the three parties managed their buys quite differently. The Conservatives held off spending at the beginning of the four-week period to save resources for a "saturation" buy at the end of the campaign. By using videotape instead of film and by not employing professional actors, they cut costs so that they could put more money into buying a greater number of spots. In contrast, the NDP sacrificed quantity in order to produce higher quality productions. As the third party wishing to appear as a government-in-waiting, professional-looking "beautiful" ads were more appropriate than ads done on grainy videotape. Ian McKinnon believes that the NDP "wasted their money on high quality production and then didn't have the guts to junk it when a change in tactics was required."[36] When polling done for the Conservatives revealed that seniors and homemakers were more likely than others to fear free trade, the Conservatives targeted these groups by buying more spots on daytime television than might otherwise have been done. Ads were booked on soaps like "The Young and the Restless" and children's programs such as "Romper Room."

The on-going success of the TV ad campaign is monitored through polling. In some cases, ads will be pulled when polling numbers indicate that the intended goal has been achieved. Ian McKinnon describes the strategy used by the Tories: "We set quantifiable targets through polling. We push a particular theme until we reach a certain number. As soon as we achieve that objective we push from there to something else."[37]

For many, the critical question about the 1988 election was whether the Conservatives were able to reap an unfair advantage because they had more money and were allowed to buy more time than the other parties. In the election's final ten days, viewers were inundated by a torrent of Conservative spots with few slots bought by or available to the other parties. NDP deputy campaign director, Robin Sears, estimated that the Conservatives had bought the equivalent of 1,000 rating points in the major markets so that the average viewer saw approximately twenty Tory ads in the final week of the election compared to ten or twelve ads for the Liberals and NDP combined.[38]

The Tory blitz featured a flight of negative ads whose purpose was to shatter John Turner's credibility. The Liberals do not appear to have had the money or the opportunity to respond to the Conservatives' brutal onslaught. As Terrence O'Malley has described the Liberal's predicament, "We were spent. We had nothing. We couldn't afford to make new commercials. All we had was what we had. The question was how was it going to hold up against the wave of attack. And it cracked."[39] According to the Liberals' chief financial officer, Michael Robinson, even when the party tried to buy time for the ads already made "the good spots were already taken."[40] The question is not whether the Tories were smarter in their buy than the other parties—clearly they had bought shrewdly—but whether parties are denied an opportunity to put forward ideas or respond to charges made against them because of lack of money or available time slots. Does the current Election Act load the dice by giving the party in power or the party with superior financing disproportionate access to the airwaves? By not giving parties the opportunity to respond adequately to claims made against them by their opponents, the Election Act inhibits rather than enhances the democratic process. It seems to be the product of a time when TV ads were more innocent and the need for scrupulous regulation to ensure fairness less compelling.

ADVERTISING TECHNIQUES

There are four types of ads that are normally used during election campaigns. While all four might be used in a single campaign, most parties will produce flights consisting of only one or two basic types during an election.[41] Leadership spots make up the first category. Sometimes called identification or profile ads, the purpose is to introduce a politician by showing voters who he or she is or, in the case of a well-known politician, his or her achievements. The politician, as an individual, is the focus of the ad; party labels, positions on issues, and arguments and appeals based on factors other than personal characteristics are secondary. If a politician is new, leadership ads can build name recognition and a positive first impression. For well-known politicians, leadership spots can soften or redefine an image by highlighting positive attributes. Robert Goodman's "hero" ads, where the politician is larger than life, bathed in flags and sunlight, and wildly cheered by adoring audiences, is leadership advertising par excellence. The "candidate on the white horse" is shown awaiting destiny and a ride to greatness.

Leadership ads are rarely used in Canada, probably because Canadians get to know their leaders relatively well through seeing them in the daily theatrics of Question Period. It's difficult to put a fresh face on images that have been bruised and battered by the routine exchanges of shouts, insults, and accusations. Nonetheless, the technique has been tried. A flight of ads done by the Liberals during the 1979 federal election portrayed Pierre Trudeau as a tough, capable leader. The intention was to have voters draw a contrast between Trudeau and Joe Clark. One was entitled "World Leaders":

Audio

In a world with tough economic and political situations emerging almost daily, Canada must have the kind of tough intelligent leadership necessary to respond.

Prime Minister Trudeau has proven himself time and time again in difficult world problems that could change the future of Canada in an instant.

He is respected. He is looked up to. He has the experience, confidence and the knowledge to guide Canada through these times.

We need tough leadership to grow. A Leader Must Be A Leader.

Sometimes selling the leader at the expense of the party or policies can backfire. During the same 1979 election that had Liberal ads showcasing Trudeau's character and achievements, the NDP tried to reap the harvest from public opinion polls that showed Ed Broadbent was the most popular leader. The party ran TV spots featuring this all-print message read by an announcer:

A lot of Liberals and Conservatives believe that Ed Broadbent would make the best Prime Minister. They say, if Ed Broadbent were the leader of their party, he'd win the biggest landslide in Canadian history. People don't have the same kind of nagging doubts about Ed Broadbent they have about Trudeau and Clark. Maybe it's time to put aside the old Liberal and Conservative myths and simply vote for the best man. If enough people did that, Ed Broadbent would be the next Prime Minister of Canada.[42]

The problem with the ad was that it reminded voters of the reason why they weren't voting for Broadbent and, in fact, made them feel comfortable about their decision. Peter O'Malley, a press aide to Broadbent during that election, remembers the horror of walking through the Kitchener market with Broadbent and being told by a vendor that although he liked Broadbent, he wouldn't vote for him because of his party.[43] The pitch based on selling leadership alone had boomeranged unpredictably.

Leadership ads, particularly those appearing in the United States, have been criticized for what are often blatant distortions of reality.

Liberal leadership ads portrayed Pierre Trudeau as a tough, capable leader during the 1979 federal election.

Ineffectual and unpopular politicians can be depicted as strong and decisive, cheered by adoring throngs. Leaders who are coldly remote and formal can be pictured in warm family scenes that give voters a sense of love and caring. A young, inexperienced politician can be made to look older, more dignified. An older man or woman can be made to seem full of youthful energy and exuberance. To counter impressions that George Bush had been weak and inconsequential as vice-president, that he was a "wimp," Bush's 1988 campaign commercials studiously portrayed him as a stalwart family man and tough defender of law and order. Image and packaging, props and pageantry—that is the substance of leadership ads. The philosophy, according to American political consultant Robert Goodman, is to "Strive for . . . an emotion, not a position. . . . Feelings decide it all. We must like this human being to vote for him. In most elections, the issue isn't foreign policy or inflation. The issue is really the human being."[44]

A second type of ad is the testimonial. In testimonial ads a leader, party, or policy is endorsed by people whom voters consider reliable or credible. Statements of support can come from someone who is well-known or in "streeters" where ordinary people, supposedly picked at random on street corners, are interviewed. Often someone who has been helped by a politician or by a policy will appear in an ad. Mothers, fathers, wives, children, and neighbours have also been used effectively. During the 1979 federal election the Liberals produced a flight of "streeters" that featured people talking about Trudeau's leadership qualities. Again, the objective was to have voters compare Trudeau to Clark. The people in the ads were a cross-section of young and old, women and men. They seemed sincere and forthright and left the impression that they had given Trudeau's record as prime minister a great deal of thought. In the 1988 election, the Conservatives used an ad to brandish the editorial endorsements they had received from newspapers across the country. An excerpt from an editorial was shown in print with a photograph of the night-time skyline of the city that the newspaper served appearing as a backdrop. The Conservatives also ran a spot taken from an interview where negotiator Simon Reisman assured voters that the free trade deal was a triumph for Canada.

A trend in the United States is for endorsements to be sentimental and heart-rending. New York Senator Alphonse D'Amato, running for the Senate for the first time in 1980, produced a spot with his mother in the starring role. She was shown carrying groceries and walking towards a modest home and talking about her son's concerns for the needs of ordinary people. The ad played a crucial role in differentiating D'Amato from the other candidates and raising his recognition level. A particularly effective ad, described in a study by Dorothy Nesbit, featured a U.S. senator walking beside a woman who described how she almost lost her leg. The senator had helped get her Social Security benefits restored when they were taken away after it was discovered that she had earned a small amount of money. According to Nesbit, "the symbolism of the repeated sequence where the senator walks beside the woman along the same path she had previously walked alone is subtle but brilliant."[45]

A third commonly used technique is the argument spot. In argument ads a case is made, an argument put forward for or against a particular policy, a politician, or a party's record. These ads remind, attack, advocate, provide facts and reasoning, and support or denounce issues, events, policies, or people. They force parties to portray a future, the positive future offered by their party as opposed to the dreary future that awaits voters should their opponents be elected. Some argument spots take a simple "selling toothpaste" approach, with a set of facts sold to voters. Others attempt to target human emotions, to touch the "hot buttons" of the electorate, by making people imagine or feel a particular problem or situation.

An ad done for President Gerald Ford in 1976 is an example of pushing a fact at voters in the hope that the point will stick and that they will remember it. The spot protrays a conversation between two women, one of whom was coming from the grocery, while the other was standing outside a President Ford campaign office:

> First Woman: Ellie! Are you working for President Ford?
> Second Woman: Only about twenty-six hours a day. Notice anything about these food prices lately?
> First Woman: Well, they don't seem to be going up the way they used to.
> Second Woman: President Ford has cut inflation in half.
> First Woman: In half! Wow![46]

Although the situation is improbable and the message delivered in a heavy-handed way, the goal was to prime voters into thinking about inflation as a serious problem and into seeing Ford as a successful economic manager. A spot made by Hal Riney for Ronald Reagan in 1984 and entitled "Bear" is, in David Beiler's view, "probably the subtlest, most allegorical political spot ever made."[47] The commercial shows a mammoth and ferocious bear approaching a man standing alone. In hushed tones the announcer explains that "There's a bear in the woods. Some people say the bear is tame. Others say it's vicious and dangerous. Since no one can really be sure who's right, isn't it smart to be as strong as the bear?"[48] The bear, of course, symbolized the Soviet Union and the unstated premise was that it was only Reagan's strong defence policy that could help the United States stay as strong as the bear.

Among the most effective poster argument ads ever produced was done for Margaret Thatcher's 1979 election campaign by the agency Saatchi and Saatchi. It showed a stark black and white photo of a long line of unemployed workers with a banner reading "Labour Isn't Working." During the 1987 British election, Thatcher's Conservatives ran a series of devastating argument ads against the Labour party led by Neil Kinnock. Labour had invested heavily in a lengthy leadership spot that featured Kinnock walking amid beautiful scenery with stirring, triumphant music as background. The ad stressed that Kinnock was a moderate, level-headed leader, someone who could be trusted with power. The Tories responded with a spot that profiled Labour's most radical candidates. The ad claimed that Kinnock was outnumbered by unsavoury extremists who would virtually destroy the country if they were elected. The Tories also ran a newspaper ad that ridiculed Labour's conciliatory policies on NATO and disarmament by showing a British soldier with his hands raised in surrender. The caption at the top of the advertisement read, "Labour's Policy on Arms." The text at the bottom of the ad stated:

Labour's policy on defence is to leave us with hardly any. They'd scrap Polaris, abandon Cruise, cancel Trident.
And insist the Americans remove all the nuclear bases from British soil.
Without the Soviets having to give up so much as one of their terrifying weapons.
So what's Labour's answer to any future attack?
Last weekend, Mr. Kinnock said it would be to use "the resources that you've got to make any occupation untenable."
In other words, let them occupy Britain first. Fight afterwards.
That, Mr. Kinnock, is not just untenable.
It's unthinkable.

Several spots done during the 1988 Canadian election were classic argument ads. The following ads done by the NDP focused on two of the party's major campaign themes: a clean environment and maintaining Canada's health care system. The first was called "Grandpa":

Audio

Grandpa: Your Dad and I swam in this lake when he was a boy.

Grandson: Why can't we swim in it now, Grandpa?

Grandpa: The lake is ruined by pollution.

Grandson: Can't we fix it?

Grandpa: First, we need a leader who isn't afraid to stand up to the big corporate polluters. Brian Mulroney promised that. But he let us down just like the Liberals.

Grandson: What are you going to do Grandpa?

"Grandpa," an NDP spot that ran during the 1988 federal election campaign, lacked the shock value needed to alert viewers to the environmental crisis.

> Grandpa: This time I'm voting for Ed Broadbent.
>
> Grandson: Can I vote for Ed Broadbent too, Grandpa?

The ad was designed to be aesthetically pleasing and to make people feel comfortable with the NDP. Some critics, however, thought that it was too soft and soothing and without the shock value needed to alert voters to the problems of a deteriorating environment. As Hugh Winsor observed during the election, "Some critics suggest the NDP's environmental spot is beautiful film but may confuse the message. Shots of billowing smoke-stacks might hit harder than a beautiful pond."[49] Ian McKinnon felt that the ad gave people "a long-distance feeling"; that it didn't hit home.[50] When the Conservatives showed the ad to focus groups, they found that although people liked the ad, perceptions about the Conservatives had not been altered.[51] Hugh Segal believes that if the same format had been used to attack free trade, the effects would have been devastating. (Grandfather: "I fought in World War I and World War II and I'm not going to give up Canada now." Grandson: "Can I fight for Canada too?")[52]

A second commercial, featuring a nurse's fears about the future of the health care system, was the NDP's most successful ad during the election because it struck voters with a patriotic yet frightful message:

> Audio
>
> This job is hard work. I love it and I'm good at it.

The NDP's most successful 1988 election ad struck voters with a frightful message about the future of Canada's health care system.

But Canada's good medicare is being threatened by the Mulroney free trade deal.

In the United States I've seen whole families wiped out by one illness. We can't let that happen here in Canada.

The New Democrats started medicare and I know I can trust Ed Broadbent to fight for it.

This time, Ed Broadbent.

The most controversial argument spot during the 1988 election was the Liberals' "erasing the border" ad. The ad raised the primal fear that Canadians have of being taken over by the United States:

Audio

U.S. Negotiator:	Since we're talking about this free trade agreement, there's one line I'd like to change.
Canadan Negotiator:	Which line is that?
U.S. Negotiator:	This one here. It's just getting in the way.
Announcer:	Just how much are we giving away in the Mulroney free trade deal. Our water. Our health care. Our culture.
	The line has been drawn. Which side do you stand on? Don't let Mulroney deceive you again. This is more than an election. It's your future.

The Liberals' controversial 1988 "erasing the border" ad raised the primal Canadian fear of being taken over by the United States.

David Morton, who headed the Liberal campaign, has described the thinking behind the ad: "What we wanted to be clear . . . was that it was the soft, concerned Canadian negotiating with the tough, more how-the-West-was-won American . . . the Canadian guy looked very serious, very good, but a little bit 'Oh, geez, am I getting taken to the cleaners here?'"[53] The ad hit an emotional chord with some voters. According to Tom Scott, the Conservatives' advertising director, the ad had a visceral effect when shown to focus groups. As Scott described their reaction, "We got it after it was aired on a Monday and showed them to groups of people who had not yet seen it on Tuesday. At first they laughed at the commercial. The second time we showed it to them there was dead silence. It got them thinking."[54] The Conservatives were forced to run a "corrective" ad that showed the border being redrawn and made the argument that nothing in the deal would affect Canada's sovereignty. The strategy behind running the counter-ad was to cloud the Liberals' message, not to ease voter's fears about Tory patriotism. As Tom Scott has explained, "The only reason we ran our ad on putting back the border was to discourage the Liberals from running their ads. It defused their ad because it added confusion in the viewers' minds."[55]

A fourth type of ad is the black or negative ad. These spots attempt to tarnish an opponent through ridicule or by a straightforward savaging of their character or record in office. The competence, motives, intelligence, and integrity of opponents is brought into question. The object is to draw blood, to inflict irreparable damage (at least for the duration of the campaign). While accusations and name calling are hardly new to politics (one is reminded that Theodore Roosevelt once described President William McKinley as having "no more backbone than a chocolate eclair" and a justice of the New York Supreme Court as being "an amiable old fuzzy-wuzzy with sweetbread brains"[56]), television conveys visual images powerfully and has the capacity to leave indelible impressions; and once an image has formed it is difficult, if not impossible, to erase.[57] Negative spots are the nuclear weapons of election campaigning, a weapon of last resort that threatens to lay waste a political process built on reasoned debate.

American studies show that while voters find negative ads objectionable, they can be effective if used shrewdly.[58] The conventional wisdom, however, is that Canadians react much differently to negative ads. Canadians like to think of themselves as less strident and more reasonable than Americans, and the view is that Canadians simply won't accept ads that "hit below the belt." For instance, André Ouellet, co-chair of the Liberal campaign in 1988, believes that "negative ads are not that important because Canadians are not as much influenced by them as Americans. . . . All of the data we've gathered, particularly in focus groups, show that Canadians hate negative advertising. . . . Brutally negative ads don't go down."[59] In practice, though, negative ads have been successful under certain circumstances. The most important factor is whether the ads reflect and are rooted in reality, that is, whether they are grounded in genuine issues and concerns. As mentioned earlier, Tony Schwartz, the American political consultant who has specialized in negative ads, believes that for negative spots to work they have to reinforce views or sentiments that people already hold. Tom Scott's view is that "the key to black ads is not to say that he's a . . . but to get the audience to think it. Canadians don't want to hear you say rotten things about the guy. But their attitude is that if the information is true, who wouldn't get pissed off."[60]

Negative advertising on television first began in 1956 when the Democrats launched a black flight against Dwight Eisenhower and his running mate Richard Nixon; but, as previously mentioned, the genre came into its own with Lyndon Johnson's campaign to demonize Barry Goldwater. It was not until 1972, however, when the Conservatives ran streeters that attacked Pierre Trudeau's record that black ads were used in a Canadian federal election. A full-scale assault came in 1979, when the Tories attempted to bury Trudeau beneath a flurry of accusations and attacks. One memorable ad in French showed a picture of a remarkably unattractive-looking Pierre Trudeau addressing the House of Commons while an announcer intoned that Trudeau was "*coupable*" (guilty) of a series of supposed crimes. After each "crime" described by the announcer, one would hear the harsh clanking sound of a jail door being slammed. In 1980 the Liberals retaliated with ads that mocked Joe Clark's competence and credibility. One of the ads that was part of this hard-hitting campaign was entitled "House of Cards:"

Audio

Joe Clark says he never had a chance to make election promises. If so, who took the chance to make election promises and then broke them?

Who took the chance to raise interest rates to record highs, to undermine Petro-Canada, to risk double digit inflation, to bring in an unfair budget with a 18¢ a gallon excise tax over and above the hefty gasoline increase?

The chances that Joe Clark has taken with Canada will be remembered a lifetime. This is the time to vote Liberal.

In 1984, the Liberals ran a flight of ads intended to place doubts in voters' minds about whether Brian Mulroney could be trusted. One spot featured a man, representing Brian Mulroney, walking through a super-

The 1980 "House of Cards" spot was part of a hard-hitting Liberal campaign designed to impugn Joe Clark's competence and credibility.

market with a shopping cart loaded with items that each symbolized an election promise. When the man approaches the cash, he is told that his promises are too expensive and that they will have to be returned. Since voters were obviously willing to trust Mulroney and were not suspicious of his promises, the ad had virtually no effect. The Conservatives had also prepared a black flight to be aired following the 1984 television debate. One of the ads reportedly showed John Turner "whispering into Allan MacEachan's ear, surrounded by all the old Trudeau guys."[61] The purpose was to depict Turner as part of the old Liberal clique and knock out the pinnings from the notion that he would bring fresh approaches and ideas. Mulroney's stinging rebuke of Turner's patronage appointments during the English TV debate made launching the flight unnecessary. Ian McKinnon has explained the process that was at work: "We had set a quantifiable target early in the campaign that a certain percentage would believe that John Turner really doesn't represent any change in the style of government. The ad was prepared with this single objective. The debate had made that measure hit that criteria. It is a spectacular example of the discipline that quantifiable analysis gives you. The purpose for which the ad had been created had been achieved by other means."[62]

Perhaps the best example of negative ads being used successfully in Canada was the Conservatives' "bombing the bridge" campaign of the 1988 federal election. After Turner's triumph in the election debates and the Liberals' subsequent rise in the polls, the Conservatives had to suddenly rethink their election strategy. The new approach was based largely on public opinion polls and what was learned from observing focus groups. When groups were asked to evaluate Turner, some people asked about his motives for opposing the Free Trade Agreement. According to Tom Scott, "the penny dropped" when strategists realized that when the Liberal leader was seen as a self-serving politician rather than as a magnanimous defender of the country's sovereignty, support for him collapsed. As Scott described it, "After the debate Turner was not viewed as a politician. He was a passionate patriot. The more like a politician he was presented, the worse he did. That was the breakthrough of the whole campaign."[63] Allan Gregg has explained the logic that lay behind the new strategy: "We saw that the bridge that joined the growing fear of free trade and the growing support for the Liberal party was John Turner's credibility. So we had to get all the planes in the air and smash the bridge and blow it up."[64] The Conservatives moved quickly to implement this broad strategy with negative ads as a central thrust.

The Conservatives can well argue that the Liberals had cast the first stone with a flight of negative spots that showed Mulroney making contradictory statements with the message "Say one thing, mean another. Don't let Mulroney deceive you again." Another spot, which ran in Quebec, told viewers that "In 1984, Brian Mulroney had us believe that his government would be honest and trustworthy. That was a lie. Never

has a government known so many scandals." The names of fallen ministers would then appear on the screen.[65]

In what might best be described as a "slur du jour" campaign, Turner
was attacked on a number of fronts. He was accused of lying about free
trade in hard-hitting speeches by Mulroney and Finance Minister Michael
Wilson. Prominent individuals such as trade negotiator Simon Reisman,
Quebec businessman Claude Castonguay, and Emmett Hall, a retired
justice of the Supreme Court of Canada, were apparently mobilized by the
Conservatives to refute Turner's assertions about the free trade deal.
Reisman went so far as to call Turner a "traitor" for attacking the agreement.[66] A four-page tabloid entitled "The 10 Big Lies," which challenged
Liberal claims, was distributed in key ridings. In addition, a whispering
campaign "waged surreptitiously in the political shadows" and aimed
principally at journalists planted the notion that Turner was opposing the
free trade deal only to get elected and that a Liberal government would
keep the agreement.[67] The "explosive shells" of television advertising,
however, were to be the main weapons used to discredit Turner.[68]

The Conservative's first salvo was a streeter whose aim was "to
reduce Turner to just another politician."[69] Seemingly based on spontaneous interviews with ordinary passersby on a street corner, one of
those interviewed was reported to be a Conservative party worker:[70]

First Person: I'm very very disappointed that Turner doesn't have
enough faith in Canadians.
Second Person: He just doesn't seem positive enough and strong
enough to be a leader for this country.
Third Person: I think that he's more interested in saving his own job
than he is in saving mine.
Fourth Person: John Turner is the type of person who's going to say
whatever is politically expedient at the time.

The *coup de grâce* was administered by a commercial whose main fixture
was a stop watch:

Audio

You're concerned about Canada's economic
future. So on Monday you'll elect a government to help us face that future.
It will take you about four seconds to mark
your ballot and four years to live with the
result.
Will it be an experienced team of competent
managers with a plan for the future or a man
with no team, no plan and no confidence in
Canada.
Think about it. Time is running out.

This Conservative ad presented Finance Minister Michael Wilson as a competent manager.

The intention was to signal voters in a dramatic fashion that time was running out. As Tom Scott explained, "This debate is going to end and it's going to end soon. It's like attorneys summing up their final arguments. We wanted to narrow the options in the voter's mind; there were only two choices, only two things to think about."[71]

The Liberals were unable to respond to the Tory onslaught by mounting counter-ads, apparently because of money. The giant wave of negative advertising was, by almost all accounts, a decisive factor in the Conservatives' mammoth victory. According to one Conservative insider, the party gained a point a day for ten days after the new ads aired.[72] An Ad Trend survey conducted by Environics in the aftermath of the election found that the Conservative spots were seen as the most influential and truthful of the campaign by the public.[73] Over one-quarter of the respondents in a Decima Research survey done for *Maclean's* said that TV commercials had helped them decide how to vote;[74] and even a 5 percent swing can make an enormous difference to the outcome of an election. The view taken by Elly Alboim is that "tracking how ads are doing is probably the best indicator of vote," and that in 1988 the ads had had an "enormous effect."[75] Ian McKinnon believes that the "Tory strategy could not have been realized without effective paid advertising."[76] The

Negative advertising paid off for the Conservatives in the 1988 "bombing the bridge" campaign.

Conservative ads had helped bomb the bridge; John Turner's credibility had been blown apart. The irony, according to the CBC's Don Newman, was that "The guy who's known as lying Brian could call Turner a liar and get away with it."[77] Four years of a deteriorating political reputation seemed to be erased by two weeks of election advertising.

The apparent success of the black ads used by both the Mulroney and George Bush campaigns in 1988 seems to have made believers out of people who had moral reservations about their use or were skeptical about their utility. Robin Sears has observed that while the NDP has always had moral qualms about using negative ads, "the demonstrated impact of that kind of advertising is undeniable."[78] He suggests that in future NDP ads are likely to have a "harder" edge.[79] Terry O'Grady believes that the NDP "learned a lesson about negative ads in this campaign. There was a definite feeling that we shouldn't indulge in that kind of campaign. If the other guys want to get dirty, that's up to them. Some of those people have now changed their opinion."[80]

Among the most controversial issues to emerge during the 1988 election was third party advertising. According to one estimate, as much as $10 million was spent on advertising by interest groups (mostly groups favouring or opposing free trade) during the election.[81] To complicate matters further, even the government of Alberta jumped on the election bandwagon with a $500,000 advertising campaign boosting free trade.[82] Although the present Election Act prohibited advertising by anyone other than political parties when it was originally passed in 1974, the National Citizens' Coalition successfully challenged the legality of this provision in a case heard by an Alberta court in 1984. When Mr. Justice Donald Medhurst ruled that the prohibition was "a restriction on freedom of expression,[83] the way was cleared for a spending free-for-all or what an editorial in *Marketing* magazine called "an unregulated advertising orgy."[84] Most analysts agree that the private campaigns were largely ineffective because the ads were unco-ordinated, had not been market tested before they were run, and lacked the subtlety, polish, and the larger strategic objectives of the party ads. According to Tom Scott, the interest group ads were simply "a lot of angry letters that got mailed."[85] Some observers, however, believe that as most of the third party ads favoured free trade, their collective weight helped tilt the election to the Conservatives. Liberal André Ouellet is convinced that the ads made the difference between a majority and minority government.[86] The great fear among party strategists is that their own ads may one day be drowned in a sea of corporate and interest group advertising; their own messages would be lost amid the clutter of so many other messages. They also worry that, unlike the political parties who have to operate according to advertising and spending rules, these outside parties have virtually no restrictions placed on what they can do.

The problem is how to reconcile the right to freedom of speech and the right that citizens have to participate in the election process. There is a need to keep elections from becoming a cacophony where no one's voice is heard. Stan Sutter of *Marketing* magazine expressed the dilemma this way: "A complete ban on non-party advertising during elections may not be compatible with the principle of free speech under the Charter, but the other extreme runs contrary to the fair play that Canadians expect in their democracy."[87] Some observers believe that in 1988 Canadians saw only the tip of the iceberg; if changes are not made relatively soon, the problem will become more intractable as the "right" of interest groups to wage a parallel election campaign becomes firmly established.

THE MEDIA'S STRANGE SILENCE

Ironically, the ad campaigns that are considered so important by party strategists precisely because they allow parties direct access to the public—unfiltered by the media—are almost entirely ignored by journalists. Although there were a number of reports and articles during the 1988 federal election describing what was in the ads and how much the parties were spending on their ad campaigns, the ads were rarely analysed in depth or criticized. Journalists displayed an uncharacteristic reluctance to discuss party advertising strategies, challenge the appropriateness or truthfulness of the "facts" presented in the ads, or make judgements. The parties were given a free ride on what has probably become the most potent and ruthless aspect of election campaigning.

Kathleen Jamieson, an American scholar who has written extensively on political advertising, was asked several times during the 1988 presidential election to comment on spots used by George Bush and Michael Dukakis. During the television shows on which she appeared, an equal number of clips from Bush and Dukakis ads were always shown and reporters always concluded by bemoaning the "sleazy" nature of the ads.[88] What frustrated Jamieson was that, "It was very difficult, given the visual structure, to make the point that Bush ads were, one, effective, and, two, lies, and that Dukakis's ads were, one, ineffective, and two, truthful."[89] By imposing the routine point-counterpoint structure, journalists had missed the main point: voters were being mislead. Canadian journalists failed to give the ads even this level of attention.

Fixated as they are on reporting the attacks, jolts, and hecklers of the leaders' tour, the latest polls and the rough and tumble of the debates, events that fit the "horse-race" criteria of election coverage, the media missed the deadly strategies unleashed in the ad war. Political parties have learned that paid media is a direct highway to voters, a highway unobstructed by the critical judgement of reporters or, apparently, by high moral principles.

NOTES

1. Frederick Fletcher, "The Media and the 1984 Landslide," in *Canada at the Polls, 1984: A Study of the Federal General Elections,* Howard R. Penniman, ed. (Durham, North Carolina: Duke University Press, 1988), p. 163-64.
2. Dorothy Nesbit, *Videostyle in Senate Campaigns* (Knoxville, Tennessee: University of Tennessee Press, 1988), Ch. 2.
3. Jeffrey Simpson, "The 15-second Tactic," *The Globe and Mail,* February 28, 1989, p. 6.
4. Jeff Greenfield, *Playing to Win* (New York: Simon and Schuster, 1980), p. 179.
5. Quoted in Edwin Diamond and Stephen Bates, *The Spot* (Cambridge, Massachussetts: The MIT Press, 1988), p. 394.
6. Nesbit, pp. 142-43.
7. John Godfrey, "Familiar Themes in 1911 Posters," *The Financial Post,* 14 November 1988, p. 13.
8. Ibid.
9. Franklyn Haiman, "A Tale of Two Countries: Media Messages of the 1988 French and American Campaigns," *Political Communication Review,* 13 (1988), 4.
10. Reg Whitaker, *The Government Party* (Toronto: University of Toronto Press, 1977), p. 229.
11. Interview with Senator Keith Davey, Ottawa, 27 January, 1988.
12. Ibid.
13. Interview with James Coutts, Toronto, 3 June, 1987.
14. Dalton Camp, *Gentlemen, Players and Politicians* (Markham, Ontario: Penguin, 1988), p. 137.
15. Whitaker, p. 262.
16. Camp, p. 281.
17. Whitaker, p. 250.
18. Diamond and Bates, p. 57.
19. John Meisel, *The Canadian General Election of 1957* (Toronto: University of Toronto Press, 1962), p. 288.
20. Ibid.
21. Interview with Dalton Camp, Ottawa, 7 July 1988.
22. Diamond and Bates, p. 105.
23. Ibid., pp. 108-9.
24. Ibid., p. 147.
25. Ibid., pp. 130-31.
26. Ibid., pp. 133-34.
27. L. Patrick Devlin, "Campaign Commercials," in *Television in Society,* Arthur Asa Berger, ed. (New Brunswick, New Jersey: Transaction, 1987), pp. 21-22.

28. Diamond and Bates, p. 209.
29. Ibid.
30. Andy Plattner, "The Key Ingredient," *U.S. News and World Report*, 29 August - 5 September 1988, p. 54.
31. Gerald Caplan, Michael Kirby, and Hugh Segal, *Election* (Scarborough, Ontario: Prentice-Hall, 1989), p. 151.
32. Interview with Terrence O'Malley, Toronto, 12 December 1988.
33. Interview with Tom Scott, Toronto, 24 April 1989.
34. Ibid.
35. Interview with Terrence O'Malley.
36. Interview with Ian McKinnon, Toronto, 24 April 1989.
37. Ibid.
38. Hugh Winsor, "Last Ad Blitz Costing PCs $2 Million," *The Globe and Mail*, 16 October 1988, pp. A1-2.
39. Interview with Terrence O'Malley.
40. Quoted in Mary Janigan and Hilary MacKenzie et al., "Anatomy Of An Election," *Maclean's*, 5 December 1988, p. 25.
41. These categories are adopted from Diamond and Bates, Ch. 14; and from David Beiler, *The Classics of Political Television Advertising: A Viewer's Guide* (Washington, D.C., Campaigns and Elections, 1986).
42. Clive Cocking, *Following the Leaders* (Toronto: Doubleday, 1980), p. 262.
43. Interview with Peter O'Malley, Ottawa, 26 May 1987.
44. Quoted in Larry Sabato, *The Rise of Political Consultants* (New York: Basic Books, 1981), p. 145.
45. Nesbit, p. 59.
46. Sabato, p. 177.
47. Beiler, p. 34.
48. Diamond and Bates, p. 27.
49. Hugh Winsor, "The Ad Battle Escalates," *The Globe and Mail*, 5 November 1988, p. D2.
50. Quoted in Winsor, "The Ad Battle Escalates."
51. Caplan, Kirby, and Segal, p. 224.
52. Ibid.
53. Graham Fraser, *Playing for Keeps* (Toronto: McClelland and Stewart, 1989), pp. 313-14.
54. Interview with Tom Scott.
55. Ibid.
56. Edmund Morris, *The Rise of Theodore Roosevelt* (New York: Ballantine, 1979), p. 610, 24.
57. Roger Aden, "Televised Political Advertising: A Review of Literature on Spots," *Political Communication Review*, 14 (1989), 5.
58. Aden, pp. 5-6.
59. Interview with André Ouellet, Ottawa, 18 April 1989.

60. Interview with Tom Scott.
61. Interview with Ian McKinnon.
62. Ibid.
63. Interview with Tom Scott.
64. "Anatomy of an Election," p. 24.
65. Fraser, p. 371.
66. Hugh Winsor, "Tories Wage a Shadow Campaign to Undermine Turner's Credibility," *The Globe and Mail*, 18 November 1988, p. A14.
67. Ibid.
68. Caplan, Kirby, and Segal, p. 192.
69. Interview with Tom Scott.
70. Winsor, "Last Ad Blitz Costing PCs $2 Million."
71. Interview with Tom Scott.
72. Ibid.
73. Martin Mehr, "Election Ads Top Polls," *Marketing*, 20 February 1989, p. 1.
74. "The Voters Reflect," *Maclean's*, 5 December 1989, p. 19.
75. Interview with Elly Alboim.
76. Interview with Ian McKinnon.
77. Interview with Don Newman, Ottawa, 9 December 1988.
78. Interview with Robin Sears, Toronto, 15 May 1989.
79. Ibid.
80. Interview with Terry O'Grady, Ottawa, 18 April 1989.
81. Charlotte Gray, "Purchasing Power," *Saturday Night*, March 1989, p. 17.
82. Jim Cunningham, "Tory Ad Budget up 85%," *Calgary Herald*, 13 June 1989, p. A8.
83. Mark Clark, "Outside Agitators," *Maclean's*, 7 November 1988, p. 19.
84. Stan Sutter, "Elections: Violating the Spirit of Fair Play," *Marketing*, 24 April 1989, p. 4.
85. Interview with Tom Scott.
86. Interview with André Ouellet.
87. Sutter.
88. Quoted in William Boot, "Campaign '88: TV Overdoses on the Inside Dope," *Columbia Journalism Review* (January/February 1989), p. 28.
89. Ibid.

PART 4
DEMOCRACY

CJR/Niculae Asciu

9

Democracy Theatre[1]

This book argues that the media have an important impact on political behaviour. Although there is no Canadian research that links the long-term effects of the media with political outcomes, the circumstantial evidence is overwhelming. Everything from Question Period to public opinion polling, from media monitoring to televised debates, suggests that the Canadian political system has been drastically affected by the power of the media. Election campaigns have become media campaigns run by those who know how to measure opinion, manipulate images, and handle reporters. The claims described in Chapter One that the media have the capacity to set the agenda and prime their audiences seems incontrovertible. Events or issues that are lead stories in the media for a substantial time period usually become matters of concern for the public, and the basis on which the performance of political leaders will be evaluated.

The notion that journalists are neutral bystanders who merely reflect what takes place in the world around them can be readily dismissed. The advent of both critical journalism and the infotainment agenda mean that news is slanted and manipulated. The ideological bias of reporters, owners, and news organizations cannot be dismissed as a factor in news reporting. This study, however, has emphasized "the village life" of journalists, the dynamics of audience demands, organizational imperatives, and the intense struggle between politicians and journalists to control the public agenda. News is a battleground over which various elites struggle for control. While many journalists may see their jobs as routine and the issues that they write about self-evident, the structures within which they work have been shaped by clashing societal forces and pressures. Front line political reporters or columnists come under direct pressure. They bargain with sources, are manipulated by the media strategies of politicians, and contend with spin doctors, handlers, and powerful peer pressures.

Sweeping changes in mass communications technology and in the attitudes of those who control and work in the mass media have fundamentally altered the landscape of Canadian politics. Indeed, an important part of Canadian democracy—the ways in which political leaders address and react to their publics—has been restructured. The speed, visualness, brevity, critical nature, and intrusiveness of the modern media have reshaped the political world in a manner that would be unrecognizable to Mackenzie King or Louis St. Laurent. The art of governing now requires different skills, the manipulation of different symbols and instruments of power, and a different public face than it did a generation ago. While very little research has been done in Canada on the impact of the media on politics, at least five plausible effects can be suggested.

First, the breathtaking speed of modern communications has collapsed the time that political leaders have to make decisions. The instantaneous nature of communications has meant that news about the overthrow or fall of a government, a sudden downturn in the stock market, an important court decision, an earthquake, or a terrorist act is transmitted across the country and throughout the world within minutes. Sometimes journalists, who constantly monitor the traffic flow on the information highway, know more about fast-breaking developments and the reactions to them than do political leaders. Journalists then have the power to bring the issues to politicians and force them to respond; and while political leaders can delay replying to new developments for hours or even days, the time available to formulate positions, seek advice, evaluate options, and build consensus has been sharply reduced. When the United States invaded Panama in December 1989, Prime Minister Mulroney and the other party leaders were expected to state their positions within hours of the attack. Not to have responded to the waiting throngs of cameras, microphones, and reporters and through them to the public was to risk appearing indecisive and not in control.

The speed with which news of events travels may also produce an accelerated "contagion effect" as people witness and learn from the experiences of others. The Soviet empire in Eastern Europe collapsed in less than 100 days in 1989 in part because news of changes in one country sparked unrest in others. A sharp plunge in stock prices in Tokyo can produce panic in Toronto on the same day's trading. One study found that a contagion effect accounted for 85 percent of airplane hijackings, with "every hijacking generating an average of two additional attempts."[2]

Second, the news format developed by the modern media places a premium on visual material. Visuals are the bread and butter of television news; they are also important to newspapers as newspapers have come to imitate television's visual appeal. Highly choreographed events and ceremonies that are designed to produce exciting visuals have become the centrepieces of political life. In particular, political leaders who have not mastered the use of television, who have low television IQs, are not likely to be successful for long. While some scholars believe that historic outcomes are shaped by powerful social and economic forces and see these new skills as mere window-dressing, there is unsettling evidence that magnetic television performances have sometimes changed the course of events. Martin Luther King, John F. Kennedy, and Ronald Reagan may have largely succeeded in gaining the political stage because they understood the new visual requirements of the media. Television certainly became the central organizing principle of Reagan's presidency. In a famous exchange between Lyndon Johnson and a CBS producer, Johnson was asked about what had changed most since his first days in Washington as a young congressman and his last days as president. Johnson replied without hesitating, "You guys. All you guys in the media. All of politics has changed because of you. . . . You've given us a new kind of people. . . . They're your creations, your puppets. No machine could ever create a Teddy Kennedy. Only you guys. They're all yours. Your product."[3] The brutal reality of the media's infotainment agenda is that political events or developments will not become leading news items unless there is exciting visual material in the form of riveting personalities or dramatic pictures.

The brevity of radio, newspaper, and television news stories has also had enormous consequences. Shorter articles, quotes, and clips are geared to the supposed attention spans of audiences and the need to provide them with jolts; indeed, it can be argued that TV viewers have become addicted to jolts per minute television and expect rapid-fire movements within and between stories. The problem is that only vague glimpses of issues are likely to reach the public. During CBC television's coverage of the negotiations that produced the Meech Lake Constitutional Accord, for example, viewers were never told what Quebec's five demands were even though they were the linchpin of the negotiations. Such basic information did not fit into the current television news format. Newspaper coverage of the making of the accord was also highly condensed and focused mainly on conflict and personalities.[4] The public was presented with slick and tightly-packaged snippets of information. It is hardly surprising, then, that there is an astonishing illiteracy among Canadians on basic issues such as free trade or the country's constitutional difficulties. Even at the height of the 1988 federal election, when the country was gripped by divisions over free trade, the majority of Canadians admitted that they knew very little about what was in the agreement. A majority of Canadians were unfamiliar with the contents of the Meech Lake Accord after years of news coverage.

News stories also have a brief shelf-life. There is a constant turnover of stories so that even important items are not in the spotlight for long. With news in continual forward motion, the public has little opportunity to focus on or grasp events before the next episode takes place. Despite the news bombardment, the brevity of news items and the short lifespan of stories may be leaving Canadians strangely disconnected from events.

A third factor is the rise of critical journalism. When journalists won the right to analyse and interpret events as tribunes of the public, they became participants in rather than merely observers of the political process. They have become a significant force in politics not only because of their editorials and investigations but also because they have emerged as the stars of the show. Television journalists are an imposing presence in their stories: they provide the context within which the actions of political leaders are described, contest the validity of their pronouncements, and always have the final word. Sometimes television news reports feature journalists describing what political leaders have said rather than allowing the audience to actually see or hear the political leaders themselves. At most, politicians are allowed ten to twenty seconds of airtime. It is small wonder that television journalists are trusted far more than the politicians whom they report on. In a similar vein, newspaper columnists routinely lampoon politicians and their policies to entertain as much as to inform their readers. They always seem bolder and more principled than the politicians they criticize, who have to balance diverse interests and make uneasy compromises.

Given the power of the media, it is almost inevitable that political leaders will face a media crisis at some point during their term of office. Once the storm sets in, politicians are at the mercy of violent winds. They endure a torrent of harsh attacks; the media dictates the issues and politicians are largely paralysed in terms of promoting their own agendas. Some political leaders are severely damaged by the crisis and have difficulty regaining their political footing. John Diefenbaker, Joe Clark, and John Turner, for example, are prime ministers whose governments were crippled by media crises.

A related fear is that negative labels and images will be applied too readily by the media and may be impossible to remove. Images can take on a life of their own and remain long after the events that inspired them have faded from public consciousness. Joe Clark took years to erase the wimp image that took hold after his world tour. It took a convincing performance by John Turner during his debate with Brian Mulroney during the 1988 election to dispel the impression—built up over years of media reporting—that he was a weak bumbler.

In order to survive in the media battleground, political leaders are continually engaged in media management campaigns. For some leaders, the media becomes an obsession consuming much of their thoughts, time, and activity; and they have developed a formidable arsenal of weapons with which to do battle. Freezing out, bypassing, letting them through the line, burning, pressing them against deadlines, the visual press release, and bargaining over editorial control are among the tactics frequently used. During elections, party leaders seek every opportunity to reach the public directly and force the media to communicate their messages. Staged visuals, political advertising, and direct mail have become principal means of political communication.

Some observers are concerned that critical journalism may be having a corrosive effect on the integrity of political institutions and structures.

As mentioned in Chapter Two, Anthony Westell has argued that the harshness of the media's criticism has produced widespread cynicism and distrust of government, and has consequently fostered greater faith in business and corporate solutions to economic problems. Confidence in politicians and in government's capacity to manage the economy and initiate and achieve national projects is certainly at a low ebb.[5]

There is also the fear that increased public scrutiny and the sting of media criticism will discourage good people from going into politics. If this is true, then critical journalism will have created a self-fulfilling prophecy, for only those obsessed with and greedy for power will enter the political fray and thus need to be constantly watched. While critical journalism does serve a useful purpose by curtailing the tyranny of politicians, there seems to be little check on the power of journalists to shape public opinion.

A fourth effect is created by the intrusiveness of the modern media. Joshua Meyrowitz believes that we are now witnessing a reversal of what was depicted in George Orwell's book *1984.* In Orwell's dark vision, the elite use technologies to control the behaviour of ordinary citizens. People are kept under constant surveillance; every aspect of their lives is observed; they live in an obsessive, stultifying world where privacy and freedom have been extinguished. In today's world, however, it is the leaders of democracies who are continuously watched, even hounded. Political leaders live in a media bubble where their every move is likely to be observed. TV cameras, radio microphones, and a throng of waiting journalists crush in on them after meetings or Question Period. Their public faces can almost never be taken off, and their private lives can be mercilessly exposed to the glaring spotlight of unwanted publicity. Dave Barrett, a candidate for the NDP leadership in 1989, found out that the line between public and private is easily traversed. A private, back-room conversation with another candidate, Simon De Jong, quickly turned into a *cause célèbre* as De Jong had been wired for a report broadcast on CBC's *The Journal*. The willingness of candidates to have themselves wired demonstrates both the seductiveness and the reach of the media.

One wonders whether John A. Macdonald's heavy drinking, Macken- zie King's bizarre communications with the spirit world, or Lester Pear- son's nervous breakdown while in uniform during the First World War would have prevented these men from becoming prime ministers today. Had the standards of moral conduct that were applied to presidential candidate Gary Hart after his affair with model Donna Rice was exposed been applied to John F. Kennedy or Lyndon Johnson, they would never have become president.

It may also be argued that the Canadian political system has become increasingly "presidentialized" by the media's obsessive focus on the politics of personality. Political parties are now portrayed as little more than their leaders writ large. Certainly the telescoping of virtually all coverage to the national campaign during elections and the importance placed on the spectacle of the leaders' debates have weakened the influence of local party organizations. Where once well-oiled local party machines and powerful local barons could deliver votes to the party leader, now the party leader is the bread-winner. The length of their coat-tails determines the fate of local candidates and even high-ranking cabinet ministers. The media have magnified the power of the leaders and diminished the influence of other players in the game.

Finally, modern communications technologies have eroded the position of political parties. Where parties once served a key function by communicating grassroots sentiments to the leadership, public opinion polls now fulfill the same purpose with much greater accuracy. Moreover, new election professionals — TV consultants, advertising people, survey researchers, direct mail specialists, and media handlers — have displaced party regulars from key campaign roles. The parties have been reduced to hollow entities that sputter to life only at election time or for leadership conventions.

This book has described the forces at work in the new landscape of Canadian politics, forces that are likely to bring even more changes in the years ahead. To some degree, scholarship has not kept pace with these changes. Even Canadian election laws lag behind in recognizing the full extent of what has taken place; for example, gaping holes exist in the rules about election advertising and public opinion polling. It is true that many of the developments have been recent: satellites, cable television, electronic newsgathering equipment, personal computers, and cellular phones only came into widespread use in the 1970s. Politicians have had to adapt to this changing media environment in order to survive. There are new rules, rituals, and instruments of power. Political leaders are aware that they cannot succeed without using and recognizing the "imposing authority" of the mass media, particularly of television.[6] Newsmaking has become a fundamental act of power in Canadian politics.

NOTES

1. The title of this chapter was borrowed from Michael Kinsley, "Democracy Theatre," *The New Republic*, 1 January 1990, p. 4.
2. Quoted in Gabriel Weimann, "Mass-Mediated Terrorism," *Middle East Focus* (March 1986), 12.
3. David Halberstam, *The Powers That Be* (New York: Alfred A. Knopf, 1979), p. 6.
4. Lorry Felske, "Fractured Mirror: The Importance of Region and Personalities in English Language Newspaper Coverage of Meech Lake," in *Meech Lake and Canada: Perspectives from The West*,

Roger Gibbins et al., eds. (Edmonton: Academic Printing and Publishing, 1988), pp. 247-60.

5. Hugh Winsor, "Fading Optimism in Coming Decade," *The Globe and Mail,* 30 December 1989, p. D1.

6. Shanto Iyengar and Donald Kinder, *News That Matters* (Chicago: The University of Chicago Press, 1987), p. 116.

Index

Canadian Broadcasting Corporation. *See*
    CBC
Canadian Facts, 187
Canadian Human Rights Commission, 76
Canadian Press (CP), 52, 73, 162
Canadian Press/Broadcast News, 87
Canadian Radio-Television and
    Telecommunications Commission.
    See CRTC
Le Canadien, 42
Candussi, Dores, 16
Caouette, Réal, 169
Capital Cities–ABC, 13
Carey, James, 52
Carey, John, 154
Carlin, Vince, 78, 111, 160
Carrington, Lord, 10
Carter, Jimmy, 81, 168, 172
Castonguay, Claude, 223
CBC, 7, 12, 18, 21, 22, 23-24, 52-53, 59, 73,
    75, 76, 80, 86, 95, 96, 98-99, 102-103,
    105, 106-107, 137, 144, 159, 161, 162,
    166, 172, 187, 191, 193, 204
CBC Newsworld, 76, 96-97
CBC Radio, 49, 144
CBC Radio News, 78, 87
CBC television, 49, 59, 73, 105, 157,
    162-163, 235
CBC television news, 57, 64
CBLT (Toronto), 103, 109
CBOT-TV, 137
CBS Evening News, 18, 62
CBS News, 99
Centre for Investigative Journalism, 14
CFCN, 11
CFTO (Toronto), 12-13
Champ, Henry, 74
Chan, Janet, 13. *See also* Ericson and
    associates
Charlottetown Islander, 43
Charpentier, Jean, 140
Charter of Rights and Freedoms, 130
Château Clique, 42
Chatelaine, 11
CHEK (Victoria), 12
Chomsky, Noam, 8
Chrétien, Jean, 104
Christie, Dinah, 59
Churchill, Winston, 72
CJOH (Ottawa), 13
Clark, Joe, 62, 82, 90-91, 104, 110, 119, 121,
    126, 129, 132, 142-143, 158, 181, 211,
    213, 220, 236
Clarkson, Stephen, 144
Claxton, Brooke, 181
Clement, Wallace, 13
CNN, 96

Cockfield, Brown (advertising agency),
    181, 203
Cocking, Clive, 139
Cohen, Bernard, 30, 50
Colby, Ken, 61
Coleman, Ralph, 140
Coles Books, 11
Colonial Advocate, 42
Comber, Mary Anne, 141, 144, 164
Comer, Harry, 170
Commentary, 58
conditioning campaign, 153-154
Connolly, Peter, 158
Conservative Party, 43-46, 49, 62, 82, 104,
    129-130, 143, 145, 153, 154, 159, 182,
    185, 186-187, 207-208, 209, 213, 219,
    220, 222
constitutional debate, 130
    and francophone journalists, 76-77
"contagion" effect, 234
Cooper, Barry, 49, 105
Coutts, Jim, 85, 111, 133, 160, 181, 194, 203
CP. *See* Canadian Press
critical journalism, 53-65
    and effects on politics, 235-237
    roots of, 54
Cronkite, Walter, 55, 102
Crouse, Timothy, 58, 89
CRTC, 22, 78
CTV, 11, 12-13, 21, 75, 106-107, 144, 156,
    162, 166, 187
CTV National News, 87, 95, 102, 109, 165
cultural model, 22-24, 25
Current Affair, A, 97

Dafoe, J.W., 44, 135
Daily Telegraph, 10
"Daisy" commercial (L. Johnson
    campaign), 205
D'Amato, Alphonse, 213
Davey, Keith, 138, 181, 203
Davis, William, 124
Day, Benjamin, 51
Dearing, James, 31
Deaver, Michael, 123, 124-125
debates, leaders' televised. *See* leaders'
    debates, televised
Deciding What's News (Gans), 103
Decima Research, 180, 182, 186, 193, 224
"Deep Throat," 82
De Jong, Simon, 237
democracy, effects of media on, 233-238
Dempson, Peter, 45, 46, 47, 71, 90, 136, 137
DePoe, Norman, 73
Desbarats, Peter, 16-17, 74
Desmarais, Paul, 106
Devlin, Patrick, 110
Le Devoir, 11, 20, 21, 44, 77, 87, 162

t from N
oct 12/06